GRACE IN PRACTICE

GRACE IN PRACTICE

A Theology of Everyday Life

PAUL F. M. ZAHL

WILLIAM B. EERDMANS PUBLISHING COMPANY
GRAND RAPIDS, MICHIGAN / CAMBRIDGE, U.K.

Published 2007 by
Wm. B. Eerdmans Publishing Co.
2140 Oak Industrial Drive N.E., Grand Rapids, Michigan 49505 /
P.O. Box 163, Cambridge CB3 9PU U.K.

Printed in the United States of America

15 14 13 12 9 8 7

Library of Congress Cataloging-in-Publication Data

Zahl, Paul F. M.
Grace in practice: a theology of everyday life /
Paul F. M. Zahl.
p. cm.
Includes bibliographical references and indexes.
ISBN 978-0-8028-2897-2 (pbk.: alk. paper)
1. Grace (Theology) 2. Christian life. I. Title.

BT761.3Z34 2007
234 — dc22

2006020128

www.eerdmans.com

This book is dedicated to

The Reverend Willi and Mrs. Ruth Stewart,

who live its theme

Contents

CONTENTS

Preface

The message of God's grace, or one-way love, has captivated me for as long as I can remember. It saved my life during my early twenties, restored my marriage in my middle twenties, then created in me a father loved by my children. Grace remade my ministry and made possible my contact with sufferers as well as with prodigals.

The message of grace has also proven to be provocative, especially in relation to other Christians. Sometimes I have been accused of being "long on grace but short on law." In other words, some have feared that my emphasis on grace is tantamount to blessing sin. The traditional word for this accusation is "antinomianism," or a teaching that is contrary to the law. Christians who stress grace — unmerited acceptance — are often accused of being "antinomian." It is almost a sure sign that you are preaching grace when people call you an antinomian.

This book is my attempt, after thirty years of teaching and preaching the message of grace, to set it out systematically, and to do this in the face of the chronic criticism grace receives. I also attempt to connect grace to some contemporary issues in world society. How does grace work? That is the theme of this book.

No apologies! One-way love is the heart of Christianity. It is what makes Christianity Christian. I hope that what you are about to read represents the *vox ipsissima Christianismi,* the true voice of the Christian religion, written without compromise or a form of words.

Certain teachers have helped me understand grace conceptually. Certain others have helped me understand grace pastorally. The man who first taught me the meaning of grace was FitzSimons Allison, during his memorable classes of the late 1970s at Grace Church in New York City. My wife and I learned the gospel of grace from Fitz Allison. We learned that grace alone achieves what the law demands and that this is true in life as well as in theology. Later, Frank Lake, who died in 1982, helped me understand grace in relation to my own concrete sorrows and sins.

Ernst Käsemann, from whom I had the chance to learn personally in the early 1990s, deepened my understanding of grace within the academic field of New Testament theology. Jürgen Moltmann, my "doctor father" at Tübingen from 1991 to 1994, made sure that I struggled with the political and economic implications of grace.

My wife, Mary, who was herself helped by Canon Anne Long's views on Christian listening within the Church of England, has been the ear of grace to me for thirty-two years. Our sons, John, David, and Simeon, all of whom now serve in Christian ministry, have each deepened my experience and my theology in relation to grace. They were my students but are now my teachers.

Three other less longstanding influences have affected this book. One is my life among the Loyalist Protestants of Northern Ireland. These are an often misunderstood if not actually mistreated people. In particular, the "Sons of William" of Maghera, South Londonderry, have given me concrete lessons in what it costs to exercise grace in relation to others with whom you deeply disagree and who dislike you. A second influence is the plays of Tyler Perry, the African American writer, which have opened up for me deep wells of grace in relation to the hurts of life as experienced, in deeply Christian ways, in Perry's community. Third, the thwarted genius of Robert George "Joe" Meek, the English independent record producer who died in February 1967, functions as a vivid and living reproach to me of what can happen when grace is *not* offered to a sufferer. I wish I had been there to comfort Joe.

Four of my students at Trinity Episcopal School for Ministry have been fruitful partners in conversation about the relation of Christ's grace to God's law. They are Jady Koch, Nick Lannon, Kate Norris, and Jacob Smith.

Simeon Zahl, doctoral candidate in systematic theology at Cambridge University; Burke Hilsabeck, doctoral candidate in English at the University of Chicago; and Dr. Dorothy Martyn, of Bethany, Connecticut, have aided me in the final editing of the manuscript. My assistant at Trinity School, Mrs. Maxine Moore, has helped me invaluably, and sacrificially, in the preparation of this book.

To all of these, and most of all to Mary, my wife, I say, thank you.

Ambridge, Pennsylvania
Epiphany 2006

CHAPTER ONE

Grace in Theology

What Is Law?

In life there are two governing principles that are at war with one other. The first is law; the second is grace. So powerful are these two principles, so virile and unquenchable, so captivating and irresistible, that all relationships, all human operations, simply lie down before them. The law crushes the human spirit; grace lifts it.

The story of the Bible is the story of this perpetual war between law and grace. Law comes in, as the apostle Paul puts it (Romans 7:21-23), and human beings become excited by it. They become excited to *resist* it. The law, which is any form of external command, provokes the opposite reaction from the one it is intended to provoke. Instead of inciting obedience or submission, it incites rebellion. It provokes revolutionary resentment.

The Bible is the chronicle of God's law in virulent antipathy with human nature, and human nature in virulent antipathy to God's law: conflict, in other words. These antipathies are reflected in real life, whether you care about the Bible or not. Imperatives produce their opposites: angry reactions. Can you name an exception to this? If somebody tells you to do something, you immediately and instinctively desire to do the opposite.

Is the law ever a gratifying thing? Does it produce pleasure? No. But the law is a true thing, an accurate summary or description of what it means to be happy and fulfilled, especially in relation to one's neighbors. If we were able and willing to follow it, the law would be the answer to humanity's problems. People who obey the law are, at least in principle, free from accusation. They are in the position of having peace in life, and also in death. But no law has been created that has the capacity to engender what it demands. The truth is, the law invites illegality. It almost cries out for it.

The law kills, the law incites, the law breeds hatred for itself, the law creates suppression. It does sometimes work to one's temporary benefit (maxims like "no pain, no gain" may help an athlete to achieve), but in the long run, the law runs out of fuel. The law does not enable us — except by mammoth and exhausting effort — to do the things it commends. The Bible declares the law to be good and right (1 Timothy 1:8; Romans 3:31; 7:12, 14, 16) but then with one great persuasive insight deprives the law of any lasting capacity to do us any good (Romans 7:24-25).

The point is crucial: law tells us the truth, the whole truth, and nothing but the truth about ourselves. It holds the "mirror up to nature" (William Shakespeare). But the law fails to convey the power to correct the maladies it diagnoses. The law is painful, like iodine on a cut, but another agent is required for healing to occur. That agent is grace.

Law in the Bible

The big idea in the Bible is the relationship of God's law to the self-absorption of the human being. Adam said to God, "I heard the sound of you in the garden, and I was afraid . . . and I hid myself" (Genesis 3:10).[1] God the Father, the ultimate father-figure of world experience, is to be avoided, by definition. His very existence is a judgment on humankind. His very voice thunders judgment, to which each of us says, like Peter, "Go away from me, Lord, for I am a sinful man" (Luke 5:8). God is purest law. Habakkuk describes God this way: "your eyes are too pure to behold

1. Biblical quotations throughout this book are taken from the New Revised Standard Version of the Bible unless otherwise stated.

evil" (Habakkuk 1:13). God's perfection is appalling because it "plumbs" (Amos 7:7-8) the depths of an imperfection distributed evenly among all human beings.

Today it is common to want to discern in texts, and certainly in the Bible, a "meta-narrative," a big idea or overarching theme. Some readers take the idea of "covenant," which is in the domain of law, as the meta-narrative of Scripture. Others have seized on "promise and fulfillment" as the grand theme. Others take "creation, fall, and redemption" as the commanding subject of Scripture.

The Protestant Reformers perceived "law and gospel" to be the governing metaphor of the two Testaments. They took so seriously the demand of God as embodied in the Ten Commandments of Moses that they actually cowered before it. This human terror before the inflexible mandate of God caused the Reformers to focus more intently than ever upon the death of Christ as the solution to human impotence. They were immensely cheered by the confidence that God had made a way for judgment to fall vicariously on a single man. For Luther especially, the law of God opened up the wound of human defeat; yet it prepared the way for the good and comforting news of the substitutive death of Christ.

We cannot understand God's grace without first understanding God's law. The scriptural view of God's perfect law is that it is the one great step toward humanity's self-understanding. Only an inflexible picture of what is required of the human being is able to penetrate to the marrow of creaturely insufficiency, and only an unbending picture of what is required of the human being is able to unveil the full and sufficient remedy for human failure. If we cheat on law, we are cheated on grace. This is why the absolute picture of law that is found in the God of the Bible is a safer interpretation of human failure than the mish-mash of extenuations and rationalizations that the law becomes in the hands of human mediation. There is a weights-and-measures relationship between law and grace: "you have been weighed on the scales and found wanting" (Daniel 5:27); but "there is a Fountain fill'd with blood" (William Cowper). A big view of God's grace — the blood that cleanses, the balm in Gilead — depends on a big view of God's law.

Did you ever see an "A"-quality film noir from Hollywood entitled

The Tattered Dress? It was directed by Jack Arnold in 1954 and starred Jeff Chandler and Jeanne Crain. It is rarely watched anymore. But there is one powerful shot in the movie — the very last shot, in fact. A lawyer has just won a case of the most obvious truth, after having been disbarred earlier in the film and having treated his own wife and children most selfishly. This man has redeemed himself, and the true culprit has just been shot and killed on the courthouse steps (it is a movie, after all). The hero, now accompanied by his reconciled wife, walks down the steps and gazes up at a large statue of the lady Justice, blindfolded and balancing the scales in her right hand. The camera dollies up and cranes back. Everyone on the steps is dwarfed and the towering statue blocks out everything else. Justice has been done. It is all that is left.

This idea is not simply Hollywood invention (although we see it through a Hollywood lens); it is a true reflection of law. Jack Arnold was a Jew who also appreciated Christianity, and he underlined the moral dimension in all of his films. The parable of *The Tattered Dress* is the parable of the perfect law. "Every valley shall be lifted up, and every mountain and hill be made low" (Isaiah 40:4). I believe that last shot, in which the figure of impartial Justice towers over all the characters and finally blots them out, is an unconditional picture of God's law, God's Bible law.

The Bible prepares the way for a discussion of law as the governing principle of everyday life, the brick wall of human impasse and frustration. The meta-narrative of law in the Bible lays the foundation for the experience we all have of law — the experience we all have of judgment — in the day-by-day conflicts of what our nineteenth-century ancestors called the "battle of life." But in doing so, the Bible's narrative also opens the way to the principle of grace, the blood and balm to this impasse.

In the Beginning

The law begins in the garden of Eden. God tells the primal couple of a spacious freedom that contains only one condition: they may not eat of the fruit of the tree of the knowledge of good and evil (Genesis 2:17). The prohibition, however, proves decisive. The sheer longing to eat this fruit overcomes them completely. The freedom of touching and tasting with which Adam and Eve are endowed includes this one No. All that is required to flout the law is one instance of it. They grab the fruit.

I once heard from the CEO of a certain institution that he had been told by the chairman of its board to make a certain decision. All it took was that *instruction* from the chairman and I knew in a moment that the CEO would go the other way. I remember thinking to myself, here's a simple directive, the only one I have ever heard the chairman give to that man. But it was an order! One little order, but an order nonetheless. The CEO refused to obey it, and that order undid him. It was such a little thing, but just as important for this man's life as the single "thou shalt not" delivered to Adam and Eve. The result was the same: disobedience, punishment, and expulsion.

We hear this story day after day. All was well before the articulation of law, but at that point the goose was cooked. It is no wonder artists as removed in time as Masaccio and Thomas Cole have portrayed the desperate moment of expulsion (Genesis 3:24). We cannot countenance the law, the dynamic of demand, so we reject it in principle. West of Eden we go, like Milton's castaway pair: "hand in hand, with wand'ring steps and slow," we take our "solitary way."[2]

From this primal disaster with the law stems cyclically every sin, every betrayal and every punishment of betrayal: Cain and Abel and Cain's punishment; the Tower of Babel; the flood of Noah; the gradual formation of a people, through Abraham, who would relate to God not on the basis of law but on the basis of faith and grace; the promises to Israel on the basis of faith and not of law; the patriarchs and the wanderings across the land; and finally the actual embodiment of law, a "position" on human waywardness that God took when he summoned the lawgiver, Moses, to the top of the mountain.

2. John Milton, *Paradise Lost* (London, New York: Penguin, 2000), book 12, lines 648-49.

The Lawgiver

God gave Moses a short but complete list of commandments, or requirements, which define the just society and happy home (Exodus 20:1-17). Each flows from the first and second commandments. The first commandment puts God as the fountainhead of all existence and creation. God is the sole source of any good and any hope, and he can be credited with every act of deliverance from trouble. The second commandment is a No to all contrary gods, the negation that underlies the prior affirmation. The next eight commandments are expressions of the will, for everyday people, of the Author of life who speaks in the first two.

The commandments to Israel, which are universal requirements of ethical existence addressed to the whole race of human beings, are law. They embody it and define it, and they are absolute in their authority. They exist and should be followed "so that your days may be long in the land" (Exodus 20:12). They idealize the social character and relatedness of living, and they are to be understood more as idealizations than as controls or levers on human freedom.

But the law, no matter where it comes from, is always the law *heard*. I hear "You shall" and "You shall not" as adversarial. This is the key to understanding human psychology and human action. All ideals and all delineations of what is absolutely good are heard and understood as accusatory statements. This is the nature of sin. The law of God, as it is with laws enunciated by human beings, is heard as being expressed in the attack mode. Say what you will about its idealistic intent, about its being the ultimate "design manual" for men and women, the law is always heard as an attack. I learned this as a child living in a family. My sister might say to me, "How do you like my dress?" and I would answer, "It looks fine." She would say back, "What's the matter with it?!" I was mystified.

Any judgment, *any* evaluation — even if it approves and speaks a blessing — will be heard as a negation. This is an absolute first principle of this book. Law is an attack. It is heard as a negation by its recipient. All laws are negation. God's law is *the* negation.

People sometimes deny this. They say that they are grateful for the criticism, that it really helped them take inventory. Or they speak of criticism as "friendly" or "challenging." I once spoke to a woman who praised "challenging" relationships with men. I asked her what she meant. She explained that some men, just by their stormy temperament or argumentative spirit, had "challenged" her, had taken her out of her comfort zone. I then asked her, partly to be "challenging," myself, whether any of these boyfriends had been permanent. No, she had to admit, none of those relationships had lasted. I pressed the point, "Would you like to be married to a 'challenging' man? Or better yet, would you like the father of your children to be such a person?" She threw me over, too, with all my "challenging" questions.

People do not wish to be challenged. People wish to be comforted. They wish to be supported. They wish to be encouraged and sustained. What people wish is to be loved.

An illustration of this occurs in a popular movie from a few years ago entitled *Bridget Jones' Diary.* After killing disappointments with men, Bridget, who simply wishes not to be alone, is told sincerely by a man, "I love you just the way you are." The scene in which he says those words to her is powerful. Despite all the social commentary about the joys of single life in hip, rich London, the audience, together with Bridget Jones, is arrested by that one sentiment. There is not a syllable of law in it. There is only grace.

Later we will look at the idea, often purveyed in Christian churches, of "speaking the truth in love." It is an empty set. It never happens. Although this form of law is loftily protested as being "within the bonds of love and affection," there is always that basso continuo of judgment in every appeal of criticism, which disqualifies such speaking from having transformative effects. Did you hear the "attack siren" blasted by the alien tripods in the 2005 version of *The War of the Worlds*? It was haunting. I could not expel it from my mind. It was the signal in the movie for mass extermination. We hear the law that way.

The law of Moses, which in my theology is the law of God, is upright and beautiful. It is "perfect . . . true and righteous altogether" (Psalm 19:7-9), but it does nothing to create the state that it requires. There is not one enabling word in its arsenal. When Moses came down from the mountain, he came down with the truth but not the means with which to apply it, save by suppression through the instrumentality of judgment.

Kings and Prophets

Scripture's meta-narrative is not metaphysical. It leaves metaphysics to the Greek philosophers. Scripture's meta-narrative is not a probing into the idea of God, nor is it the interpretation of a humanly interested Reality that lies behind the mask of repetitive historical events. It is not a hymn to cosmogony, nor a prelude to Spinoza. Scripture's meta-narrative is not fundamentally concerned with what we think of as scientific inquiry.

Scripture's meta-narrative is ethical. It concerns itself with our human conflict with the divine requirement. Yes, Scripture is almost uniformly religious — that is, its main character is God. This character is locked in an ethical battle with antagonistic and resentful men and women. Will human beings submit to God's law, the Mosaic Decalogue? Or will they run in the opposite direction?

Without exception, human beings run. When the Jews are finally settled into the Promised Land, the land of Canaan, they demand a king (1 Samuel 8:4-5). They do not wish to bear with God's own mouthpiece, the prophet Samuel. Later, they had been chronically uncomfortable with God's other mouthpieces, the judges. One after another, each judge started well, then either went bad or was repulsed by the people. In the Old Testament books there is not one sure minute of acquiescence, unconditional relatedness, or obedience before the law of God. The cycle goes from mandate to rebellion to catastrophe to mandate again, and then the great "wheel in the sky" turns for the next generation. It is not a pretty picture.

When the prophetic voice is stilled and the voice of human kings becomes dominant, the cycle begins again in earnest. From King David to Solomon to the division of the monarchy and the kingdoms to the pincers of northern and southern aggression, the big idea of the Old Testament is autonomous protest against God's Word, followed by collapse. The big collapse occurs in the year 587, when Jerusalem is destroyed and the people exiled.

The prophets deliver hope, not in themselves, but in the God of grace, who forgives the law-exhausted failures of the people. This hope comes not only from the major prophets like Isaiah and Jeremiah but also from the minor prophets such as Habakkuk, Zechariah, Micah, Joel, and Hosea. Each of these prophets understands the fruitlessness of the law to amend their people's shattered existences. Each of them is forced into the corner of speaking grace, the complete book of new beginnings in the light of pathos and repentance. Their message, again and again, is heard by a remnant of the people. The Psalms, too, and sections of what we today call the "wisdom literature" release them from the law and into the favor of God's grace. The people hear a new song — not consistently, but often enough to provide hope.

The last stirrings in the Old Testament of this new song, the song of grace, occur in Daniel and in Malachi. These books affirm the great principle of promise. God will provide a grace that triumphs over his judgment, they say, and this grace has to do with a once and future king from God. He "will turn the hearts of parents to their children and the hearts of children to their parents" (Malachi 4:6). The "father problem" of the Old Testament, the unending ethical conflict between parent and child, will be healed at last. But this message is all a little vague. It is a little dreamy. It is all a little "hopeful."

One thing we know for sure from the prophets. The law did not effect what it demanded. It could not deliver what it mandated. The law on its own terms is a discredited thing by the end of the Old Testament. How could you say otherwise from the texts themselves? Failure to live it and failure to want to live it are the result of centuries of use. We do right to hear the Old Testament's gloomiest interpretation of human existence: "I, the Teacher, when king over Israel in Jerusalem, applied my mind to seek and to search out by wisdom all that is done under heaven; it is an unhappy business that God has given to human beings to be busy with. . . . What is crooked cannot be made straight, and what is lacking cannot be counted" (Ecclesiastes 1:12-15).

Law is true. It is also impotent and counterproductive. It produces its opposite.

Four Lives

The lives of Jesus, the Gospels, are interesting because they all tell the same story, the story of a single hero. Each of these lives provides its own reflected insight concerning him. Together, they provide a united view of him, a "check" on each of the individual views, because the Gospels are really one story told in four different voices.

The law ran out of energy during the Old Testament. Its battery acid spilled out on the roadway again and again. From the garden to the wilderness, from the judges to the prophets and the kings, the law proved unable to generate acquiescence and obedience. "Happy are those," announces Psalm 1. To which Malachi replies, "But who can stand when he appears?" (3:2). The whole of the Old Testament is a free-fall from original blessing, a plunge that is arrested at the moment of false hope in the possibility of willed obedience. Moral failure after moral failure tramps through the pages of Scripture. This failure is not just the fate of individuals. It is the fate of an elected nation. "If my people would only do thus and so, then I would restore, redeem, renew, relieve, reward. . . ." The sentence fades into an everlasting *et cetera.*

The Old Testament ends in defeat. We can agree that there is some hope in its end, a projected hope. There is the idea of a coming deliverer, who will save the people from their sins (Matthew 1:21). But this hope is a future thing, a maybe thing, and it is sadly shadowed by the great dark history of their past, a past of unending resentment and unfulfilled dreaming.

But Emmanuel does come (Matthew 1:23). He is born, and the law is both fulfilled in him and ended. How does this happen?

Jesus taught that the law is true diagnostically and in its entirety. Not once in the Gospels did he loosen the law of God. In fact, he tightened it (Matthew 5:19-20). Jesus said that an angry thought was tantamount to the criminal act of murder (Matthew 5:21-22). He asserted that a lustful fantasy is equivalent to adultery (Matthew 5:27-28). He allowed for no conditions, not one that would extenuate, rationalize, or excuse marital divorce (Matthew 5:31-32). Theologians sometimes call Jesus the *Mose Mosissime* ("the ultimate Moses"). He said that he came to fulfill and establish the rigor of the law right down to the dotting of its i's and the crossing of its t's (Matthew 5:17-18). When it comes down to it, Jesus was extremely interested in the law. Most of his polemics and debates took place against the Pharisees, who were regarded as consistent but merciless defenders of the law. Christ out-lawed the Pharisees (Matthew 5:20)! Yet he also flouted the law in such a public manner that it earned him instant controversy, intense resistance to his teaching, and finally the death of a martyred prophet.

On the one hand, Jesus spoke of the law as an instrument probing to the innermost reaches of the human will and inner mind. The law penetrates to the exact, inward motivation of a person. The law penetrates the external "dome" over a person's real life. It looks into the "whitewashed tombs" (Matthew 23:27). It calls sinners to account (Luke 5:32) and separates the living from the dead (Luke 16:19-31).

In the light of the law, all that men and women can do, declares Christ, is to repent (Matthew 3:2, concerning John the Baptist; Mark 1:15; Luke 13:3). Repentance is not the same thing as restitution or a changed heart. Repentance is felt sorrow, sorrow in your very marrow, for what you have been and done. Repentance not only covers shame at what you have done but also includes shame at who you are, as in the parable of the Pharisee and the tax collector (Luke 18:9-14). Repentance is not a disposition in relation to the future. It is a disposition in relation to your personal past.

Not long ago I read a newspaper article about an executive at Boeing. The reporter asked him to name the secret of his success, and he said, "There is nothing you can do about the past. The only thing you can do anything about is the future." Christ saw life differently. For Christ, the only thing you can do anything about is your past. God alone can deal with your future. If you have repented of your past, if you have taken an inventory of the full extent of hurt, victimhood, malice, and self-service that describe your achieved life, if you have said the one single needful word, "sorry," then that is all. There is nothing more. The future, which Paul would later call the "fruit of the Spirit," flows totally from the "sorry." The past resolved gives the present its only chance. The future is the Spirit's job.

How else can we explain Christ's one-line attraction to sinners, "I have come to call not the righteous but sinners" (Luke 5:32)? Unlike the Pharisees, who judged the world from the platform of the law, Christ ended the law for people who lived in its failure. Christ abrogated the law, and intentionally. He and his disciples picked corn on the Sabbath, and when they were challenged by the Pharisees, Jesus said, "The sabbath was made for man, not man for the sabbath" (Mark 2:27, RSV). He watched as forgiven people leapt into new skins and led new lives full of praise and love. This is because he embodied the acceptance that the law had denied them. He saw these people, such as the cleansed lepers (Matthew 8:2-3; Mark 1:40-42), exchange calcified skins of sublimation and depression for skins that contained the seeds of love's fruit. Against such natural and spontaneous fruit of the Spirit, such fruit as Mary Magdalene and Zacchaeus bore, there could be no law!

Jesus taught that the law's stranglehold on humanity was finished. I do not mean that Jesus was a "liberal" in the contemporary sense. I do not mean to say that Jesus cast off the law as simply one big and needless inhibitor of human potential. Not at all. I mean that Jesus recognized the inability of the law, which shows us exactly who we ought to be, to provide its own fulfillment. Christ did not say that the law is bad. He said instead that the law is wholly good. But most importantly, he said that the law is no skilled mechanic. It cannot fix what it has broken.

This great and actualized insight of Christ's ministry, which made his Galilean spring a unique moment of human emancipation, created the principle of compassion and the power of grace. Paul would soon put words onto the things Jesus did. Paul would articulate what in Christ's life was a blessing on the Magdalene, a touch to the leper, a lifting of the child, a pause at the blind man, an inconvenient conversation with a hypochondriac. Paul would put words on these actions. He would provide a way of thinking about Jesus' mode of doing.

But before that, before the interpretive brilliance of the apostle Paul, Jesus was required to put the law in the grave. He was forced — although he, being free unlike the rest of the human race, acquiesced to the forcing — to put his body on the stone table. He was forced to undertake the destruction of the law within the flesh and bones of the only thing he "had," his subjectivity. Christ had to answer personally to the law.

High Noon

When Christian theology affirms the "end of the law" (Romans 10:4), some people become nervous. They are afraid that such talk, talk of the end of the law's control over the human race, suggests *antinomianism.* That is a big word asserting that the law is bad. An "antinomian" is someone who is against the law. There is a lurking fear in Christianity — in life! — that grace is the opposite of law and will lead to license.

There is an excellent British movie entitled *The Day the Earth Caught Fire* (1961). In this movie, word gets out that the world is going to end because its orbit is taking it too close to the sun, and everybody "goes crazy." There are mad orgies in the streets, and London spirals down to total drunken chaos. These scenes capture English fears concerning the "end of the law." Are you saying, these fears inquire, that Christianity removes self-discipline and order from the human equation? Are you implying that Christians are free to do exactly what they like? Where does that lead? It must lead to Britney Spears and Jerry Springer!

The answer to these questions is No. This theology of everyday life is not saying that the law is bad. The law is good. God's law is good perfectly and describes the ideal human social environment. What I am saying, and what the Bible teaches and demonstrates, is that the law cannot deliver what it promises. We are made in such a way that we instinctually rebut and act against the law in all its forms. If someone tells me to do something, I immediately oppose it. It is my nature to do so. "Don't tell me what to do!" is a cry from the DNA of the human species.

It is not the content of the law that rankles. It is the mode of its address. We will not stand for it. Before the First World War, an ancestor of mine was threatened with being drafted into the German army. He apparently shot off one of his fingers to avoid it. Other men in his family emigrated to America so as not to be drafted. It would have been different if they had wanted to enlist, if the cause had been one in which they believed. But the law produced its opposite. This is the point about the law. Paul never tires of saying that the law is "holy and just and good" (Romans 7:12). But Paul also never tires of saying, "If a law had been given which could make alive, then righteousness would indeed come through the law" (Galatians 3:21).

Thus we arrive, in surveying the presence of law in the Bible, at High Noon. The High Noon of Jesus Christ's approach to the law of God occurs on Good Friday. The human race exists under judgment. Jesus spoke of a "baptism of fire" with which he was going to be baptized (Luke 12:49-50). He spoke with gravity of the wrath to come (Matthew 23:33, 38). He saw the people of Israel standing under the most imperative accusation for their historic and cyclical exclusion of the prophets (Matthew 23:29, 31, 34; Luke 11:48-51; 13:28). He spoke of his death as "a ransom for many" (Matthew 20:28; Mark 10:45). He spoke of his own personal "Passover" as his body given and his blood "poured out for many for the forgiveness of sins" (Matthew 26:28; Mark 14:24; Luke 22:19-20). Christ's grim assessment of the judged character of human performance came out again and again in his parables. To minimize the vicarious sacrificial nature of the death of Christ, the High Noon on Calvary when Christ faced God's irreducible law, is to miss the unifying drama of the Bible.

Observe that High Noon does not minimize the law, as people sometimes understand the gospel to be doing. That *would* be "antinomian." Rather, Christ's death maximizes the law. It states that death alone is sufficient to answer the accusation of God's perfect law.

We know this inside ourselves. I was trying once to please a secretary who worked in a church I was serving. I sensed that she did not like me and that she was probably comparing me to my predecessor, so I undertook to win her. I brought her little presents, tried to be funny, took her out to lunch, but no dice. The sour feeling remained. Then I tried to dress more like my predecessor. He had been a sharp dressed clergyman, and it is true that I was indifferent to my clothes. I asked my wife to help me dress better, and I actually started to look good. But the sour feeling remained. I tried every trick in my book to win over this woman, but no change. Then a member of the Vestry took me aside, kindly in fact, and said, "Look, as long as you're not him, she will never like you." That was the truth; I was the wrong man. She would have been satisfied only if I were to become someone else, someone specific, and also perfect, in her mind.

On another occasion, I was getting some heat from my colleagues in a theological seminary. It concerned a very small matter. I could not understand the vehemence of it, especially given the fact that I was new and they didn't know me yet. Then an outsider, a professional educator, said to me privately, "You don't understand. From their point of view, the only good dean is a former dean."

Those experiences were both instructive. Nothing I could do was sufficient to deter the accusing voice of judgment. The condemnation had less to do with any actions I might perform, "good" or "bad." The condemnation had to do with who I was. "I" was the problem.

This brings us to the heart and soul of the Bible's High Noon. Jesus Christ was our substitute. He "bore the sin of many" (Isaiah 53:12). I do not need a helper only. I need something more than an advocate. I certainly need a mediator when it comes to defending my life. But what I need the most is a substitute.

The High Noon of Scripture's story of the law involves a personal substitute by which the extreme accusation of the law against the human race is absorbed in its absolute and total character by an innocent person. This is the famous "once for all," the "righteous for the unrighteous" (1 Peter 3:18). Unless you take seriously the principle of substituted guilt to its full extent, then the death of Christ seems an incongruent and disproportionate sentence and solution.

Why did Christ die? He died to atone for the sins of the whole world. This idea will be developed later, for it is crucial to the logic and application of all Christian theology. For now it is enough to say that the High Noon of Christ involves a substitution for guilt, by which the accusation directed by the law against the imperfection of the human kingdom is taken off the many heads of the guilty and placed on the one head of the innocent.

This theological anchor draws criticism. Some say it is unfair. How can an innocent person bear the guilt of a criminal? It offends our sense of fairness. But it really doesn't! Rather, it asserts the unconditional necessity of the guilty being punished. It does not relieve the burden of this criminal guilt by denying it or attempting to lower its impact or significance. The substitutionary High Noon depicted in each of the four lives of Christ takes the weight of guilt seriously and loses not a crumb of its crushing substance. After all, if there is not a way out from moral guilt and judgment, what possible hope could people have? The alternative to the High Noon of moral substitution is despair, madness, and, most obviously, death.

Paul Taught What Jesus Did

One of my theological teachers was Ernst Käsemann. During the last few years of Käsemann's life, I lived in Tübingen, Germany, and was able to ask him many questions about the teaching of Paul. Käsemann had lived history, as a resister of the Nazi regime under Adolf Hitler, and had also taught history, as a theologian of early Christianity and especially of St. Paul. Käsemann had almost single-handedly initiated a view of Jesus of Nazareth that became known as the "second quest for the historical Jesus." But his governing interest was in the theology of Paul, within the context of the earliest forms of Christianity in the Mediterranean world. One of Käsemann's best maxims — and he coined several — was this: Paul taught what Jesus did.

Käsemann believed that Christ upset the religious teachers of his time and place because he understood himself to have authority over the law. Käsemann underlined Christ's welcoming the repentant, his actual encouragement of former law-breakers to join his movement. Käsemann saw Christ as inaugurating a new dimension of human experience in which the binding and controlling power of law, which he saw in almost demonic terms, was ended.

This particular German historian of earliest Christianity saw an acute discontinuity between the Judaism of Jesus' day and the teaching that Jesus himself presented. In the exorcisms of Christ, in the authority of Christ over demons, Käsemann observed that Christ personally ushered in a new era. Käsemann made a point of calling Jesus "the first Christian" and broke with his more famous teacher, Rudolf Bultmann, on this point. Bultmann had argued that Jesus of Nazareth was a Jew, theologically speaking. It was only the resurrected Christ that Bultmann regarded as a Christian. Käsemann could not have disagreed more.[3]

I believe the New Testament sees Jesus as the offender of custom and tradition and the embodiment of forgiveness to all who have broken the law. He comes to fulfill the law (Matthew 5:17) by quenching the attack on the human spirit that the law unleashes through the ferocity of its diagnosis. Christ died on the cross having interpreted his death beforehand, at the Last Supper, as an atonement for human sin. Only atonement could make the death of Christ understandable and palatable to his students and followers. Otherwise it constituted suicide for them. If his death had not counted for something extraordinarily important, their cause would have been a mighty hoax, a wincing joke to the world.

It is Paul who interpreted what Jesus offered in his life and death. Sacrificial terms come to the fore in Paul, words like "redemption" and "atonement" (Romans 3:24-25). Legal concepts such as justification and acquittal (Romans 5:16, 18), taken from the courtroom, also appear in his letters. The climax of Paul's thought on the law and its relation to Christ occurs in Romans 10:4: "Christ is the end of the law so that there may be righteousness for everyone who believes." What Paul means is that Christ's death signals the end of law in its power to accuse *(lex semper accusat)*. The death of Christ renders anachronistic all attempts to satisfy the law by means of performance or achievement.[4] Christ is the end of merit.[5]

Everything else fails. Nothing is good enough. As C. F. Alexander said it in her old hymn, "There Is a Green Hill Far Away": "There was no other good enough to pay the price of sin/He only could unlock the

3. For a summary and discussion of Käsemann's relationship to Bultmann, see my *Die Rechtfertigungslehre Ernst Käsemanns* (Stuttgart: Calwer Verlag, 1996), pp. 105ff. There is nothing in English yet concerning the details of Käsemann's break with his teacher.

4. I realize that some interpreters, especially within the school of thought known as "the new perspective on Paul," wish to see the Greek word for "end" here, which is *telos,* as meaning "fulfillment" or "consummation," rather than "conclusion" or "cessation." But the context requires "conclusion" or "cessation."

5. Joachim Jeremias, *New Testament Theology* (New York: Charles Scribner's Sons, 1971), p. 217.

door of heav'n and let us in." Mrs. Alexander understood what St. Paul taught about what Jesus did. Paul envisioned the defeat of Christ as the transfer of a massive, shared guilt, one that is equally distributed within and among the human race. He envisioned Christ's death as a victory. It was the victory of substitution.

Others have wished to interpret the cross differently. Some have seen it as a paradoxical statement of the power that resides in the acceptance of defeat, in voluntary weakness. This is a powerful idea as well as true to life. Some have seen it as God's defeat of the devil within the matrix of a stratagem. This so-called "Christus victor" interpretation is a head-trip, a sort of fantasy that sounds good until you look for concrete examples of it in everyday life. "Christus victor" is the "Harry Potter" among the theories concerning the death of Christ.

Others have accepted the legal language and paradigm of Paul's writing about that High Noon on Good Friday, but they have argued that it is just a partial reading of Paul, a "subsidiary crater" within a much larger landscape. One can certainly discover in Paul a few other manners of speech concerning the death of Christ in relation to the law. But these other languages are simply vestiges of what all preachers do: find as many metaphors and illustrations as you possibly can, in order to cast your net to as wide an audience as possible.

The ground floor of Paul's theology is Romans 10:4: "Christ is the end of the law." This ground floor is held up by great bricks of atomic substance in the following words from the third chapter: "For 'no human being will be justified in [God's] sight' by deeds prescribed by the law, for through the law comes the knowledge of sin. But now, apart from law, the righteousness of God has been disclosed, and is attested by the law [in the five books of Moses] and the prophets" (verses 20-21).

Paul taught what Jesus did. Given the total inability of the people it oppresses to effect their own freedom, the end of the law comes through the instrumentality of one man's sacrifice of substitution.

St. John the Revelator

Everything I have said so far is broad-brush. It lays the foundation for a systematic theology of everyday life that is grounded in the principle of grace over and against the principle of law. This one question — What is the law? — is one of the largest conceptual questions in the world. What I am doing here is summarizing the direction of the Bible's teaching. But short is good. We groan under great masses of words these days. Everyone wants to express himself or herself. I discover that almost no one actually wants to be brief. This has something to do with self-assertion and the bottomless pit of our human search for identity. When I ask clergy to keep their sermons brief, they look at me like I am curbing their right to exist. But short is good. So this is a short overview of the Bible's use of the principle of divine law.

But we are not quite finished. St. John of Patmos, the mighty Revelator, has something to add to this picture. His voice is the last we hear in the New Testament. At the end of the 2005 *War of the Worlds,* Ray Ferrier (Tom Cruise) tries to arrest a soldier's attention. He wants to point out a good, if grisly, omen. He sees flocks of vultures closing in on fallen alien tripods inside of which their pilots are either dead or dying. These vultures are come to feast on dead predators from Outer Space, and they signify deliverance. They signify the end of the alien extermination of the human planet. The aliens have been laid waste by earthly microbes.

There are similar scenes in the classic finish to the Bible. St. John of Patmos wrote the Revelation, a phantasmagoric portrait of the end of the world, from the vantage point of exile on a tiny island off the coast of Turkey to which he had fled in order to escape martyrdom at the hands of the "politically correct" Roman government. The Roman government's sense of its sovereignty was repelled by the religion that claimed unique authority. It could not stand the religion of Christ. In the service of tolerance (for all religions were tolerated provided they saluted the imperial power in some formal way), Christianity was vomited out. During this period, John, who had been a disciple of Christ and had become a kind of senior statesman of the Christians at Ephesus, wrote his second big book. He envisaged the death of the Roman Empire, with waves of blood accompanied by birds of prey (Revelation 19:17-21).

What is striking within the Revelation of John for this discussion of the law is that it insists on the unconditional judgment of sin and law-breaking (2:23; 6:16-17; 14:9-11; 16:4-7) as well as the triumph of God's grace and mercy (3:12; 7:16-17; 21:4-6; 22:17). No lawbreakers are allowed within the New Jerusalem (21:27), and there are no tears, no regret, and no mourning there (21:4). The guilt of the world is washed away by the blood of the Lamb (7:14), and the effects of guilt are refused any final home.

The Revelation of John is filled with judgment. It abreacts the wrath of God in the blood of the Lamb and then re-creates the human world into a judged and utopian place. There is nothing gradual about this transformation, no idea of process or progress. Human malice is judged and barred from entry — end of story. Cleansed spirits, to whom the law has done its worst but whose accusation has been swallowed by the one Substitute, populate God's enduring city.

Schoolchildren used to have to memorize Vachel Lindsay's poem "General William Booth Enters into Heaven." It is a vivid and rhythmic combination of lampoon (of the Salvation Army) and mercy (to the refuse of society). It richly sums up the message of the Bible about the law. It truncates nothing, takes no shortcuts in its demand for full repentance from sin on the part of sinners. Yet it is at the same time pure grace. To its final view of human destiny this book will return again and again:

General William Booth Enters into Heaven

[To be sung to the tune of *The Blood of the Lamb*
with indicated instrument]

I.

[*Bass drum beaten loudly.*]
Booth led boldly with his big bass drum —
(Are you washed in the blood of the Lamb?)
The Saints smiled gravely and they said: "He's come,"
(Are you washed in the blood of the Lamb?)

Walking lepers followed, rank on rank,
Lurching bravos from the ditches dank,
Drabs from the alleyways and drug fiends pale —
Minds still passion-ridden, soul-powers frail: —
Vermin-eaten saints with mouldy breath,
Unwashed legions with the ways of Death —
(Are you washed in the blood of the Lamb?)

[*Banjoes.*]
Ev'ry slum had sent its half-a-score
The world round over. (Booth had groaned for more.)
Every banner that the wide world flies
Bloomed with glory and transcendent dyes.
Big voiced lasses made their banjoes bang,
Tranced, fanatical they shrieked and sang: —
"Are you washed in the blood of the Lamb?"
Hallelujah! It was queer to see
Bull-necked convicts with that land make free.
Loons with trumpets blowed a blare, blare, blare
On, on upward thro' the golden air!
(Are you washed in the blood of the Lamb?)

II.

[*Bass drum slower and softer.*]
Booth died blind and still by Faith he trod,
Eyes still dazzled by the ways of God.
Booth led boldly, and he looked the chief,
Eagle countenance in sharp relief,
Beard a-flying, air of high command
Unabated in that holy land.

[*Sweet flute music.*]
Jesus came from out the court-house door,
Stretched his hands above the passing poor.

Booth saw not, but led his queer ones there
Round and round the mighty court-house square.
Then in an instant all that blear review
Marched on spotless, clad in raiment new.
The lame were straightened, withered limbs uncurled
And blind eyes opened on a new, sweet world.[6]

Law in Society

Theology has something to say about ethical and moral activity in society. This is obvious to a religious believer, but it is not obvious in the "public square" today. Within the public square, it is commonly stated that law exists independent of divine or theological sanction. Thus in the running controversy over displays of the Ten Commandments on public properties in the United States, one school of thought seems happy to see eight of the ten displayed, but not the two (or possibly three, depending on your translation) that invoke God. "Thou shalt not murder" is fine, just don't preface it by invoking God. Cannot the law and its principles of social equity and fairness exist independent of an external, transcendent authority?

Theology has something important to say about the social or civil injunctions of the law. This is because the Bible understands human resistance to it! The Bible knows about the indelible character of human resistance to being told what to do. By "resistance," I mean the perpetual tale of personal resistance to any form of address that involves demand. The law, even the law when it is thoroughly unhinged from theology, accuses, and it accuses always. The principles of law in secular dress are not any different from their theological framing in the way that they are *heard*. "Don't envy" is just as unpalatable to the concupiscent side of me as the theologically grounded, "God says . . ."

If I am told to drive 45 miles per hour on the Ohio River Boulevard

6. Vachel Lindsay, *General William Booth Enters into Heaven and Other Poems* (New York: Macmillan, 1917), pp. 1-4.

when it seems obvious to me that 60 m.p.h. is perfectly reasonable, then I will resent the limit as set. I will constantly fantasize about a higher speed, even when I do not act this out. I reason to myself, "This speed limit is obviously designed for the sake of small townships that are hungry, are *dying*, for revenue." Then I start to dicker in my mind: "50 is fair, 55 is definitely fair." Then I see a poor fellow pulled over by a patrol car. And I seethe and obey the rule. But is my heart in it? Do I inwardly grasp the reason for this limit?

How different things are at a busy intersection along the Florida Panhandle beach road where I see two patrol cars parked on different sides of the road *twenty-four hours a day*, their roof lights turning every second! I ask someone why those cars are always there. It turns out that several people have been killed there in the last two years. In fact, a month ago two high-school cheerleaders were on their way home from their after-school jobs when they were run down at that intersection by a drunk driver. Both young women were killed. My eyes tear up. Bless those patrol cars. Bless those officers who have to sit there in four-hour shifts. Bless those poor innocent lives taken in a second by a drunkard. Theology illuminates this comparison. Theology can serve to shed light on the law that accuses as well as the law that lives out of loss. Let me explain.

The Social Characteristics of Law

Christian theology teaches that law has two outstanding characteristics: (1) it makes no exceptions and is therefore entirely merciless; and (2) it is incapable of producing the motivation to obey it. This is what Paul taught and Jesus did.

On the one hand, law takes the whole loaf. It mandates the whole person, the submission of the entire human being to the whole divine demand. Immanuel Kant understood this when he posited the "categorical imperative": I ought never to act except in such a way that I can also will that my maxim should become a universal law *(Groundwork of the Metaphysic of Morals)*. His idea was that anything a person does that has moral significance must be universal rather than situational or contextual. Moral action of any kind has to be repeatable in every conceivable place and time. This is a biblical way of looking at the law, because Kant saw law as non-contextual, as having divine and final character. One cannot extenuate law or rationalize law or try to adapt law to fit new conditions. Kant's law, like Moses' Decalogue, is absolute.

Its universality makes the law into a hard engine of human control. The problem here is not the law's inflexibility, which is right and good. The problem is its second characteristic, its inability to produce the obedience it requires. As I tried to demonstrate with speed limits, we instinctively fight the law. We use a thousand arguments to criticize it and flout it. Speed limits do not come naturally. You see this concretely in the driving manners of many young men and women. They are incapable of sticking to them. The 25 m.p.h. sign is a red flag.

The law is a red flag. In society it does nothing to control the "theater of blood" (Vincent Price) that makes the world go round, save by rigid police restraint. It is also defeated by the inward resistance, which we have already plotted in Scripture, to anything like a social "ought."

Here is another example. The whole world tells you not to smoke. Right now it is almost the worst thing you can do, except maybe hunt a fox. To smoke is to alienate and somehow actually intend to kill the people around you. People actually believe, and believe passionately, that you can contract cancer from cigarette smoke fifty yards away.

I am not a smoker. But I am tempted to become one now. Smoking is tempting because everybody tells me not to do it. I drive down city streets in February and see groups of workers on their breaks, smoking in the bitter wind. The chance of these people catching pneumonia and dying is about ten times the danger they pose in the short term to others or to themselves. When you see those poor, huddled bands of banished office workers, it makes you want to stop the car and jump out and join them. I want to become a smoker because the world calls it anathema.

This is the failure of the law in society. It cannot alter anything. Just review the headlines in the newspaper. We are always seeking to bring under control some problem in our society. It could be a drug like methamphetamine or ecstasy. It could be low SAT performance by high school boys. It could be single-parent families or pregnancy among very young girls. It could be AIDS in central Africa. It could be repeat-offender child molesters. It could be suicide bombers in English cities. You name it. The big problems of society vary from generation to generation.

I happen to like "exploitation" monster movies from the 1950s. *I Was a Teenage Werewolf* (1957) is an excellent little movie. The social problem it seeks to unmask with the help of the monster-movie genre is "juvenile delinquency." No one talks about "juvenile delinquency" anymore. In the 1950s, many people wrote impassioned articles about the kind of man they thought James Dean was. (There is a touching innocence, by the standards of the Columbine High School massacre or *South Park,* to *I Was a Teenage Werewolf.* The teenage rage it unmasks is just an old-fashioned aggression that comes of inert fathers and needy unsatisfied youth.) Could the law deal with "juvenile delinquency" in the 1950s? Is the law today sufficient to control the inbuilt aggression of adolescent boys? It never has been, and it never will be.

The law in society is a double message. It calls for perfection but stimulates rebellion. It creates the very thing it wants to control. The law is a dud. Social reformers have seen this forever. They have seen terrible ills and have worked tirelessly to correct them. They have been appalled by injustices and done everything to challenge them. Yet year after year, one injustice gives way to another.

Consider Bolivia. The U.S. government has helped to stamp out the coca-growing culture there in order to hinder the drug trade in our home country. But the result of this extermination of one bad thing has been another bad thing: the complete collapse of the Bolivian peasant economy. This collapse has brought down the government, tied all social hope to repossessing foreign-owned natural gas and other resources (the sale of which only hastens global warming), and created terrible despair in an already despairing nation. The heart of the law is neutral: it is an "ought" that stimulates its opposite. It is a taskmaster that never creates peace or satisfaction in the life of men and women. You can see why reincarnation is such an appealing bid: maybe in another life I could finally appease the "ought."

Law and the Motivation of Loss

Christianity provides an essential insight into the powerlessness of law to effect change. It is the insight that demand always creates resistance. It is a Newtonian principle. Human resistance to law is in direct proportion to the strength of the demand.

The former Soviet Union is in a shambles. The birth rate has sunk to almost zero; vast sectors of the country are rusting and rotting; violent crime is almost everywhere; the few who are rich are getting richer while the many poor are getting poorer; and terrorism in the former Soviet Union finds no deterrent. But only two decades ago the country was under lock and key. The Communist Party and its members held absolute control. There was no freedom and no expression of dissent. Anything free was underground, suppressed entirely.

When this absolute law was removed and the Party's hold collapsed, the real facts of suppressed rage, chaos, and dispiritedness emerged. They burst out. The result was collapse. Many Russian cities now have a "Blade Runner" feel. The only sure way to get things done is to have a Mafia boss help you.

I use this example to illustrate that the chaos is in direct proportion to the degree of suppression — the degree of law — that kept things "under control." Another formula: If you add to the degree of suppression the length of time for which it was in effect, you can roughly calculate the degree of rebellion that surfaces. Socially speaking, the law is both inept and finally creative of the very behavior it seeks to amend.

Christianity now brings a second insight to bear: the insight of grace. Grace is the point of this book. But we are not quite there yet. Right now it is enough to recognize the inflated claims of the law. The police cars on twenty-four-hours-a-day duty at the tragic intersection on the Florida Panhandle, on the other hand, convey the seed of what I shall say is the theology of everyday life, the fact that only grace creates the fruit and consequence of a law-abiding life. When you pass the patrol cars at that intersection, with their unfailing lights, it is not the law you see. You see the response that a cruciform loss created, the loss of two young girls on their way home from after-school jobs. The police cars at the intersection are in fact *not* the expression of law. They are the expression of love issuing from a broken heart.

This point is vital. On the one hand, law creates resistance to itself. On the other hand, grace, which we will define next, creates the fruits and consequences of love. These fruits (the expression is from Paul's letter to the Galatians 5:22-23) look like the law's requirement. They come, however, from a different source. They look like two police cars watching every single civilian car creep around the corner, just waiting for an infraction. But they are not. They are a whole community's labor of love emanating from deepest grief. They are not resented. They are not bargained against. They are not "authorities" to elbow up against. They are, oddly and beautifully, expressions of the grace of God.

Law in Everyday Life

Before we observe the vitiating effects of law in everyday life, two other ideas have to be introduced. They are vital for this argument, and they are vital for understanding the way Christianity works.

The first idea is the *dynamic or operational principle according to which Christianity works.* This book is not about the metaphysical or philosophical ideas of Christianity. It is not about the so-called "doctrine of God." It is not about the Trinity as a normative description of God's unity in plurality. This book is not about anything related to essences or pure being or ontology or anything like that. This book is about how Christianity *works.* I am not suggesting that we be anti-intellectual. Nor am I saying something experiential at the expense of something reflective. What I am saying is that the gospel of Christ is a dynamic or operational principle.

It is perfectly fine to say that God is such and such a thing, or such and such a person. But the value of the idea is in its application. I am interested in how God's perfection affects us. In other words, I am interested in God as the source of law. What is the word that God's character as lawgiver says, in experienced reality, when we hear that he in himself has eyes "too pure to behold evil" (Habakkuk 1:13)? What is the effect of that? (It is dreadful.) When, on the other hand, we hear that God's Son "welcomes sinners" (Luke 15:2; 5:29-32; 19:7), what is the effect of that? (It is glowing.)

The gospel of Christ has to do with guilt and with the ashamed response of imperfect people to a perfect God. The gospel represents a transaction involving guilt and the shame of being caught in the reality of human being and human action, which is powerfully self-deceived. The gospel is about the relation between law, which is crushing, stunning, and wrecking, and grace, which is restoring, repairing, and re-creative. The gospel is *not* about substance or matter, the chemistry of divine essence and its impartation. The gospel *is* about force and effect, punishment and rehabilitation. The focus of this book is on the gospel, the leverage of Christianity in relation to human resistance and brokenness, and not on the creeds, which affirm conceptual truths concerning God. The focus of this theology of everyday life is on how Christianity works.

The second idea that needs introduction now is the relation between "the Law" and laws, the relation between God's law absolutely given and understood, and the infinite forms of this law that are embodied in numberless "laws" or standards under which people suffer. This second idea in understanding the influence of law in everyday human experience is *the unity of God's law with human laws and standards.* This is an important point that some resist. This is because they find that it puts God's Ten Commandments on a par with human standards and thus brings God down to our level.

What we have to do in order to relate the concept of divine unbending law to human experience is to speak from analogy. The point is an old one: you cannot understand God, who is not understandable to human beings on his own terms, without reference to human (thus accessible) experience. I say this without apology. You cannot understand God apart from perceived, true, real life experience. Without connecting God's law, for example, with the innumerable "laws" that people place on themselves, God's law is a concept. It is an abstraction.

We can state this as a thesis: the principle of the divine demand for perfection upon the human being is reflected concretely in the countless internal and external demands that human beings devise for themselves.

In practice, the requirement of perfect submission to the commandments of God is exactly the same as the requirement of perfect submission to the innumerable drives for perfection that drive everyday people's crippled and crippling lives. The commandment of God that we honor our father and mother is no different *in impact*, for example, than the commandment of fashion that a woman be beautiful or the commandment of culture that a man be boldly decisive and at the same time utterly tender.

Take the idea that a man should be decisive as well as outwardly expressive of his feelings, or that he should lead *and* be the passive sidekick for a strong woman. You may be thinking that this trivializes law by equating it with ever-changing, culturally conditioned "laws." But I am saying that they are the same thing.

How is this possible? How can Sinai law, with its ennobling demand for personal and social rectitude, be equated with the world of fashion or the world of psycho-sexual politics? But that is my point: they function exactly the same way in human experience. Men become bowed down and paralyzed in fact by demands from the other half of the human race, and women are utterly freighted by the conflicting demands to be a perfect professional and the mother of dazzling children. The weight of these laws is the same as the weight of the sublime moral law. Law, whether biblical and universally stated or contextual and contemporarily phrased, operates in one way. *Law reduces its object, the human person, to despair.*

This theology of everyday life makes no distinction between the law of God and the laws of human interaction individually felt and socially expressed. Law and laws constitute a unity in their effect!

Why is this idea resisted? It is resisted because it brings the faith of Christians too close to home. If the demand of God has to do directly with the subduing and depressing demands of one's father or mother, or the guilt one feels in relation to one's siblings, or the high pressures of a job or a boss, then this Christianity might actually touch somebody. It might actually relate to people. Someone near me commented about a devout evangelical Christian in her family: "She is wholly sold out to the gospel just so long as it doesn't come anywhere near her real life."

This book is an attempt to bring the gospel of law and grace into direct encounter with the real and tangible stress of living a life within the swooning, human world. In order to look at the way law makes itself present in everyday life, and especially in everyday family relationships, it is an unconditional prelude to affirm the unity of God's law and human standards, whatever they are. I am not talking about the material claims of Christianity regarding the nature of God, except in their consequence for operational experience. I am talking about how it works. A theology of everyday life perceives that the pressure to be a "good Christian" and the pressure, for example, to be a "good husband" are the same in their effect.

Christianity works through the law embodied within the inward human laws that cause stress and guilt. St. Paul says this in Romans 2:14-16:

> When Gentiles, who do not possess the law, do instinctively what the law requires, these, though not having the law, are a law to themselves. They show that what the law requires is written on their hearts, to which their own conscience also bears witness; and their conflicting thoughts will accuse or perhaps excuse them on the day when, according to my gospel, God, through Jesus Christ, will judge the secret thoughts of all.

This passage has given much concern to people who wish to distinguish absolutely between God's law and the laws of human beings. But Paul is saying exactly what I am trying to say: everyone carries laws within themselves. There is no core distinction between the laws of the non-Mosaic Gentiles and the law of the Mosaic Jews. Inner conscience, inner stresses of demand, are the same thing as God's law that requires perfect submission.

The law plays out in startling and appalling ways in everyday life. Every time a person feels "uncomfortable" before somebody in his or her family; every time a grown child bristles at a parent's "advice"; every time a husband tries to change his wife; every time a Christian tries to "speak the truth in love" in order to straighten out a friend — it is the same old story. It is the law in its wounding persona.

I think we could go so far as to say that the law is the origin of every clash that takes place between people in their emotional life. I hear it time and time again: "He is judging me"; "She is always trying to change me"; "I wish they would just take me as I am"; "If he only knew what I am really like, or where I have really been in my life, he would say 'forget it, this whole thing is a mistake.'" Ask yourself, what poisoned the well between you and this other person? When did things start to go sour between her and you? At what point did you begin no longer to feel at home with him? I would ask whether the break is not almost always the result of some form of judgment.

In its devastating impact on love, God's law is not a sublime thing. It turns love into a duty. It imperils the freedom of love in favor of doing something we are supposed to do. Again, ask yourself: When in that relationship did I soar in my love? Did it have anything to do with the "ought"? It never does. The relationship was elated when I loved her from a full heart, when I held nothing back. I needed to hold nothing back. I gave my whole self to her from the heart, and she did to me.

You see this in marriages. Marriages continually return to points of contention that arose in the earliest days of the relationship. They continually come back, on the minus side, to points of contempt and withholding that were on the docket from the start. Conversely, in order to be restored, marriages have to return to that "first love," to the moment of recognition that got it started in the first place. This is usually a point of physical contact or breakthrough, but behind this contact was some sort of deeper embrace. It was grace.

The bar to grace, and almost always the prelude to it, was the law. One's problems with other people have to do with the threat of accusation, with what we can safely call the "no confidence" problem. That was the point of the law. One felt awkward, or untalented, or just out of sync with the "in crowd." It was all law, like the Sissy Spacek character in the film *Carrie* (1976). Carrie is an extreme wallflower, ruthlessly teased and hoaxed. She is teased by the prom queens and by the "jocks" in her class. Her plight is all the more poignant in the light of her mother's evangelical Christianity, which is law-based and even snaps to the point of psychosis. Carrie's pathetic story is a parable of human laws intersecting with divine law, at least as interpreted by her and her mother.

Carrie's vengeance, on the other hand, is in direct proportion to the degree of law that has stunted her life. In short, everyone gets murdered. Her wrath is in proportion to the degree to which her life has been maimed by the law.

Later, I will describe the operation of grace in singleness, in marriage, with children, with parents, and with siblings. For now, it is enough to say that the law dispossesses love in every place to which it speaks. Naturally the *intent* of the law is to move us to goodness. In a sense, the intent of Carrie's law was to move her to beauty and poise and to becoming queen of the high-school prom. The intent of her mother's law was to move her toward sanctity before God. In both cases, the law backfired. It always does. Law creates the opposite of what it intends to create.

Can you not detect this in yourself? You want with everything in you to see that your child is happy in his or her marriage, fulfilled in his or her work, protected in his or her happiness. You aim to control that. You start out as a parent in high hopes of controlling the environment of the child. But your control is resisted. (If it isn't, you haven't noticed.) Control gives birth to its opposite. So many cases of extreme adolescent rage I have observed in ministry, so many cases of suicidal behavior among teenagers in relation to eating, have issued from a "type A," controlling home. Both in theology and in everyday life, the law results in its distorted underside: resentment, passive-aggressive behavior, protest, and hospitalization.

The Curse of the Law

The law downs that soaring airplane which carries every aspiration for human freedom. Law is the great depressant. Let me repeat, it is not a depressant because it is wrong in itself. Law depresses because it stimulates the opposite thing to that which it intends. In a recent book by the comedian Robert Klein (*The Amorous Busboy of Decatur Avenue: A Child of the Fifties Looks Back,* 2005), the author takes a sentimental journey into his old neighborhood in the Williamsburg section of New York. He recalls a sign on the side of a building that read, "Absolutely No Ball Playing Allowed." Klein observes that the sign's existence was the absolute red flag provoking all young boys in the neighborhood to bat every conceivable projectile against it. The sign stimulated mass attack.

The law is like that. But there is something more to its atrocity. The law is actually a curse. The "cursing" characteristic of law, a squeamish, shocking word, is expressed by St. Paul in the letter to the Galatians: "For all who rely on the works of the law are under a curse; for it is written, 'Cursed is everyone who does not observe and obey all the things written in the book of the law.' . . . Christ redeemed us from the curse of the law by becoming a curse for us — for it is written, 'Cursed is everyone who hangs on a tree'" (Galatians 3:10, 13). Paul is drawing on two images from the book of Deuteronomy (27:11-26 and 21:22-23), in which a curse is pronounced on all persons who do not fulfill all the requirements of the law, and the public exposure of a hanged man or a crucified man constitutes a curse on the man.

What is a curse? It is a malicious prayer or imprecation intended to put someone's whole life and everything in it under a dark cloud, the evil eye of a steady pitiless fate. In Greek tragedy, mortals and their offspring are cursed when they offend the gods. The children of such mortals, and their children's children, are sentenced forever to their irresistible fate. When you see the word "curse," think of Medea and Jason. She hated him so much that she poisoned her children to spite him.

This is the curse of the law, its double-barreled shot of malignant power. It curses even when the recipient of the law is impotent to obey its commands.

St. Paul does not leave us there. He moves in Galatians from the law's darkest curse to "the blessing of Abraham [that] might come to the Gentiles" (3:14). But we cannot proceed there flatly or glibly. We have to stay with the curse, the curse of the law. For us, who cannot "observe and obey all the things written in the book of the law," there is not the cursing in words, but rather the "spider-pit scene" in *King Kong* (1933), the censored footage that depicts a group of sailors who have been shaken into a deep crevasse being eaten by giant crab-like spiders. The law throws you off any degree of poise or balance you may have achieved. It makes a mockery of the very idea of achievement. It slams you down into a mudhole and leaves you there without any hope of getting out, at the mercy of giant spider-creatures that feast upon you in their own time.

The law is a curse. It doesn't just knock you down; it kicks you while you are down. Moreover, the law is a curse for all people, non-believers and believers. Christians suffer under it just as much as non-believers and vice versa.

Without grace, law has no future. Its future is nothing more than total immurement within a mud-hole or some kind of wild flight. The law, of God and of men and women, of super-ego and depressive reaction — the law of God in operational unity with the "laws" of inner space — has no future. On its own terms, the law has no future.

Side Bar: Is This Antinomianism?

Before moving forward to define grace, and grace specifically in relation to law, an objection has to be faced. Whenever I say "the law has no future" or observe the impotence of law to create the virtues it requires, including for Christians, objections start to fly. These objections claim that such a negative gloss on law as I am suggesting is antinomian. "Antinomianism" is the formal word for any teaching that is critical of law or undermines or overturns the law. Antinomianism is regarded as the opposite of law and order, which would turn a religion such as Christianity into an excuse for "license," which usually means sexual libertinism and promiscuity, not to mention drug use, thievery, casual violence à la Mad Max, "Girls Gone Wild," and a total breakdown of law and order. It is safe to say that whenever grace is preached in relation to the law, preachers of grace are — wrongly — labeled "antinomian." Ironically, being accused of antinomianism is a sort of badge of honor for those who preach the doctrine of grace, because this reaction means that the doctrine of grace is hitting home. The accusation means that grace is making law-bound people uncomfortable.

Nevertheless, what I am stating here concerning the law is not antinomian! Christianity on the understanding espoused here, which I believe is St. Paul's in principle and Christ Jesus' in action, is the way by which God's law comes to expression and fulfillment in life. It is not the opposite of that. What we have seen all along is that the law is "holy and just and good" (Romans 7:12). What the law requires is exactly what men and women need in order to be wise, happy, and secure. But the law cannot pull this off. The problem with the law is not its substance. The problem with the law is its instrumentality. The law is not up to the task it sets for itself. If the law says, "Jump," I sit. If it says, "Run," I walk. If it says, "Honor your father and mother," I move . . . to Portland. If it says, "Do not covet" (Romans 7:7-8), I spend all day on the Home Shopping Channel.

To see into the failure of the law to instill its good within human beings is not to be antinomian. It is rather to see the character of law as what we today call a "set-up for failure." The law is a set-up for failure. This is true despite the fact that the law is right in everything it asks.

Only this way can you understand the many times Paul had to defend himself against the charge of antinomianism. He observed the intrinsic insufficiency of law to change people. Yet he still believed in the rightness of the changes that the law presses on us all. In New Testament religion, questions should never be posed in relation to the law's content, but only in relation to the law's capacity to bring its content to expression.

Christianity's insight of unfathomable weight is that we have to look for another means for the law to work. There must be another means for it to accomplish what it purposes: the happiness, goodness, patience, and kindness to which it aspires. On its own terms, law is a failure and possesses not a second of a future. It has no shelf-life. On the other hand, in relation to God's Good News of a legally judged and dead man, the law has the brightest future in the world. As the pop group Timbuk 3 put it in 1986, "The Future's So Bright, I Gotta Wear Shades."

What Is Grace?

A short definition of grace is hard to find. "Unmerited favor" is the classic one, but "favor" sounds old-fashioned. "Undeserved love" is another try, but then, what love is really deserved? The minute "deserving" comes into it, the romance and emotion, all the feeling, melt away. A jawbreaker definition of grace is the old anagram that defines grace as "**G**od's **R**edemption **A**t **C**hrist's **E**xpense." Don't expect to get too far when you use that one!

What is grace? Grace is love that seeks you out when you have nothing to give in return. Grace is love coming at you that has nothing to do with you. Grace is being loved when you are unlovable. It is being loved when you are the opposite of loveable. The cliché definition of grace is "unconditional love." It is a true cliché, for it is a good description of the thing. It just sounds a little 1970s (as in "Have a Nice Day!"). Yet the words are apt.

Let's go a little further. Grace is a love that has nothing to do with you, the beloved. It has everything and only to do with the lover. Grace is irrational in the sense that it has nothing to do with weights and measures. It has nothing to do with my intrinsic qualities or so-called "gifts" (whatever they may be). It reflects a decision on the part of the giver, the one who loves, in relation to the receiver, the one who is loved, that negates any qualifications the receiver may personally hold. In 1965 Joe Meek produced a would-be pop single that was sung by Bobby Rio and The Revelles and was entitled "Value for Love." It was a great tune, but, like almost everything Joe Meek produced, it only grazed the Top Thirty. The lyrics were wildly false. The singer keeps telling the girl she should go for him because he is "good value for love." He is "worth" her falling for him. Sure, Bobby Rio! That line never works. It never will. It is all weights and measures. Grace is *one-way love.* That is the definition for this book. Grace is one-way love.

The one-way love of grace is the essence of any lasting transformation that takes place in human experience. You can find this out for yourself by taking a simple inventory of your own happiness, or the moments of happiness you have had. They have almost always had to do with some incident of love or belovedness that has come to you from someone outside yourself when you were down. You felt ugly or sinking in confidence, and somebody complimented you, or helped you, or spoke a kind word to you. You were at the end of your rope and someone showed a little sympathy. This is the message of Otis Redding's immortal 1962 song, "Try a Little Tenderness."

Later in the book I shall offer several illustrations of how grace works, with children and with husbands and wives and in singleness and with parents and with brothers and sisters. It is true in life that grace, one-way love, has the power to turn despair into hope. It is almost always some form of grace, some outside source of unexpected and unhoped for compassion and kindness, that creates the change from discouragement and despair to endurance and perseverance. Grace as one-way love is thus the opposite of law. Law depresses and incites. Grace enlivens and enables.

Grace is one-way love. Take an inventory of yourself. Watch other people about whose happiness you care. You will see it over and over: one-way love lifts up. One-way love cures. One-way love transforms. It is the change agent of life.

Grace in the New Testament

To understand grace in the Bible, we need to begin with the New Testament. This is because Christians see the shape of grace as being uniquely visible in the New Testament character of Christ. After the New Testament picture of God's grace in Christ has been scanned, we shall go back to the Old Testament and see where similar pictures of grace emerge within the biography of Israel.

What is grace in the New Testament? The phrase "one-way love," which is an attempt to put into simple words an idea that eludes quick description, could be misunderstood. It could be misunderstood as a love that is not returned or that exists in no relation to the response it craves. It could be understood as unrequited love.

What the phrase points to is the fact that love, in order to be received without guilt or expectation of return, must be received in a one-way operation. For instance, if I think that anything is expected or demanded as the result of a compliment, then the compliment loses its force. Instead of complimented, I feel manipulated. Grace depends on the fact that its origin is wholly outside myself. This is the heart of love: it comes to me from outside myself. Moreover, while it almost always elicits a response, which is my love in return, it comes toward me without any reference to my response. One-way love does not deviate on the basis of its goal. It is determined solely by its source.

Romance makes this clear. Almost any teenage boy will tell you that when a pretty girl shows interest, he will always go along. I am not sure I have ever met a young man who is able to turn down the advances of a pretty or sexy woman. The fact that she likes him, or indicates that she does, is enough to ensure his response. It doesn't matter whether she is right for him, or has good qualities, or displays any kind of rational compatibility. If she likes him, he swoons right there on the floor.

This is an important idea. One-way love is the change agent in everyday life because it speaks in a voice completely different from the voice of the law. It has nothing to do with its receiver's characteristics. Its logic is hidden within the intention of its source. Theologically speaking, we can say it is the prime directive of God to love the world in no relation to the world's fitness to be loved. Speaking in terms of Christian theology, God loves the world in a kind of reverse relationship to its moral unfitness. "God proves his love for us in that while we still were sinners Christ died for us" (Romans 5:8).

In the dimension of grace, one-way love is inscrutable or irrational not only because it is out of relation with any intrinsic circumstances on the part of the receiver. One-way love is also irrational because it reaches out to the specifically undeserving person. This is the beating heart of it. Grace is directed toward what the Scripture calls "the ungodly" (Romans 5:6). Not just the lonely, not just the sick and disconsolate, but the "perpetrators," the murderers and abusers, the people who cross the line. God has a heart — his one-way love — for sinners. This is the problem with Christianity. This piece of logical and ethical incongruity and inappropriateness is the problem with Christianity.

It is also the New Testament account of grace: God's one-way love is a love that acts independent of all response to it yet at the same time elicits a response. "We love because he first loved us" (1 John 4:19). That is the premise of this book. *Grace works independent of its response, but typically engenders it.* Right from the start, in the Prologue to John's Gospel, we hear that "the law indeed was given through Moses; grace and truth came through Jesus Christ" (John 1:17). "God did not send the Son into the world to condemn the world, but in order that the world might be saved through him" (3:17).

What Christians call the incarnation, which is a secondary development in theology that rides on the one-way love of grace, is the expression of a prior love for the world. The world is understood to be the devil's playground of competing human power allegiances that ebb and flow and never reach stability. The human world is overwhelmed by bigger powers than we — namely sin, the flesh, and the devil. But "while we were still weak, at the right time Christ died for the ungodly. . . . God proves his love for us in that while we still were sinners Christ died for us" (Romans 5:6, 8). God's approach to the world is an advance upon a hostile sector of the universe. This fact is grace, and grace is the overarching paradigm of the New Testament.

We can view this paradigm from the beginning of the New Testament to its end. Grace is the womb from which the incarnation is born. In the beginning, the initiative to love is from the outside in. The life that Jesus led is the purest picture of initiating grace that we have. He calls men and women who are the opposite of elite. Jesus did not call the Matthew McConaugheys and Joan Didions of his day. "Can anything good come out of Nazareth?" (John 1:46). He consorted instead with the worst people of his day. Christ's calling of Matthew the tax collector was countercultural (Matthew 9:9-13). The blessing of the "unclean" act performed by a woman "who was a sinner" drew censure from the Pharisees (Luke 7:36-39), a tribe that has not left the world to this day. Jesus' placing of human needs above divine law in the interest of fulfilling divine law aroused furious resentment. He said, "The sabbath was made for humankind, and not humankind for the sabbath"(Mark 2:27).

Christ's repeated "mission statement" that he came to call not the righteous but sinners (Luke 5:32; Matthew 9:13; Mark 2:17) is the exact shape of grace. Christ was not a sinner himself, for he was the divine embodiment of perfect law. But his direction was to sinners and to sinners uniquely. This is expressed in his encounters with the other tax collector, Zacchaeus (Luke 19:1-10); with the paralytic whom he healed, contrary to the law, on the Sabbath (Mark 2:1-12); with the woman who had been suffering from hemorrhages for twelve years (Mark 5:25-34); and with the persistent blind beggar outside Jericho (Mark 10:46-52).

The labor of one-way love expressed in the life of Christ is also succinctly, and devastatingly, enacted in his relation to Peter. Peter is a neon sign above the entire New Testament. His story beams the grace of God to sinners and never runs out of light. Peter misunderstood Christ and once even embodied a Satanic temptation (Mark 8:31-33). Peter tried to push Christ to do the short-term thing (Mark 9:5-6). Peter lost his trust in Christ when he stepped out of the boat (Matthew 14:28-31).

Peter is therefore at the center of the New Testament's drama concerning grace. Worse than anything he did during Christ's three years of teaching, Peter denied his relationship with Christ when it really mattered (Matthew 26:69-75; Mark 14:66-72; Luke 22:54-62; John 18:15-18, 25-27). The denial of Christ by Peter is one of the worst breaches of faith in the Gospels, second only to Judas's denial. It was insistently warned of in advance, and it was carried out at the single loneliest point of need in Jesus' life. It was indefensible. It was repeated, denied, and defended — yet strangely not judged.

"Neither do I condemn you. Go on your way, and from now on do not sin again" (John 8:11). This is the one-way love of grace in the life of Christ. As he forgave Peter, so the Lord forgave the woman taken in adultery. He did not throw a stone against her. His apparent imperative in John 8, "Go on your way, and from now on do not sin again," is not an imperative. It is a descriptive. Few who have ever been forgiven a crime possess the inward desire to offend again. It was obvious that she would not sin again. And if she did, she would be forgiven again; and the chances of her offending again would be reduced by half. Under grace, imperatives become indicatives.

What I am saying is that Jesus' life was a labor of grace. This is boundlessly evident in the four Gospels. It is also the reason why he was crucified and why his approach to religion was abhorred. The Pharisees were just as bad as they are portrayed. How often I hear them whitewashed or cleaned up, as solid citizens who were much less heartless than they are portrayed. I realize that this is partly true. They were certainly not inhuman. They were casuists, people who bend the law to fit around themselves. They talked about extenuating circumstances and exceptional cases and special needs. But *they lived by the deception that the law is able to effect change.* This is where Jesus cut the tie to their conceptual reality. He related to ritually disqualified people and boundary crossers with single-minded direction. Unlike the law, Christ's approach always worked. The people whom he treated under the sign of grace broke down. Each of them had his or her nervous breakdown. Being loved one-way, without reference to their response, they always said Yes. This Yes is the breakdown that arrives with undeceived diagnosis in the presence of love. Zacchaeus broke down. Mary Magdalene broke down. The woman who was "freed from [her] ailment" (Luke 13:12) broke down. St. Peter broke down (Luke 5:8; John 21:17). Every one of the original disciples broke down (Matthew 26:56). "All fall down."

Grace has a domino effect. It is at the bottom of the house of cards that is human identity. It is the ground floor of our striving after love. When grace comes in, when it rewrites the script, when its light shines in the basement of the house that is ourselves, unbuilt to God, grace demolishes and creates. It does what it promises. Unlike the law, which produces the opposite of what it demands, grace succeeds. It produces the fruit, to use the New Testament metaphor, of a law-congruent life.

In the light of Christ's gregarious life, we have to look now at the way he died. It was not gregarious. It was a barren summation of the one-way love that permeates the Bible.

The Death of Christ

The execution of Jesus on the cross was not a victory. It was not a successful procedure. It is not an overstatement to call it the collapse of a revolutionary movement. Pertinently for today, it is completely unacceptable in incident, and also in principle, to the Muslim world. Jesus, God's prophet, though not his final prophet, cannot be regarded by Muslims as having died as the result of his movement's failure. He cannot be regarded as having lost.

Christ's defeat is the negation of his significance in terms of the law.

His death is an irremediable thing. Even in light of the great "rabbit pulled out of a hat," the famous resurrection on Easter Day, the death of the movement with the death of the man is the final commentary on grace. Grace came to nothing!

Moreover, Christians have always interpreted Christ's death as accomplishing its opposite. They have negated the negation, calling the defeat a victory, and valued it as the site of grace in the world where grace is most plainly displayed. This is an amazing victory of the absurd over the obvious. Grace is the victory of the absurd over the obvious. "For God's foolishness is wiser than human wisdom" (1 Corinthians 1:25).

Christ's bloody death represents the final stage of man and woman's need for deliverance. It is a stymied need, but it is also the abject and bottomless need of human beings. When the chips are down, the chips are really down. Christ died, and the outreach of extrinsic intervention perished with him.

Listen to the most gracious of the psalms, which imports the grace required to reimagine the death of grace at Jerusalem:

> If I say, "Surely the darkness shall cover me,
> and the light around me become night,"
> even the darkness is not dark to you;
> the night is as bright as the day,
> for darkness is as light to you. (Psalm 139:11-12)

The crucifixion of Christ on *Good* Friday means that dark is not dark if God is there. Dark is dark in the absence of God. But in the presence of God, darkness becomes light, just as a tragic loss in everyday life becomes bearable if someone is there to love you through it.

The grace of God assumes the worst concerning the human situation. It assumes the lowest possible reading of our anthropology. To that idea, the deepest rung of theological anthropology, we shall return later. But the grace of God understands that the world is in an either-or situation from which only a miracle can save us. To people who take the low road on the question of human nature, the death of Christ is not a problem. It is a tragedy. It is a disappointment. It is poignant particularly because God, or God's intention, was involved. But the death of Christ is plausible. It is what we would expect.

For me, Christ's cry from the cross, Psalm 22, is the apogee of grace, for it could be answered only *from* grace: "My God, my God, why have you forsaken me?" (Psalm 22:1; Matthew 27:46; Mark 15:34). If Christ had not died, or if he had been defeated in a more regular manner, as in "old soldiers never die, they just fade away," there would be no grace to the situation. Had he won, there would have been no grace to the situation. Had he lost the skirmish but won the war, or lost the war but won the skirmish, there would have been no grace to it. Grace, which is one-way love, happens only at the point at which hope is lost. At that point, there was no love left in him, no love left from him.

The death of Christ portrays the human world's worst fears for itself. Its lack of light, its transparent darkness, make it the perfect template for grace. For people who live from grace, it is not a surprise, nor is Easter itself a surprise. Christ's death is grace-directed because, as The Brooklyn Bridge sang so plaintively, "It's the worst that could happen, to me" (1969).

Easter Day

The resurrection of Christ is the perfect instance of one-way love. This is because it is an actual case of life from death. It is all action on God's part, and no action on Christ's part. It is not healing, and it is not recuperation. It is a case of life from the dead.

The grace involved in the first Easter is noted by St. Paul in Romans 4. Paul underlines the theme of grace as life from death in a dense and theological verse:

> [God] raised Jesus our Lord from the dead, who was handed over to death for our trespasses and was raised for our justification. (4:24-25)

Paul connects the death of Christ — this instance of intense beleagueredness, which depicts the human dereliction in its truest, darkest colors —

with his being raised. The being raised answers the forlornness of the death in terms that Paul calls "justification."

There is a connection here that requires explanation, as it is the fulcrum on which we turn from the facts of Jesus' Good Friday and Easter to the interpretation placed on those events by the grace-preaching apostle to the Gentiles. St. Paul is saying that human beings need to be justified, which means that human beings need to live a non-accused life. They need to have the certainty that before God they are innocent.

In all of Scripture we have seen that law always accuses the human being *(lex semper accusat)*. God as law is undeviating. The accusation is always in front of us, and the whole human drama of finding false hope in secondary things is a form of flight from that accusation. Thus we need fundamentally to be non-accused in order to look back up at him whose "eyes are too pure to behold evil" (Habakkuk 1:13).

The reason why the first Easter is a meaningful instance of grace is that it sets Christ's resurrected body in this gap between the total war of God's law and the fight-or-flight of quivering men and women. By raising this perfectly innocent man, whom we understand to be the perfect expression of God, and by putting that man between us and our irrefutable accusation, God "justifies" us. Thus "Jesus our Lord . . . was handed over to death for our trespasses and was raised for our justification" (Romans 4:24-25).

We are not required to be interested in the metaphysical possibilities inherent in the first Easter. I am not focusing on its significance as consolation, nor on its encouragement that we will not be alone when we die. What this theology of everyday life seeks to emphasize is the grace of the first Easter, by which our helpless need as pathetic, predatory human beings is given a remedy.

God did not leave us comfortless. He left neither us nor him hanging in the air, on the one cross of Christ or on the infinite number of crosses people make for themselves and for each other. The dereliction of human experience, which I take to be the universal fact of life, the great misfire of our existence between what we wish would have happened to us and what has actually happened to us, is engaged by the solemn God of life both in the abandonment of Christ at his last moment and by God's bringing him back in order to bring us back with him in innocence.

This now swings us toward the interpretation that Paul sought to place on the life and death of Christ. There was grace within the interactions Jesus had with the people he met. There was grace in the desolate death to which his grace-in-action life led. There was grace in the "justification," the restoration of innocence, that Easter brought about. There is a new freshness to everyday human living, which the grace of Easter and Good Friday imports. How does this grace work?

Grace in St. Paul

Ever since the late 1800s, Christian theologians have tried to diminish the radical nature of St. Paul's approach to life. Among these in the early days were Johannes Weiss (1863-1914), Wilhelm Wrede (1859-1906), and Albert Schweitzer (1875-1965). So strong is the dose of grace that the apostle gives in his letters that a numerous school of revisionists has been birthed. This birth takes place again and again in every generation of New Testament scholars, but under different names. They do not like the discontinuous nature of Paul's ideas, the discontinuity of Paul's ideas with "Second-Temple" Judaism. Therefore they wish to domesticate his teachings on grace by chaining them to a cultural context rather than liberating them for service in the present world.

Their argument goes as follows. Paul's teaching on the grace of God as expressed in the metaphor of "justification" is part of his larger interpretation of the life and death of Christ. But it is only a part! The justification metaphor is actually subordinate to the metaphor of "participation in Christ," not to mention various pictures of the imminent return of the Lord to the earth. What Paul meant to do with his grace metaphor of justification, his "forensic" or legal illustration of Christ's significance, was to provide a conceptual license to preach his message to non-Jews. He meant primarily to give to non-Jews, or Gentiles, the space to be real Jews yet with Christ as their Lord. This space could be achieved by removing the "curse of the law" in terms of specific points of ethnic identity, such as circumcision, Sabbath observance, and the Jewish dietary laws. For these revisionists of Paul, the grace metaphor of justification was Paul's means of opening a door to Judaism, with Christ as a part of Judaism, to non-Jewish people who would otherwise resist the more alienating specifics of Jewish everyday life. This is what the revisionists say, and this view has held steady, within differing scholarly circles, for more than a hundred years.[7]

This is an emasculation of St. Paul. It is a kind of "Holocaust denial" that flies so brutally in the face of the evidence that one can only ask oneself, Why are these people saying these things? What is the intention behind their words? Such questions must be asked, and asked repeatedly, because the evidence on the pages of Paul's letters is so contrary to the new interpretation.

It is true that Paul uses several visual images and illustrations concerning the life and death of Christ. Like all preachers, he is ever in search of a good illustration or simile. He is ever in search of a way to connect to the people around him. He juggles several of these pictures in order to interpret the "big idea," which is the abandonment of Christ the innocent on Good Friday and his grace-justification on Easter Day. *But Paul's overarching paradigm is the paradigm of grace-justification.* It simply consumes more pages than any other paradigm. Count the chapters in Romans, add to that the chapters of Galatians and Philippians, and it is clear as glass that the most expansive and loved portrait of Christ's achievement comes to the fore in those books.

I would reject as secondary the images that many Pauline scholars today regard as primary, such as "participation," "body," and "covenant." They rush to discredit the grace-justification emphasis, yet they miss the key development of it in practice. Scholars tend to miss what is obvious to ministers: grace-justification preaches! It preaches to the abandoned and those who pant for mercy. It preaches to criminals and perpetrators. It preaches to victims and to women. It preaches to children and to the oppressed poor. It preaches to oppressors and abusers. It preaches to people

7. See my "Mistakes of the New Perspective on Paul" (The John Wenham Lecture, Tyndale House, Cambridge, UK), *Themelios* 27, no. 1 (Autumn 2001): 5-11.

caught in the act. It is thoroughly non-partisan, non-sectarian, and non-ethnic. It tears down denial. It is thus a threat to walls and veils of excuse. I understand the rejection of Paul's message of grace-justification, on the part of at least two generations of scholars, to be a classic instance of denial. Somehow the word of grace that is kryptonite within the ideas of Paul has met a wall of lead, a hardened form of protest that has become sufficient to silence its power and its hearing. This book is an attempt to let the grace-word of the New Testament, and of Paul, be heard again.

What does Paul say concerning grace? His quintessential teaching about grace-justification is found in Romans 3. There Paul establishes the impossibility of human beings changing their world. Paul draws on several dark verses from the Psalms and the prophets to describe a Malthusian chaos of aggression and spite (Romans 3:10-18). So established is this chaos, built on self-defensiveness and self-serving, that there is absolutely no hope for us to change the world on the basis of our own strength. The law holds out no hope for correction. Thus Paul writes, "'No human being will be justified in his sight' by deeds prescribed by the law, for through the law comes the knowledge of sin" (3:20).

Grace, Paul continues, is the only hope for the human race. "All have sinned and fall short of the glory of God; they are now justified by his grace as a gift, through the redemption that is in Christ Jesus" (3:23-24). This is theological language that admits the impotence of law before the success of grace. It is always a four-word sentence from God: law fails, grace succeeds. Grace does what the law cannot do.

How this happens is sketched out in Romans 7. There Paul shows the native recidivism of human beings, their relapse, who perpetually do what they say they do not want to do, and fail to do the things they say they should do (7:19). Nowhere is grace more succinctly preached than it is in Romans 7. Once again, as in Romans 3, the impasse of existence is revealed: "Wretched man that I am! Who will rescue me from this body of death?" (7:24). To this, the word of grace resounds: "There is therefore now no condemnation for those who are in Christ Jesus" (8:1). The dead end of law succumbs to absolution. This is the continual note in Paul's voice. Grace, which is absolution, is the second and defining word from God, after the first word of judgment. It is not a word that is said just once or even twice or three times. It is said every hour. The absolving word never fails and never halts. The "eternal return" of Romans 7, by which men and women always go back to square one of their bound repetition-compulsion to sin, is allied with its grace-full replay: "There is therefore now no condemnation."

This is the center of Paul's idea of grace. It meets a need that never changes, and in itself it never changes. The "big crater" on the landscape of Paul's thought is the repeated grace-word of absolution.

Paul's treatment of grace in his letter to the Galatians is controversial and radical. Contemporary proponents of the "new" Paul, who regard justification as a "subsidiary crater" on his theological landscape, want to understand Galatians as an occasional letter dealing with one particular problem.[8] This problem is the relation of Jewish Christians to Gentile converts within a single Christian community. Paul's task in Galatians, they wish to say, is to interpret the law in such a way that the Gentiles do not have to be circumcised. In this sense, the letter is an epistolary skirmish within a sort of "culture war," which should not be freighted or over-interpreted beyond its local context. It should not be universalized.

This contemporary approach to Galatians flies completely in the face of what the letter actually says, and I stick to Paul's language. Paul regards the law as a curse (Galatians 3:10-13). He regards the grace of God as an invasive and strongly new intervention, through which trust in God rather than in human performance is at the heart of the human relationship to God. He writes:

> Therefore the law was our disciplinarian until Christ came, so that we might be justified by faith. But now that faith has come, we are no longer subject to a disciplinarian; for in Christ Jesus you are all children of God through faith. (3:24-26)

Bound slaves to the law, we were unable to secure release until the intervention of the Lord. "While we were minors, we were enslaved to the el-

8. For a full survey and discussion of the "new perspective on Paul," see James D. G. Dunn's "The New Perspective on Paul: Whence, What, Wither?" in his *The New Perspective on Paul: Collected Essays* (Tübingen: Mohr Siebeck, 2005), pp. 1-88.

emental spirits of the world. But when the fullness of time had come, God sent his Son, born of a woman, born under the law, in order to redeem those who were under the law, so that we might receive adoption as children" (4:3-5).

Paul then catalogues the things the law condemns, which he calls "works of the flesh" (Galatians 5:19-21). He compares them with those things which the law cannot produce but against which there is no law. These things he calls the "fruit of the Spirit" (5:22-23). He prefaces this with a cry for freedom that sounds like a manifesto: "For freedom Christ has set us free. Stand firm, therefore, and do not submit again to a yoke of slavery" (5:1). Every word of Paul's letter to the Galatians demolishes the law as having any enabling or creative powers to get people to change. At the same time, every sentence of Galatians sustains the content of the law. The problem is always how to get there, how to effect what the law requires. Only grace does that.

The connection Paul makes in Galatians between grace and freedom reminds me of something Pen Densham said. Pen Densham was the producer of *The New Outer Limits,* a television show based on the original *Outer Limits,* which aired in the early 1960s. Densham was asked how it was that the early seasons of *The New Outer Limits* were so good, so fresh and new in concept and design. He said, "I learned that creativity on my team did not stem from dictation, it stemmed from emancipation." In other words, he did not preach the law to his creative team but gave them the creative freedom to go for their vision. He offered grace to his team, and they came up with "fruit" — the fruit being many arresting productions for television.

Pen Densham didn't know it, but he was speaking like St. Paul in Galatians. Liberty derives from grace, and it produces the things the law demands but cannot form. This is Paul's timely and universal word to both the Jewish and the Gentile Christians of Galatia. His message was contextual for the Galatians, supra-contextual for all Christian churches, and universal for all conflicted people — right down to the artistic team behind *The New Outer Limits.* In other words, Paul's message was designed for real people living in the ancient place of Galatia. But it burst that context in being able to address all Christians. And it offers insight for everyone, Christian and non-Christian, who has ever struggled against accusation and been hammered by stress.

The last salvo from Paul concerning grace comes in his letter to the Philippians. There he talks about himself. He inserts himself personally into the "big idea," and thus makes his idea biographical:

> [I] have no confidence in the flesh — even though I, too, have reason for confidence in the flesh.
>
> If anyone else has reason to be confident in the flesh, I have more: circumcised on the eighth day, a member of the people of Israel, of the tribe of Benjamin, a Hebrew born of Hebrews; as to the law, a Pharisee; as to zeal, a persecutor of the church; as to righteousness under the law, blameless.
>
> Yet whatever gains I had, these I have come to regard as loss because of Christ. More than that, I regard everything as loss because of the surpassing value of knowing Christ Jesus my Lord. For his sake I have suffered the loss of all things, and I regard them as rubbish, in order that I may gain Christ and be found in him, not having a righteousness of my own that comes from the law, but one that comes through faith in Christ, the righteousness from God based on faith. (3:3-9)

I quote this section at length because it carries an important principle. Paul includes himself within what theologians call the "meta-narrative," the big idea that overrides all others yet includes the author. For the apostle himself, the law had proved inhospitable. It had burdened him. The burden was not just conceptual; it was false. It was a spurious foundation for personal identity. It crumbled, and a new "righteousness," an identity before God that is acceptable to God, took its place. Paul lived this grace himself.

The passage from Philippians connects with a painting from the Reformation era that now hangs over the altar table in the Parish Church of Weimar, Germany. In this painting, which depicts the crucifixion, the artist, Lucas Cranach, stands under the cross. Onto his bald head the blood of Christ is dripping, actually splashing. The artist looks out at the viewer. He has portrayed himself as being a part of the drama. The grace of God, issuing from the bloody side of Christ, belongs to the artist, too.

It does not belong only to first-century spectators. The Christian impulse is to see oneself as part of the divine history, now and always.

Several years ago the actor David Morse told me that he had responded to some sermons I had given at Grace Church in Lower Manhattan. I asked him, "What made the difference?" He said, "What you were saying made me feel like I could be an actual part of God's plan for the world I live in now." This is the same principle, from St. Paul to Lucas Cranach and now to us. The one-way love of grace supplants and supersedes, replaces even, two-way and half-way ideas of love. They do not work. Grace makes the change.

Grace in Jeopardy, in Hebrews, James, and Second Peter

Grace, the one-way love of God, comes under criticism in three of the later letters of the New Testament. It is often considered amusing, within historical theology, that the Reformer Martin Luther expressed exasperation in relation to three passages in the New Testament that seemed to him to take away the very gift grace had given in the letters of St. Paul. Luther's exasperation was not unjustified. Three passages are in question, and we should not avoid them, even in this short survey of what I have called the "big idea" within the New Testament.

The first passage is in the otherwise atonement-permeated letter to the Hebrews. It reads thus:

> If we willfully persist in sin after having received the knowledge of the truth, there no longer remains a sacrifice for sins, but a fearful prospect of judgment, and a fury of fire. . . . Do not, therefore, abandon that confidence of yours. . . . For you need endurance, so that when you have done the will of God, you may receive what was promised. (10:26-27, 35-36)

Grace is in a little trouble here because the text says that the great gift of God, the "sacrifice for sins," no longer applies if we sin deliberately or consciously after we have become Christian. In other words, I can spoil and ruin God's work myself, and on my own. God cannot be trusted to bring his work in me to fulfillment and completion. I can play a crucial part in its progress: I can pollute what God has cleansed.

This particular word from Hebrews damages grace. It implies that God brings us to a "knowledge of the truth," but afterwards it is up to us. A fully expressed doctrine of grace seems to be reversed in this passage, at least for Christians. It is therefore at odds with the theology expressed almost everywhere else in the New Testament. What shall we do with it? We probably have to understand it as a small piece within a large mosaic.

The second section of the New Testament that has caused problems for the lifeline of grace is found in the letter of James.

> Do you want to be shown . . . that faith apart from works is barren? Was not our ancestor Abraham justified by works when he offered his son Isaac upon the altar? You see that faith was active along with his works, and faith was brought to completion by the works. . . . You see that a person is justified by works and not by faith alone. (2:20-22, 24)

These sentences seem to have been written in opposition to Paul, for they hark back to the same example of the faith-alone, grace-alone patriarch Abraham whom Paul had invoked in Romans and Galatians. But James comes to a different conclusion. James concludes that Abraham's faith was sufficient only in that it issued in the "work" of his sacrifice of his son Isaac. The concept is semi-Pelagian. James is not against faith; he is just against faith *alone.* He believes that faith alone is wrong. He believes that faith accompanied by works is the answer to the unpalatable mystery of God's grace. James attaches a condition, the condition of consequence and result, to that trust which is faith in the grace of God.

James sounds reasonable enough. Faith produces works, or, as Paul had said, faith engenders the fruit of good living. But the words "works" and "fruit" are different in tone. They convey a different sort of progress or development. The "works" of James condition the faith that he (half-heartedly) salutes. The "fruit" of Paul is the unconditioned result of the faith occasioned from grace. Faith-alone is the position of St. Paul. Faith-annexed-to-works is the position of St. James. These positions are incompatible. Again, what can we do with this? Anyone can hear the note of dissonance.

The third and most explicit rejoinder to grace in the New Testament comes in the second letter of Peter. In Second Peter, something different occurs. Paul's writings come under attack!

> So also our beloved brother Paul wrote to you according to the wisdom given him, speaking of [salvation] as he does in all his letters. There are some things in them hard to understand, which the ignorant and unstable twist to their own destruction, as they do the other scriptures. You therefore, beloved, since you are forewarned, beware that you are not carried away with the error of the lawless and lose your own stability. (3:15-17)

This particular dissent from Paul, which is the most pointed dissent with another canonical writer within the New Testament, is serious. It accuses Paul in his theology of grace of being guilty, potentially, of creating lawlessness and instability among Christian people. Both in Second Peter and in Hebrews, it is understood that non-believers, once they become believers and accept the Christian way out from the law, are on their own. There is fear being expressed here that Paul's ideas on grace could undermine their striving after self-mastery.

This way of thinking has had a long life in Christian history. We hit people with the law (that is, with a proper diagnosis of their fallen condition), and they get softened up for grace. Grace is then offered and everything changes. But *now,* in the new sphere of the so-called "Christian life," they are hammered once again by the law. Once saved, in other words, people are on their own again, to work and prove.

This is standard stuff in Christian history, and it is loaded with potential for making a person want to "hand back his ticket." The hidden "leaven of the Pharisees" (Matthew 16:6, 11; Mark 8:15; Luke 12:1) is right here, in these passages within Hebrews, James, and Second Peter. The leaven has never stopped growing within the Christian movement.

I have to add that much of Hebrews, a fair amount of James, and some verses in Second Peter are inspirational and convey grace. But a few missed and dissonant notes, like the ones we have heard above, are significant. They have gathered momentum over many centuries. Go to almost any church service that is directed to "Christians," and you will more frequently find yourself in the world of James and Second Peter than in the world of Paul's one-way love.

The Canon within the Canon

When I first heard the phrase "canon within the canon," I got nervous. The phrase seemed to imply that the Bible contains within itself more than one big idea, that you more or less choose the particular big idea, or "canon," that you like, and then you are free to interpret everything else in the light of that canon.

Thus, for example, your canon within the canon could be law and grace in their distinct relation. People sometimes say that the Protestant Reformers took law and grace as their canon within the canon, through which they interpreted everything else in the Bible, including the passages that conflict with it. Another canon could be the covenant people of God and the agreement and disagreement of this people with the God of their covenant. Looking at the New Testament, another canon within the canon could be the concept of "participation in Christ." Many interpreters today are working with that one. Or you could take the character of the Holy Spirit, especially in the New Testament, and understand the whole story from the birth of Christ through the persecution of the church to be the driving action of the Spirit. There are several possible canons within the canon.

Isolating canons within the canon is a dishonest project potentially. What can happen is that you become seduced by a single idea and then try to force all the other data through it, like a magnifying glass capturing the sun. This trick can burn you, in other words. It can make you guilty of one-sidedness and reducing the texts to a false unity. It can take a various truth, a prism of insights, and reduce it to a single color. The problem with canon-within-the-canon thinking is that it can miss an accurate and whole picture of the truth.

The idea of a canon within the canon also goes against the grain of current cultural thinking. Current cultural thinking is into "nuance" and the "diversity" of the human voice. Unity is out; plurality is in. The "one" is out, and the "many" are in. Anything that applies a single light to the data is suspect. But regardless of political correctness, if a canon-within-the-canon approach misses the whole truth, it must in any case be wrong.

This systematic theology of everyday life *is* a modest form of a canon within the canon. In this case, I am saying that the canon within the canon of grace covers just about all, but not absolutely all, the biblical data. Where there is law in the New Testament, it is law as distinct from grace, and it demolishes the foundations of anything else but grace as response. Where there is grace in the Old Testament, it is grace as distinct from law, which demonstrates the eternal relation in God between his two words, the No of the law and the Yes of the gospel. There is a lot of grace in Isaiah and Jeremiah, and there are overwhelming representations of it in the lives of the patriarchs and Moses. Similarly Christ's Sermon on the Mount is mostly a word that mows down law. It puts the listener in her or his place, scattering us into "broken pieces on the ground" (James Taylor), of which all human achievements ultimately consist.

It is possible to place the overwhelming measure of Bible stories and Bible characters and Bible prophecy and poetry into a "canon within the canon" of grace into relation to law. I see no other "big idea" that encompasses so much of the material. Are there exceptions to this? Three passages in Hebrews, James, and Second Peter have been noted. Is this really a problem? No, because those three are small exceptions within a document that can be interpreted overwhelmingly and credibly within the canon of grace as it relates to law. Moreover, Hebrews, James, and Second Peter are *obvious* exceptions. They stand out because of their inconsistency with the overall pattern of total reliance on grace in the face of law. Second Peter takes off the mask, in fact: the author says how critical he is of Paul, or at least of misinterpretations of Paul. Peter is open concerning the dissonance. He admits in his own words to being troubled by a main writer of the book to which he is another contributor. The author of Second Peter is trying to explain away the problem I am talking about.

Don't let the phrase "canon within the canon" get to you! The point is, which canon or "big idea" produces the biggest and most sustaining reading of the Bible? Which canon within the canon takes account of the greatest number of texts? No canon takes account of all the texts. *I believe the law and grace canon covers almost every verse of the Bible.* The few problem passages I have underlined are small asteroids in a night sky of Andromeda galaxies.

Grace on Patmos

The way something ends is important. It passes a judgment on what went before. It comforts you concerning the credibility of the steps that preceded it. It is good for the person, or the project, because ending well confers satisfaction.

This is true of books. It is true of movies and art. As I said, I am fond of the second incarnation, from the 1990s, of the television show entitled *The New Outer Limits.* It had a moral earnestness and a surprising ability to break through the veils of political correctness in an eye-popping way. But it also had one besetting sin: it surprised too much. It almost always pulled the rug from under you at the last minute. Some underlying "back story" or dark fact would surface at the end, and you would be shocked. The problem with this was that it made you gun-shy the next time. Every time I watched a new episode, I would brace myself for a horrible plot reversal at the end.

This is to say that the Bible, in contrast, concludes its long narrative of grace on an exceptionally high and helpful note. It is not like one of those *New Outer Limits* episodes. We saw already how the last book of the Bible, the Revelation to St. John, understands the requirement that law be invoked to its last drop in order for grace to be summoned. The elders with their robes washed "in the blood of the Lamb" (7:14) and the City of God in which tears will be no more (21:4): these images do not deny reality. They are wholly truthful expressions of the sin (i.e., the blood) and the sorrows (i.e., the tears) of the world. Secured within these boldly accurate images are also images of grace, the one-way love that washes, cleanses, and comforts.

Grace concludes the story of the Bible. We can stand alongside one arresting image and lay down the case for God's scriptural grace. We can lay it down with confidence.

> Then the angel showed me the river of the water of life, bright as crystal, flowing from the throne of God and of the Lamb through the middle of the street of the city. On either side of the river is the tree of life with its twelve kinds of fruit, producing its fruit each month; and the leaves of the tree are for the healing of the nations. Nothing accursed will be found there any more. But the throne of God and of the Lamb will be in it, and his servants will worship him; they will see his face, and his name will be on their foreheads. And there will be no more night; they need no light of lamp or sun, for the Lord God will be their light, and they shall reign forever and ever. (22:1-5)

Three ideas in this passage convey the grace of God. The first is the image of fruit. In grace everything is naturally produced. Everything springs without artifice. Everything comes spontaneously. It requires no "tweaking." The healing of the nations, according to John, is the result of the growth of fruit. This is grace and not law.

The second idea in this passage is the final end of mediation. "They will see his face" (22:4). To quote an old gospel chorus, there is "Nothing Between." In the law, everything is always mediated. I am doing everything I can to squeeze a response from the judge of my life. I am always putting something out there to make the judge approve. That is the law. Everything is between. It is not so with grace. Grace enacts the end of mediation. The human being at the close of Revelation is face to face with God. There is nothing between, and there is no fear. That is the grace of intimacy. It is what the world wants, and it is promised here without qualification.

The third idea here at the end of Revelation is the total finish to nuance. "There will be no more night . . . for the Lord God will be their light" (22:5). One of the marking characteristics of life under the law is *nuance:* that ambiguity, multivalence, plurality of interpretation, with its grays and smudges. Looking on the world from the standpoint of law is to create a million partial truths and contradictory insights. An "innocent" man is shot on a London subway car, but every police officer within ten miles is packing a sub-machine gun in the face of suicide bombers. We say we need "heightened security," yet the moment it is employed the world points a finger and says it takes away our rights. The world under law is a total mixed message. It is a Yes and a No at the same time, all the time.

It is not so under grace. Under grace, reality is "not according to ordinary human standards, ready to say 'Yes, yes' and 'No, no' at the same time. . . . Our word to you has not been 'Yes and No.' For the Son of God . . . was not 'Yes and No'; but *in him it is always 'Yes.'* For in him every one of God's promises is a 'Yes'" (2 Corinthians 1:17-20). Christianity spells the end of nuance, the end of ambiguity as a governing principle. Paul made the point propositionally that John of Patmos expressed visually. We no longer live under a Yes and a No simultaneously. That is the world's approach. It is the world's approach because of the law, which is always a little of this and a little of that. The law is gradualist; nothing is ever complete and done. There is never any pure satisfaction, not a bit of it. The law is the dedicated enemy of completeness. It is not so with grace.

Grace on Patmos was fruit from a root, not a "genetically altered" production. Grace on Patmos was a pure relation, nothing between. Grace on Patmos was light without any black holes. This is the conclusion of New Testament religion. It is the definite last word in a "canon within the canon," which is really the whole canon of Holy Scripture.

Grace in the Old Testament

To trace the history of one-way love in the Old Testament, Christians need to travel *backwards* from the New Testament. This is because, for Christians, the New Testament portrait of Jesus is the unique biblical portrait of God's one-way love. This love is not so focused in the Old Testament; or rather, it exists there in competition with a few other notions of love.

In the Old Testament, grace as one-way love in the Christian sense oscillates between instances of its full expression and instances of what Christians call semi-Pelagianism, or half-way love. Semi-Pelagianism is the technical term for the idea that God loves us as we are but we have to bring something to the table.

Pelagianism, named after a fourth-century British teacher of theology, is the idea that, in order to receive God's love, we have to be worthy of it. God will love us if we are proven worthy recipients of his love. *Semi*-Pelagianism, on the other hand, is half-way love: we need him to love us, but our response to his love is very important. God loves us; all we have to do is accept that love. In short, he will love us a lot if we love him a little.

Semi-Pelagianism, a Christian term, describes some of what is affirmed in the Old Testament concerning the relation between God and Israel. To put it another way, the Old Testament is less Christian than the New Testament — which sounds obvious — and Christian interpreters of grace in the Bible need to begin with the New and travel backwards.

Most everyday Christianity is semi-Pelagian. It is a two-way street with three lanes. Two lanes come from God, and one lane comes from us. This is not grace. It holds a slice of grace, we might say, but not the whole loaf. For grace to be grace, there must be one-way love. For grace to be grace, it is necessary that I play no role whatsoever in that love.

All you need to do is look at yourself when you are in a crisis. Look at yourself when you are in a box canyon of your own making. Look at the external circumstances of the thing. Most criminals, for example, when they are finally caught and shut up in a prison — let's say a Turkish prison, to really get the idea — are open to grace. Only one-way love can help them. I see many people who are living in the inner equivalent of a Turkish prison. I see men who dislike women because they are women, and women who fear men because they are men. I see people entrenched in decades of amassed resentment that lies just below the surface. For such people, who live under overmastering states of feeling, grace simply has to be a one-way street. Semi-Pelagianism will not do. Nor will Pelagianism do, the idea that grace is a one-way street proceeding from me. The love of God, the true love of anyone, in fact, is a one-way love that travels from the deserving to the undeserving.

I say this because there is always a little push in the Old Testament, and to some extent, as we have seen in three instances, in the New Testament, toward semi-Pelagianism. You get the idea in some of the prophets that, if the people of God would just discipline themselves, then God would respond with "love and happiness" (Al Green). This is expressed in the famous condition of 2 Chronicles 7:14: "If my people who are called by my name humble themselves, pray, seek my face, and turn from their wicked ways, then I will hear from heaven, and will forgive their sin and heal their land." Christians have to call that grammatical condition an instance of semi-Pelagianism. Second Chronicles 7:14 describes a truth that, when it is heard, turns into law. It is absolutely true that moral rectitude is required for God to exist in experienced relationship with his people. But when this absolute truth contains a requirement, it starts the fire of resentment and rebellion. The "If my people" command is semi-Pelagian in practice. It is superseded by the grace that Paul taught in the New Testament and that Jesus lived.

Another example of semi-Pelagianism in practice is the invitation from Malachi: "Return to me, and I will return to you, says the Lord of hosts" (3:7). This reflects a truth in description, for we are far apart from God, and the distance must be bridged by means of ethical innocence on the part of us who are most certainly not ethically innocent. But when this description becomes a prescription, when it becomes law, it is no good. Or at least it is no good to you and me in practice. Instead of making me want to "come close," it makes me want to run the other way. As Genesis 3:10 puts it: "I heard the sound of you in the garden, and I was afraid, because I was naked; and I hid myself." This latter statement, Adam's admission of his shame before God, is the true condition of man and woman before the imperative, which is God as law. At the point of the imperative, there is no desire to "return to me."

To find grace in the Bible, you have to look for one-way love. The first place to find it is in the patriarchs. Abraham, the founding father of Israel, is a man of absconding disbelief (Genesis 15:2, 3; 17:17; see also 12:10-20). Yet God speaks to him and for him. Abraham is old and unbelieving, and God gives him a son through his ancient wife, Sarah. Abraham in earlier years had lied, and lied again, about Sarah when he was passing through foreign countries with his family. He had actually put Sarah into the king of Egypt's harem in order not to be killed for her beauty's sake (Genesis 12:14-20). But God forgave and forgave, then forgave again.

Later, Jacob, who is one of the most self-serving and wily characters in the Old Testament, is forgiven and restored (Genesis 33) and used for good and for the good of the future. Abraham and Jacob are recipients of one-way love. They are recipients of grace.

The judges are examples of this also. Gideon is reduced in force and resources to almost nothing so that his victory over the Philistines can be attributed only — and I mean *only* — to the Lord (Judges 6–8). It is only grace that saves Gideon, and not his own hand at all. God is frequently described as "jealous" for the sake of his one-way love. He wishes no human being to receive or to take a single atom of credit for what he has done. This uncomfortable lesson is repeated over and over again in the Old Testament.

The prophet Samuel and the first king of the Israelites, Saul, are constantly given this description of God's grace as one-sided. If Saul or his men for one moment suggest that any of the credit for their success belongs to them, they are one-sidedly, and ruthlessly, judged. After being forced by God to give up his kingship, Saul is cursed by Samuel: "As your sword has made women childless, so your mother shall be childless among women" (1 Samuel 15:33). Saul is cursed because he tried to take his problems into his own hands. But God desired to solve Saul's problems. There is no synergism, or shared achievement, in the theater of grace.

One-way love: it is the theme song of Old Testament religion in relation to biography. A pure example of this is the call of Moses the lawgiver. Moses complains that he is not a public speaker. He is timid and tongue-tied. God questions him with overwhelming justice: "Who gives speech to mortals?" (Exodus 4:11). God will do for Moses all that is required. Nothing that Moses has by way of natural gifting, which is a ridiculous term as we shall see more and more, will contribute to what lies ahead. The only thing Moses has brought to the equation is murder and slipperiness. Not only is Moses not the one who will finally bring the great release to its conclusion — as he will be held back at the entrance to the Promised Land — but he is weighted down by his past. Moses is a prime case in point for the system of one-way love that is God's grace. God insists that Moses renounce every human effort in favor of the one divine effort.

Here is the anatomy of grace in the later books of the Old Testament. Grace as one-way love comes out of nowhere into a world determined by two-way love ("I will love you if you will love me") and half-way love ("I will love you but I need a little sign, just a little one"). Grace as one-way love appears within the prophecies of Isaiah, Jeremiah, and Ezekiel. Isaiah conceives of a messenger from God who will embody the principle of bringing nothing to the table before the face of God:

> For he grew up before him like a young plant,
> and like a root out of dry ground;
> he had no form or comeliness that we should look at him,
> and no beauty that we should desire him.
> He was despised and rejected by men;
> a man of sorrows, and acquainted with grief;
> and as one from whom men hide their faces
> he was despised, and we esteemed him not. (53:2-3, RSV)

The messenger will be so separated from human merit that his success can only be regarded as the sole achievement of grace.

Isaiah sees the one-way love of God for the messenger reflected in the extreme exclusion that the world delivers:

> By oppression and judgment he was taken away;
> and as for his generation, who considered
> that he was cut off out of the land of the living,
> stricken for the transgression of my people?
> And they made his grave with the wicked. (53:8-9, RSV)

The alienation of this man, on whom God has set his grace, makes Isaiah's prophecy a unique performance concerning the reality, and Godengenderedness, of one-way love. Nothing human or worldly is in play. God will have to raise him from the dead.

Later the prophet Jeremiah goes forward with this grace-line when he predicts a period of history in which law-keeping will no longer be focal or useful. God will make the people, from his own grace, *want* to do good rather than see the good in terms of requirement. Jeremiah foreshadows the New Testament's focus on inward religion:

> The days are surely coming, says the LORD, when I will make a new covenant with the house of Israel and the house of Judah. It will not be like the covenant that I made with their ancestors when I took them by the hand to bring them out of the land of Egypt — a covenant that they broke. . . . But this is the covenant that I will make with the house of Israel after those days, says the LORD: I will put my law within them, and I will write it on their hearts . . . for I will forgive their iniquity, and remember their sin no more. (31:31-34)

This is the end of the law (Romans 10:4), because the law is no longer needed. Duty becomes choice; demand becomes desire.

The prophecy of Ezekiel speaks about one-way love in Ezekiel's metaphor of muscle-bone-and-flesh resurrection. In Ezekiel 37, the prophet sees the Israelites as dead men. They are bones in a field full of bones. There is nothing there but "the bones of the dead" (as in Matthew 23:27). But the prophet sees them brought to life by the Spirit of God (Ezekiel 37:7-10). This is the portrait of a love that has nothing to do with amelioration. The bones are dead. They are not the remains of the day. They are actually dead. But then they are reanimated.

One school of thought in Islam believes that Jesus did not die on the cross but was extremely ill when they took him down. His disciples carried him to India, where he finally died of the wounds he had received at Jerusalem. This is a fascinating commentary on death and resurrection. When the Spirit of God asks Ezekiel, "Mortal, can these bones live?" (37:3), the answer is, obviously and non-Islamically, No. Grace is about life from death, or better, life to the dead. When the Spirit raises the dead men's bones to life and puts muscles on them and pumps blood into their muscles, the paradigm is not sickness and recovery. The paradigm is death and resurrection. That is the quality of grace. It responds to nothing whatsoever from our side, not a scintilla, not a sign of life, not the receptive wink of an eye. Grace is one-way love. It comes from outside.

Grace suffuses the Old Testament voice of God and its effects. Grace permeates Genesis. It discovers the guilty Moses and makes of him a mouthpiece for the perfection of God. Grace is at the bottom of the well for every judge and patriarch of the earliest times. Grace makes David the adulterer into the second founding king of the people. Grace puts the work of God at the fore in the reign of every king of Judah and Israel.

After the climactic reversal of fortune represented by the Babylonian captivity (587 B.C.) is fully felt, grace is understood to be the sole way forward. Ezekiel understood this. So did Isaiah before him, and Jeremiah too. The minor prophets are grace-intoxicated, although there are pieces of semi-Pelagian thinking in a few sections. The idea sneaks in that if we could only consecrate ourselves fully to God, he would come and heal us. You can see this in Amos, who, for all his powerful social criticism, seems to believe that human obedience is the ground floor of divine return. Semi-Pelagianism finds a following in the so-called "inter-testamental literature" before the time of Christ, and it permeates what scholars now call "Second-Temple Judaism," that form of Judaism into which Jesus was born.

We detect an uncertain voice in the closing verses of the Old Testament:

> Remember the teaching of my servant Moses, the statutes and ordinances that I commanded him at Horeb for all Israel.
>
> Lo, I will send you the prophet Elijah before the great and terrible day of the LORD comes. He will turn the hearts of parents to their children and the hearts of children to their parents, so that I will not come and strike the land with a curse. (Malachi 4:4-6)

Grace is foreseen in the form of the "great and terrible day of the LORD." And it is only God who can change hearts, the hearts of reactive children and stubborn parents. But the imperative does exist within a relationship that invites obedience. The implication of impasse between a requiring deity and a hopelessly tangled humanity is an uncomfortable one.

The themes of law and grace are mixed, finally, within the great book of theological praise, the Psalms. On the one hand, there are Psalms 51 and 32:

Have mercy on me, O God,
  according to your steadfast love;
according to your abundant mercy
  blot out my transgressions.
Wash me thoroughly from my iniquity,
  and cleanse me from my sin. . . .
Purge me with hyssop, and I shall be clean;
  wash me, and I shall be whiter than snow. . . .
Create in me a clean heart, O God,
  and put a new and right spirit within me. . . .
The sacrifice acceptable to God is a broken spirit;
  a broken and contrite heart, O God, you will not despise.
(51:1-2, 7, 10, 17)

Happy are those whose transgression is forgiven,
  whose sin is covered.
Happy are those to whom the LORD imputes no iniquity. . . .
I acknowledged my sin to you,
  and I did not hide my iniquity;
I said, "I will confess my transgressions to the LORD";
  and you forgave the guilt of my sin. (32:1-2, 5)

On the other hand, there is Psalm 119, which travels a distance toward the semi-Pelagian view of humankind in relation to God:

I have chosen the way of faithfulness;
  I set your ordinances before me.
I cling to your decrees, O LORD;
  let me not be put to shame. . . .

You have dealt well with your servant,
  O LORD, according to your word.
Teach me good judgment and knowledge,
  for I believe in your commandments. . . .
If your law had not been my delight,
  I would have perished in my misery.
I will never forget your precepts;
  for by them you have given me life. (119:30-31, 65-66, 92-93)

The Old Testament preaches both law and grace. You have to be able to tell the difference between God's attacking voice of the law, his inhibiting and deposing voice, his voice that kills; and God's revivifying voice of grace, his creative and loving voice, his voice that makes alive. The New Testament aids us to distinguish between these two voices.

Side Bar: Grace in Systematic Theology

Systematic theology has its detractors. They come from two sides. One side is uncomfortable, even intimidated, by the word "systematic." They argue that God, who is by definition unable to be pinned down or limited by a logical journey of thought, could never be captured by anything so rational as a "systematic theology." "Systematic" sounds like the opposite of "mystical," "experiential," or "personal." Or they say, when I tell them I am a systematic theologian, "Whoa! That's above my pay grade." What I think they mean is that the word "systematic" sounds removed from their lives, as if it were the province of ivory-towered eggheads. Thus contemporary religious people reject the term because it is too rational or they reject it because it is intimidating. But their rejection is unsatisfactory. You cannot reject a claim because it is consistent or thoughtful. That is anti-intellectual, the strategy of an ostrich. Nor should you reject systematic theology because it sounds a little threatening.

There is a second front from which the attack on systematic theology originates. This is from the theological "right," from sincere and consecrated people who would rather be known as "biblical theologians" than as systematic ones. This group, and it is a large constituency within the Christian community, fears that systematic thinking about theology will become the product of human thinking rather than thinking that issues from divine revelation. These people wish to know that one's theological expressions originate only and uniquely from within the written Word of the Bible. Human attempts to create and impose systems are suspect. After all, is this not what the medieval church tried to do: substitute human-derived ideas for God's written Word?

What this book, this systematic theology of everyday life, attempts to do is develop the theme of grace in a consistent manner, beginning with the Bible, and apply the Bible's view of it to a wide range of everyday human problems. For myself, I discern within Scripture a deeply consistent or "systematic" understanding of the grace of God working on the world. The grace of God in relation to the law of God is the "long and winding road" (Paul McCartney) that forges coherence from the many books and eras of the Bible. There are some minor bumps on that road, such as the book of Esther, which does not mention God, as well as the three passages already cited from Hebrews, Second Peter, and James. But these contrary parts of Scripture are few. They stand out! We should interpret their minority report in light of the overwhelming majority report of God's law-fulfilling grace. We can do this as we stand beneath the overwhelming evidence of Scripture.

My point is that a systematic theology of grace is also a systematic theology of the Bible. There is not a problem between the two. It is just that I wish to put in boldface the one word of grace, which, like an underground river, flows in and through the many biblical words of Holy Scripture.

I cannot interpret the Bible in the way that Muslims interpret the Holy Qur'an. It is not necessary to give the same exact weight to every single verse of the Bible. We should always see the trees in light of the forest. We should always permit the whole to shed light on the part. If and when biblical theology applies to Scripture the Qur'anic method, according to which every syllable is equivalent to every other syllable, then it has lost contact with the main tradition of Christian exegesis by which we weigh verses partly according to their thematic weight.

No one is going to say that the genealogies of Christ, important as they are in establishing his messianic identity within a historic human (as opposed to a ghostly theological) family, are just as weighty as John 3:16. I hope that no one is going to put Christ's "dark" saying concerning "that fox [Herod]" (Luke 13:32) in the same category as "Come to me, all you that are weary and are carrying heavy burdens" (Matthew 11:28). Rather, we need to interpret the "harder" texts from the evidence of the "easier" texts. This is not a fast-and-loose approach. It simply places the emphasis where Scripture itself places it, on human sin (under the law) and God's grace (through the gospel).

That is why this systematic theology of everyday life is also a biblical theology of everyday life. A systematic theology of grace "earths" Christ's crucified grace in the difficult conditions of everyday living.

Grace in Society

"Little children, keep yourselves from idols" (1 John 5:21). This is the abrupt ending of the first letter of John. Endings are important because they should leave you with a fundamental point. Great pop songs never fade out; they end with a jolt. Joe Meek's first big success in Britain was titled "What Do You Want to Make Those Eyes at Me For?" (1959). It shocked every disc jockey in England that year because of its surprise ending, the first of its kind in a pop record. The song ended. The sound simply went completely off. Then, five long beats later, just when you were lifting the stylus off the turntable, the refrain came back, twice as loud as before! The listener never forgets it. The same is true of St. John's out-of-the-blue warning at the end of his letter. It flies from its context and hits you in the face with its sublime No to the context in which we all live, to the world and its gods. What does John mean when he says, "Keep yourselves from idols"?

John is referring to the driving forces outside people that seek to direct their ideas and demand their allegiance. From the Cable News Network to QVC, from the *Atlanta Constitution* to the *San Francisco Chronicle,* from the radio show you put on at the start of the day to the music you listen to in bed at night — all these things shape you in terms of the world.

In the New Testament, the world is the aggregate of externally induced metaphors and conditioning influences that destroy the freedom of human beings to think and feel for themselves. Many people do not realize that they are being controlled by a thousand alternating currents of other people's notions, the sum total of which comprises "the world." But they are being controlled. They are being deeply formed. St. John drops us off the cliff at the close of his letter by putting us face to face with the simple, ineluctable power of the world. He also writes in 2:15: "Do not love the world or the things in the world."

The world detests grace. The world loves law. At least, it thinks it does. The world hates pardon and release from demand. It rejoices in retribution and the kind of demand that provokes suicide. Understood in this way, we know why the world crucified Christ and martyred the prophets. The world took the touching idealism of the young students in *Les Miserables* and stamped it out. The students were all killed in a complete massacre. The world caused Romeo and Juliet to commit suicide, but it was all a mistake. Do you remember the song "It's a Mistake" by Men at Work (1983)? It is about nuclear holocaust, fear, and a red button. The red button is pushed, but "it's a mistake"! This is what the world, which in New Testament terms is the devil's playground, enjoys. The world consists of big, big mistakes.

Because of the world's thrall (an old but concise word) to the law, which accuses the poor "sons and daughters of Adam and Eve" (C. S. Lewis) of ever new abuses and crimes, the grace of God provokes a never-failing resistance. When a man who committed a crime professes conversion to God, the world does not accept this. The world hates his profession of faith and tells the man he is a hypocrite. When the Jim Brown character in Tim Burton's *Mars Attacks* (1996) says he has "embraced Allah and cleaned up his life," we are meant to be skeptical. (He had been a Las Vegas bouncer and general no-good.) But the film shows that it really has happened. The character offers his life, in a Christ-like posture on a tarmac cross, for the other main characters. It is a heart-stopping moment in an otherwise trivial (but extremely cool) movie.

Tim Burton meant it that way. "Muhammad" or "Christ": the world doesn't like to hear that a man has turned from its own influence to influences outside its closed system of narcotic manipulation.

Grace is one-way love. Society demands two-way love. Society requires quantity and value and "evidence" of the pound of flesh. In human society grace has a bad day every day. This was first expressed conceptually when the philosopher Aristotle composed his *Nicomachean Ethics* in the fourth century B.C. Aristotle taught that a man is defined by his deeds: a good man is good because he does good deeds. This is the only way to gauge moral worth. Measurement becomes everything. Progress becomes everything. Amelioration becomes the law of life. I would say that Aristotle is the safe harbor of absolute worldliness in the world of thought.

Grace is the opposite of Aristotle. Grace takes a different approach to criminal justice. Grace takes a different line on what forms human identity. Grace rewrites the meaning of achievement and career. Grace is not utopian; in fact, it is *dys*topian. What I mean is that utopian ideas of society call on hard work and human dedication to create a new society of fairness and equity — the same old story. Grace, on the other hand, recognizes the wholly dystopian and hellish character of life in the world under the law and posits an alternative view of reality.

Another theme arising from grace in society is the theme of *single* message versus *double* message. A principal reason why grace gets such a hard time in the world is that it is an unequivocal word. It is not, as we have seen, a mixed message, a No and a Yes (2 Corinthians 1:17-20). Just as the law is a No in its essence, so grace is a Yes in its essence. The world has a hard time understanding this. It is too good to be true. How can love be one-way? How can grace end-run its way around standards and yardsticks? It sounds unfair.

It is unfair, but it is completely unfair. It is the other side of the law, which is a total grappling, a totally unsuccessful and failed grappling, with judgment. Because the law is completely fair, grace has to be completely "unfair." The atonement makes grace "fair," as is apparent in the teaching concerning the cross. But from our point of view, from the standpoint of its recipient, grace is unfair.

The "unfair" character of grace makes it *persona non grata* in the cut-and-thrust of the battle of life. Nobody welcomes grace. At the same time everyone pants for it; everybody wants it every second of every hour. Grace is an either-or proposition; it is not both-and.

If we apply grace to issues in social thought, the world's rejection becomes clear. Take criminal justice. Grace believes in absolution and release. It most certainly does not believe in capital punishment. Once a young man who worked for me was arrested for allegedly shooting another young man to death. It was all over the papers: "Arrested for Capital Murder." I could not believe it. It chilled me, that adjective "Capital." There simply would be no way out if he were sentenced. Yet the world yearns for retribution.

I compare the feeling of horror I had then with the feeling of elation I had on first seeing the ending of *Intolerance* (1916). At the end of D. W. Griffith's epic film, Christ comes again to the world. The effect is created by an optical superimposition. What the inspired director shows is a prison teeming with convicts, all dressed in prison stripes. They look up and the prison walls start to fall. They emerge, every one of them, into the absolving light of the one releasing God. The release is total. I don't think the image — and it is the last image of the movie — is intended metaphorically. Another quick frame in the montage shows men fighting on a battlefield, their long bayonets skewering each other with brutal relish. Overhead, the brightly lit cross of the Second Coming suddenly appears and they drop their weapons. There is no "peace process" here. It is finally all over.

Griffith's great images are apocalyptic. They are the visual images through which the artist depicts the grace-full end of history. The vision is inspired because it is either-or. There is either war or peace, imprisonment or release.

Jesus went to his hometown synagogue and announced "release to the captives and recovery of sight to the blind" (Luke 4:18; Isaiah 61:1). In all his dealings with accused people, he illustrated his non-gradual reception arising from grace. His approach to people was one-way love. Moreover, it was not a compartmentalized one-to-one exchange. It had implications for the larger field. Christ's expression of grace has implications for deterrence in relation to criminal justice and for our ideas concerning war. These implications are one-sided. When Jesus speaks of peace, it is total. When he speaks of forgiveness, it is not a shadowy thing or a metaphor. The social consequences are extreme. This is why Christianity is subversive. "These [are] people who have been turning the world upside down," say the accusers of the Christians in the book of Acts (17:6). The words are apt.

Consider another social idea and look at it through the lens of grace: the "good" of *career* as the world assigns it. The world puts a high measure on professional achievement. Career is regarded as an important thing. Success in one's profession is thought to be a definite mark of the satisfied life. Both women and men now accept this, or generally accept it, as something for which to strive. I am amazed at the extent to which career success is universally regarded as a key to identity. The fact is quite funny to anyone who lived through the 1960s. In that transitional time, success in the professions was thought to be selling out to the "establishment" — to the "military-industrial complex."

I remember the visit of the father of a friend of mine to a fraternity house on the campus of the University of North Carolina. The boy was from Greenwich, Connecticut, and his dad showed up looking exactly like our 1960s undergraduate idea of a businessman from Greenwich, Connecticut. It was May of 1970, right around the time of the Kent State shootings. One of my fraternity brothers turned to me and said, "Have you ever seen such a pig in your whole life?" There was a ripple of disgust in the dining room as the man, our "brother's" father, walked through. Today, on the other hand, college fraternities are considered the height of "red-state" thinking. Everywhere, from Brown to Stanford, from USC-LA to USC-Columbia, the "I-Banker" is the acme. Almost every student I know on a college campus thinks that the real thing is to be a trainee with Morgan Stanley or Goldman Sachs. In less than forty years, there has been an about-face away from huge suspicion of the professions to total adulation and competitive jealousy for places within them.

Everyone wants a career. Everyone thinks it is the thing to do. Whether this is fashion or not, grace turns it upside down. Not only is career, from the standpoint of grace, a mighty joke — for a career spits you out as rapidly as it sucks you in — and not only is it dominated overwhelmingly by the principle of law as it fixes your path, but grace declares that real "work" is created only when it springs from belovedness. Grace declares the end of all "career paths" that envisage a concrete goal. In grace, work — the best and most enduring work — is "fruit" as unstudied and uncontrived as the peaches in Chilton County, Alabama. The irony of grace is not only that it sabotages any interview you might have with a Wall Street law firm but that it actually prepares you to do the best work you will ever do if you should actually land the job. For when work is produced from natural desire and motive, rather than from the idea of actions resulting in proposed consequences, the best work is done. This is because the subject of the work, the "I" of all human endeavor, is not its end. That "I" is dead; it was dead on arrival the day grace arrived on the scene, irrespective of your gifts, talents, and givens. Under grace, career advances only one way: away from the wreckage of the "I" and the absence of any fixed need for achievement.

Justice, punishment, career: these are just three of the social sectors for which grace has high implications. More will be covered in later chapters. But the big field for grace, the place where it has got to have free reign for any happiness to reign at all for more than ten minutes, is the field of personal relationships.

Grace in Everyday Life

Grace has the power of the mallet. Every other prong and heavy-lifting device that seeks to change people is an expression of law and accomplishes the opposite of what it intends. People fear that grace will give permission to be bad. This is the classic fear: that grace will issue in a license — "007" — to do whatever you want, without consequences.

Yet that never happens! In fact, the opposite happens. When you treat people gracefully, they always end up doing the right thing. It comes naturally. Their righteousness grows like fruit, as Jesus predicted (Mark 4:20; Luke 6:43-45; 8:15; John 15:5).

What does grace look like? Let's say I am talking on the phone to somebody who is a real talker. I know this phone call is going to take at least a half hour. Inside, I am resisting it on every front. Somehow I give way, however, and fifteen minutes into the conversation the person says, "Look, I know you're busy and I'll let you go. But thanks for listening." Had I tried to get off the phone, had I tried to impose the law (in this case my own law) and forced the conversation to end, I would never have gotten off. Even if I had gotten off, I would have felt guilty about it for the rest of the day. Grace lets be.

Maybe you write a lot of e-mails. Take this *Dilbert* exercise: do you ever find yourself fretting over the wording of an e-mail? You overcorrect it; you make mistakes at the keyboard; you keep going back to make sure it's right. When this happens, you can be sure that the person to whom you are writing is a figure of the law in your life. The person to whom you are writing has some kind of judging power, and it is this power that puts your e-mail under threat. I recently did an inventory of the e-mails I wrote on a particular day, and I noticed that three of them had caused me discomfort and vacillation. Each of the three was written to someone who in my mind was potentially accusatory. On the other hand, the messages that came naturally and were even on the fun side of my work, these flowed like water. In those, I was responding to grace — in the others, to law.

Consider your wardrobe. Whether you are a woman or a man, how you look is probably at least a little important. Most of the time appearance seems to matter very little to me. I wear the same old corduroys and polo shirt and loafers. In the winter I wear a blazer, and in the summer I wear a seersucker jacket. Every so often, however, I take more pains. But it is rarely love that causes this checking up. When I take pains with my clothing, it is almost always out of law. I know this because it is so uncharacteristic. I watch my lapel pins, afraid that they may signal a controversial cause. I may look too "preppy," or maybe my tie is not acceptable — no outrageous "Jesus" ties allowed, and also none that stem from questionable organizations like a college eating club or a Protestant fraternal organization. In my case, grace is there when I am not worried about the way others will size up my appearance. Law is present when I begin to second-guess myself.

Take your workplace. You know that grace is operating there when you are not worried about running into the wrong person on your way to the restroom. The corridor at work is a lightning rod for law, and also for grace. More typically, you worry about running into the wrong person or maybe passing their cubicle when they are actually there. You might actually have to talk to that person, that painful person who raises every hackle you have. When people quit their job, they usually quit because of somebody in the workplace who is judging them or "making their life miserable." Most people who like their work do so because they feel free to be creative and are not being managed or controlled. This feeling has everything to do with grace and nothing to do with law.

Take your daughter-in-law or your son-in-law. Perhaps your daughter-in-law does not like you. Somehow she has decided that you do not approve of her. The other day I heard a woman rake her son-in-law over the coals in his absence. He does not have a "Mount Pleasant [South Carolina]" background, I heard her say. Then she added, "I don't know him very well, anyway." No wonder! The poor boy is not from the right neighborhood. Surely he must know how his mother-in-law feels. Neither of them is going to come anywhere near each other as long as that sort of law-based thinking prevails. I am certain, by the way, that he judges her, too. But there is no hope as long as the law defines their relationship. Many daughters- and sons-in-law relate well to their spouses' parents; in those cases there is grace. Often the law has infected a person's relationship with her natural parents, and the daughter-in-law has transferred her feelings about her parents to her spouse's parents. I see this all the time in families. Few extended families are not dealing in some way with their experiences of the law.

Take your own child. You live in Trenton, and he moved to Portland. The fact is, he could not get far enough away from you. He would not put it this way himself, but you represented the law for him. He understood you as a judge over his life: *lex semper accusat* (the law always accuses). This broke your heart because you never meant to come across as accusatory. But you did. So now he lives in Oregon, land of "physician-assisted suicide."

But there is still hope. Reconciliation is possible. You fly out there;

you do not grovel but you apologize instead. You apologize especially when he and the woman with whom he lives have a child. You roll up your sleeves (staying at a motel nearby, not their house) and help them. You do not throw stones and you do not open old wounds. But you really help him; you help them, right when your son really needs you. This is grace. Three years after that weekend, you receive a call: "Mom and Dad, Cheryl and I want to move back to New Jersey. We want our little boy to know his grandparents." This is grace. Tacked on to that surprising, thrilling conversation is a little postscript: "By the way, we didn't tell anybody, but we got married last month. We even found a nice minister to do the service."

We could say that there are three prime relationships in life, in addition to work. The first is with your parents; the second is with your siblings, if you have them; and the third is with your children, if you have them. These are the blood-relationships. Grace makes the difference in all of them.

If any of the three relationships, especially the first, is law-driven, there is no relationship. There is no relationship because torn relationship means no relationship. On the other hand, if any of these three relationships, especially the first, is based on grace, there is everything good and fruitful there. It is that simple and that pregnant.

Because of what Christianity calls "original sin," which is only another expression for a realistic portrait of the human being and the human situation, almost every relationship in the world is assailed by the law. Every relationship is fragile because it exists under the law. There are a few non-neurotic, non-law-based relationships in life, but they are few and far between. Just count on your fingers and toes the number of non-judgmental people you know. Grace comes from outside of us. It is one-way love. Grace is the intervention that draws people away from the law. It has worked in your life. You had a teacher once, an uncle once, even a mother once, who drew you away from the law. When this happened, everything changed. As a character in *Close Encounters of the Third Kind* (1977) said, "The stars came out last night and sang." Colors returned to nature and feeling returned to the anesthetized parts of your life.

Grace against the Curse: "Deeper Magic from before the Dawn of Time"

The law is a curse. We saw this earlier from St. Paul's letter to the Galatians, and we saw it in the reference to crucifixion in the book of Deuteronomy. We see this in life. Law curses everything it touches. It is an ironic curse, because it intends to bless. It means well.

Often this is true in love. We mean well. We really do love someone. We really do wish to bless them and not curse them. But our love is wrong somehow. It is possessive, or it springs from an intense need on our own part. Have you known examples of love that was sincere but somehow got mishandled, tainted with self-love?

Take the example of the possessive widower who cannot let go of his daughter. He would be just as happy if she never grew up, never left home, and stayed with him into his extreme old age. He needs her that badly. She is his fixed object of love. His love has become a bent love, however, a misconstrued love, and it results in destroying the very one in whom it believes. It is like the novel *The Collector* by John Fowles (1963). Its main character collects beautiful things, like butterflies. But he decides he needs to collect a beautiful woman. He imprisons her and wants only to admire her within his little museum. The man is not Hannibal Lector, but the result is the same: the beloved's destruction.

Love, when it is processed wrongly or confused with self-love, is a curse. Think of Norman Bates in *Psycho* (1959). This utterly split-personality killer thought he was doing right. Listen to Norman's own words at the end of the movie, Robert Bloch's epitaph on his famous character: "Don't they know? I wouldn't hurt a fly." The law is like Norman Bates. It thinks it will do us good. It desires to do us good. But in fact the result is always that "the trespass multiplied" (Romans 5:20). It makes worse that which it seeks to control.

Grace has the opposite effect. If law is the "deep magic from the dawn of time" (C. S. Lewis's phrase from *The Lion, the Witch and the Wardrobe*), then grace is the "deeper magic from before the dawn of time" (also Lewis's phrase). Grace is required to counteract the curse of the law. In Lewis's story, the law has frozen the world. Every animal, every human, every living thing lives within this frozen world. The White Witch wants it this way. She keeps the world frozen in place. She presides over the fatal rule of law. When Aslan, the Christ-like figure, challenges her and her minion, the freezing law, he must pay for it. He is executed under the law. The "deep magic" of the law has been in charge forever and must be reckoned with. No one can remember a time when its sway was not complete and unchallenged.

But Aslan is raised from the dead. The Emperor-Beyond-the-Sea intervenes with grace and justifies the one-way love of the Lion. Grace melts the frozen world because of Aslan's one-way love. Aslan dies in the place of the law's victims (the frozen, once-living beings who sit covered in sheets of snow and ice). He dies in place of one particular sinner, the selfish and even vicious Edmund, who betrayed Aslan as well as his sisters and brother. The one-way love of the Lion delivers the world, and the curse of the law is lifted. The world is unfrozen! Grace is the end of the curse over life. It is the end of the law. This is why Paul writes as an exclamation his words in Romans 10:4: "Christ is the end of the law."

What Is the Relation between Law and Grace?

Grace and law are the driving forces of the world. They exist in a relation, but it is not a both-and relation. It is not a little bit of one and a little bit of the other. The two are resolved in a one-time resolution that is connected to a single historical instant, the death of Christ. In the way we receive them, however — in the way they play out in everyday life — they are completely separate. In human historical experience, there is no such thing as grace in law, although some wish to believe there is. Neither is there law in grace, although some wish to believe there is.

Resolving the Opposition of Law and Grace

The law of God is absolute, and the grace of God is undeviating. These are two irresoluble forces. They are also irresoluble in everyday life. If a person gives me a compliment but is also holding over me some idea that I have to express appreciation, then his compliment means nothing. If I am being pummeled verbally, but my attacker holds out the tiniest carrot of kindness, it is simply confusing. Do you remember the torture sequence in George Orwell's novel *1984*? Winston Smith was subjected to intolerable psychological torture in Room 101 only to be embraced by his torturer with promises of cherishing and hope. That was law tinctured by grace. The result was that Winston fell apart. His entire personality was undermined and finally liquidated.

If grace and law are irresoluble, if they are inherently contradictory, then how is it possible to live? If there is no resolution, then our lives in reality are lives of total despair before the insuperable and impermeable "hill of legality" (John Bunyan). Nothing we can do will satisfy the law. Of course, we will long for release. We will be one continual teardrop in hopes of rescue. (There was a 1980s pop group with a great name, "The Teardrop Explodes.") But rescue will never come. The law will not permit it.

So what does the Bible mean when it says, "Righteousness and peace will kiss each other" (Psalm 85:10)? It is the idea, in a kind of plaintive promise, that God's demand, or his righteousness, will one day coincide with his mercy. Hope is held out, especially in Isaiah, for a resolution of the two irresolubles. The mechanics, however, of such an impossible dream are sketched only roughly: "The righteous one, my servant, shall make many righteous, and he shall bear their iniquities . . . because he . . . was numbered with the transgressors" (53:11-12). To dream the marriage of law and grace! This is what a few of the Old Testament prophets do. They "dream the impossible dream" *(Man of La Mancha)*. For Christians, the heart of religion is the impossible dream made real. The old words for the impossible dream and its coming into reality are "the substitutionary atonement of Jesus Christ on the cross."

With the arrival of these words upon the scene, one might wish to put up one's hands in horror. Oh *that!* The crutch of all traditional Christians: the intervention of a divine forgiveness so devoutly to be wished for but so completely elusive in life. But is there any other resolution possible for the impossible conflict between grace and law?

Grace is what everyone wants. No one enjoys the stress of demand. It is terminally exhausting. When the President of the United States asks a Supreme Court nominee why he or she wants the job, the only true answer should be a refusal: I do not want the job! The *lex-semper-accusat* character of the scrutiny under which the nominee will exist during the next four months of her or his life is hell on earth. Law is hell on earth. It is as rigidly fixed as the lot of every person who has ever lived. Grace, on the other hand, is what everyone desires. One-way love is the object of all human craving.

If there is no resolution to the conflict between grace and law, then suicide is the right thing to do. In fact, many more people take their own lives than is publicly admitted. A higher number of family members take their own lives, in one way or another, than is ever "released." I have learned this from thirty years of parish ministry. Suicide is a sort of tragic "wising up" to the true state of affairs. For this reason, Christian faith must bear witness to the resolution of grace and law in the substitutionary atonement of Christ.

The death of Christ on the cross is an event that took place in a specific place and time. It was a death and not an illness, which is to say it snuffed out life and therefore hope, as humans conceive it. This death took place on the cross, which made it a public event and also a judicial event. A man was tried and found guilty of a crime deserving capital punishment. He was then exposed, for everyone to see. From a Christian point of view, and probably even from a secular judicial point of view, his death was unjust. The event was public, exposed, unjust: a miscarriage of the law.

There is a sentence in the New Testament that can properly be described by the overused word "lapidary." It is in 1 Peter 3:18 and reads: "Christ also suffered for sins once for all, the righteous for the unrighteous, in order to bring you to God." This is an interpretation of a concrete event that was already an instance of a terminating, unjust, and public execution. The execution operated in favor of unrighteous people on the part of a righteous man. It was a substitutionary atonement. The resolution to the problem of grace in relation to the law took place in connection with this substitutionary atonement.

What is atonement? It is someone giving up something in order to satisfy the demand of someone else. It is even a little more than that, for atonement has to do with guilt. In atonement, the demand of the other is proper. It is the result of an original injustice. Something valuable must be offered in satisfaction. "John Barleycorn must die." This is the territory of once-popular sociologists such as Joseph Campbell. Campbell was always talking about atonement-motifs in world religions, from "lord of the harvest" agrarian sacrifice to the drowning of young girls by the Incas. Campbell, like his forerunner, Sir James Frazer, saw a fascination with myths of atonement in religions throughout the world. The fascination of these myths lay in their resonance with the occurrence in Christianity of such ideas. "Christ died for sins once for all, the righteous for the unrighteous."

Christians do not need to be uncomfortable with Joseph Campbell's thesis. I agree with it myself. In the face of a demand, there has to be something one can give up that is sufficient to satisfy the demand. What can I give up? The resolution of grace and law inherent in the Christian religion gives up the Son of God on the cross of Christ. It presents the death of the innocent in place of the guilty. This is atonement thinking, and it is properly capitalized (i.e., Atonement) because it is a proper noun in the Christian context. It is a proper noun because the New Testament regards it as final: "once for all." Atonement resolves the irresoluble conflict between grace and law. It is the end of the law, as St. Paul states it in Romans 10:4. The incomparably stressful demand of the law is answered perfectly in the death of the innocent. This is the heart of Christianity.

When I first read the enigmatic ghost stories of Montague Rhodes (M. R.) James (1862-1936), I struggled with the "back story," the real mechanism of the plot. James gives you tiny clues and strange details of what is happening behind the scenes in his stories. You always feel slightly thrown off the scent. Behind the sudden deaths and mysterious apparitions, what is going on? It is hard to say exactly. M. R. James wrote an essay entitled "Ghosts — Treat Them Gently!" in which he explained what he had tried to do in these weird tales. He said that the author of a "weird tale" has to have clearly in view the actual thing that is going on, the mechanics, the explanation, so to speak, of the supernatural event. But the reader only receives the intended chill, later.[9]

This is a good way to understand the atonement of Christ. Almost immediately after it happened, something awesome was believed to have taken place in relation to the event, the death of Jesus of Nazareth as a criminal under Pontius Pilate. What was it? God knew. Nobody else really knew. St. Paul was given to know later, as someone who had definitely not been there. The "back story" was given to the author of Hebrews, too: the interpretation of a veiled event as the mechanism by which God would forgive the sins of the world. It was given to St. John also. The mechanism of the resolution of grace and law, a resolution that must be posited in order that human suicide not be the result of their conflict, is the atonement of Christ, "for all time [the] single sacrifice for sins" (Hebrews 10:12).

The substitution involved in the atonement is an even further point. The atonement has to consist of a substitution. Here many people stumble, because it seems too good to be true. In order for the atonement to resolve the conflict between grace and law, it must consist of a substitution. Here again, First Peter displays sublime brevity: Christ died "once for all, the righteous for the unrighteous." The word "for" signals the substitution. This death was a final advocacy. It was a final substitution for our guilt.

This substitution is an unpopular idea. People become incensed when they are told that their sin, or (perhaps more immediately) the sin of someone who has hurt them and wronged them, can be conquered by an outside intervention that is a direct substitution for that guilt. How dare God? How dare God, or anyone for that matter, substitute himself for that dreadful person who hurt me so badly? It is unfair!

I ask people, What if *you* were the perpetrator? What if you were the one who had committed the crime? Are there not examples in your life when you were not the victim, but rather the perpetrator? The substitutionary atonement of Christ is a mechanism for perpetrators. It

9. In Montague Rhodes James, *Casting the Ruins and Other Ghost Stories* (New York: Oxford University Press, 1998), pp. 349-52.

carries grand implications for victims, but its prime focus is on perpetrators. This is to the good. Yet some people react to the teaching with feelings of its unfairness. The world and its many victims regard the substitutionary atonement as an experiment in "cheap grace." It is not cheap. To the perpetrator, the sinner, it "gets you off the hook." Christians have always clung to this "one-sided" release from the accusation of the law.

Substitution is more than a metaphor. It is one person in the place of another. During the days of "Camelot" in Washington, D.C., the JFK years, there was the constant "Teddy Kennedy factor." Teddy Kennedy had apparently cheated in an undergraduate exam at Harvard by paying someone else to take the exam for him. This was cheating, no question about that. The example of substitution that this incident provided was more important to me than the uproar his infraction generated. Teddy Kennedy apparently wanted what everyone wants: someone to do the hard thing for him so that he would not have to do it himself.

What is wrong with that in principle? What is wrong with wanting it? Who does not desire a substitute? Oscar Wilde's short novel *The Picture of Dorian Gray* is a masterpiece concerning substitution. An immoral young man is able to transfer his sins onto a magical portrait of himself, which is hidden in an unused room of his house. Dorian Gray stays young forever, but his picture ages. It becomes not only old, but scabrous. Haunted by this image of himself, the forever-young hero finally stabs the painting in the hope of ridding himself of its visualized guilt. But in doing so, he stabs himself. The man Dorian Gray falls down dead, old and withered and "loathsome of visage," recognizable only because of the rings he wore.

The problem with human substitution is that it cannot be pulled off. There are some instances of it, for example when a soldier in combat falls on a grenade in order to absorb the explosion that would kill his comrades. But the overwhelming portion of our longing for a substitute cannot be fulfilled. There is no one to do it. There is no one who can do it. The law, which makes me despair and wish that I could call upon a substitute, overtakes me. There is no substitute for our suffering. So the law overtakes me. I fail my bar exam, three times. I choke after I am promoted and fall on my face. I am unable to do the high-pressure job I thought I always wanted. I am not handsome enough to draw her attention.

All this is to say that substitution is necessary if the atonement is to have effect. If it is to do anything, atonement must involve substitution. Thus when St. John says of Christ, "Here is the Lamb of God who takes away the sin of the world" (John 1:29), it must be added, "the righteous for the unrighteous." Substitution is the mechanism behind the atonement. It is the back story. Substitution enables the law to afflict Christ instead of me. It puts him in the crosshairs and not me. It is unfair, in any worldly way of looking at it.

Listen to how St. Paul, who never saw Christ in the flesh and who only afterward discerned the mechanism behind his death, described the substitutionary atonement:

> There is therefore now no condemnation for those who are in Christ Jesus. . . . For God has done what the law, weakened by the flesh, could not do: by sending his own Son in the likeness of sinful flesh, and to deal with sin, he condemned sin in the flesh, so that the just requirement of the law might be fulfilled in us. (Romans 8:1, 3-4)

Divorcing Law and Grace

To the degree that grace and law are resolved in the substitutionary atonement of Christ, to the same degree they are separated in experience. Grace and law are completely distinct in everyday life. The moment we recognize this, instances of grace become transformative. The moment we blur the distinction, all attempts to hear or speak grace become futile.

This separated experience of grace and law from life is confirmed by the Bible: "The law indeed was given through Moses; grace and truth came through Jesus Christ" (John 1:17). Moses was given one thing: the law. Jesus Christ was given another: grace. The biblical distinction is true in everyday life.

Here is an example: Suppose a woman marries someone who really loves her. But he has a couple of personal sensitivities. He does not like a mess. In fact, he is a little obsessive about order. He is always picking up after her and implying, by doing so, that she is a slob. This sensitivity of his did not seem very important at first. Other aspects of their life together were good. But the older he gets, the more anxious he becomes when she is just being herself. It is a problem between them, if you want to know the truth. He is becoming more "type A" in relation to the house, and his wife feels like becoming more "type B." Sometimes she just wants to take the trash and strew it out in the middle of the living room. She is that aggravated by his attitude.

Initially, this marriage had grace in it. But the law, beginning with a fairly small thing, took over. The more he judges her, the more messy she wants to be. "Law came in, with the result that the trespass multiplied" (Romans 5:20). We know, from the gospel of grace, that if he would just stop noticing (she calls him "Mr. Notice-It-All"), she would probably start picking up her things. Grace begets grace. Law begets resistance.

Here is another example: you start using words with me like "accountability," or, if you are a practicing Christian, "discipleship." You start to "speak the truth in love" in my life. You tell me that you intend the criticism you dole out to be for my own good. You tell me there is really love beneath the lecture. But all I can hear is the lecture. My receptors, as an ordinary original sinner, are wired to pick up the law. Tell me one thousand times that your law is in the service of love. I will even tell you I believe you. But I don't. There is no law in existence that can be heard as grace by sufferers and sinners. The cliché is true: we need unconditional love.

You can learn about this absolute separation between grace and law if you listen to your children. Children never respond well to a lecture. Is there a case on record of children responding well to a lecture? They may assent by a reluctant nod or a sort of grudging silence. But it is all resistance. When you are dying, it will come back to you. Your children will tell you the incidents that made a difference to them. They will tell you the moments when they heard the true voice of parental love. Believe me, it was rare. It was rarer than you ever thought. It took place in connection with your daughter's divorce and the way you didn't say a word of "I told you so" when she walked in the door with her six-year-old daughter and no more husband.

Or maybe the grace came out after your son's car crash. Rod Rosenbladt, a Lutheran theologian, tells the true story of wrecking his father's Buick 8 when he was sixteen years old. Rod was drunk, as were all his friends who were in the car. The first thing Rod's dad asked him over the phone was whether he was all right. Rod said yes. He also told his father he was drunk. Later that night, Rod wept and wept in his father's study. At the end of the ordeal, his father said one thing: "How about tomorrow we go get you a new car." Rod says now that he became a theist in that moment. God's grace became real.

When Rod tells that story, there are always a few people in the audience who get mad. They say, "Your dad let you get away with that?! He didn't punish you at all?" And Rod says, "No," adding the following: "Do you think I didn't know what I had done? Do you think it was not the most painful moment of my whole life up to that point? Do you think the law wasn't cutting me down to nothing?" Rod's father spoke the word of grace in that moment. In that eternal encounter, for it reflected the mechanism of God's grace, there was no law. The law's dominion came to an end. Grace superseded it.

The two accounts, grace and law, must be kept separate. No commingling! Grace is never law, nor is law ever grace. Grace is the chemistry of the new life, and law is the *modus operandi* of the old life. When you mix grace and law, the solution is no longer grace but casuistry, which is worse than law in law's purity. The principles of grace and law must be kept strictly separate.

Consider this in politics. The partition of Ireland in 1920 was the only way to have peace between Protestants, who composed about 30 percent of the population, and the triumphant Roman Catholics, the other 70 percent. The two groups needed to be separated. Had separation not occurred, the Protestants would have been wiped out. There was no mercy at that time from the ascendant Nationalist or Catholic community. Partition had to take place. The Protestants were forced to hole up in the north, and the Catholics remained in the much larger south. The cry of the hour was, "Divided we stand!" Partition guaranteed that no more Irish Protestants would be burned out of their houses in the middle of the night. Partition promised to Protestants some protection. It also gave their neighbors to the south the vast majority of the country, the city of Dublin, and, most importantly, freedom from the British government. Divided we stand.

I am eager to maintain a sharp separation between grace and law. In experience, I am not helped by compounds of the two. Law is good because it shows me how things really stand. Law obliterates my illusions and shows me the truth. But law is also a stress from which there is no release. Nothing I am able to do endows me with peace if its aim is in any way to appease the force of law. The law is divine and speaks, in my own unconscious mind, with an iron voice. Its voice makes me as anxious on vacation as it does in the office. A few years ago, there was a *New Yorker* cartoon of a vacationing middle-aged businessman and his wife sitting on an island beach. He is engrossed in taking notes, and she observes, "Dear, are you doing your daily list here, too?"

Joe Meek, the independent producer of pop music who shot himself in 1967, once recorded himself singing the words to a song entitled "Happy Valley." "No problems there," it goes, "I'm a goin' to Happy Valley, gonna get there today." Joe's unearthly, depressed voice singing this impossible lyric is one of the most affecting and disturbing recordings he ever made. He sounds like the "wretched man that I am! Who will rescue me from this body of death?" (Romans 7:24). He is singing irresistibly and sympathetically of a grace of which his life offered him not one atom.

If we separate grace and law, which life experience does for us, it has the result paradoxically of *reunifying* the two. When grace is heard and received, when it is not confounded in any degree by the law, it paints a masterpiece: a person unconditionally affirmed who becomes instantaneously the expresser of love, joy, peace, meekness, kindness, and creativity. This graced human being becomes the flesh-and-blood example of the thing the law had wanted of him. Yet the law is gone from his or her mind. Grace produces the appearance of what the law says it wants, but only when grace is able to act unilaterally. Looking at this man or woman, who has been given grace unconditionally, we see established in him or her the very faithfulness and chastity and hopeful spirit that the law had sought to pound into that person.

In everyday life, the divorce between grace and law creates the new being (Ephesians 2:14-16), a person formed solely by grace but looking like the law-providing Moses. Grace and law must always be treated like a divided Ireland: "Divided we stand."

Is Grace against the Law?

The relation between grace and law is resolved historically and also conceptually in the crucifixion of Christ. The crucifixion of Christ is the union of law and one-way love. But in everyday life there can be no relation between grace and law.

This is a strong statement. It comes under threat both from nonreligious people and from religious people. Here is an example of the former. In 1995 a Canadian film crew produced a one-hour television program entitled "The Conversion." It told the story of a character named Henry Marshall, who shoots three people at an office Christmas party out of resentment for having gone to prison for a white-collar crime actually committed by his boss. Henry escapes and finds refuge in a country inn. There he keeps himself quiet, nursing a bullet wound in his side. There he also meets a man named Lucas, who seems to know all about him and tries to help him. Lucas has compassion for Henry, who is bitter and bleeding, and tries to reason with Henry about the roots of compassion. There is a lot of talk. Out of nowhere, Henry notices that his wound is gone and that Lucas now has it, bleeding from his side. His identity has been switched with Lucas's. When the original Lucas, who now looks like Henry, is arrested, the original Henry goes free. As Henry leaves the inn and looks into the Christmas sky, he sees a falling star and an angel. Beautiful music fills the soundtrack. No one who saw "The Conversion" will ever forget how it moved them to tears. It was like *It's a Wonderful Life* meets *My Dinner with André,* with music by Enigma.

The show created a stir. It created a controversy, in fact. Fans made a lot of chat about it on the Internet. Jason Warren, who runs a website concerning this kind of material, said the show was completely unfair because it held out forgiveness to a criminal character who had murdered three of his co-workers. Warren wrote that the episode's "Christian belief system," by which a bad man is forgiven "for no reason," made it problematic.

It *was* problematic in any worldly sense. The show presents the idea that Henry Marshall can be forgiven for his crime and that he is just an ordinary person who has gone off the tracks. Lucas, the Christ figure, loves him and also knows everything about him. Moreover, Lucas takes Henry's wound into himself and switches identity with him right down to the fingerprints. As many of the show's fans said, the episode was "Christian" and unfair. How can you forgive a man like that?

It is not only the world that detests grace. The Christian world also finds the absolution of grace to be a bitter pill. Every time you preach or embody grace, some Christians will accuse you of "antinomianism," the idea that you are against the law. When Tyler Perry's African American movie *Diary of a Mad Black Woman* (2005) became an overnight success, it was roasted by white critics, even as it rose to be the number-one movie in America. The *New York Times* called it "Amos 'n Andy meets Cinderella in Sunday School." I expected the secular press to have problems with this somewhat vulgar but explicitly Christian drama of redemption. What I did not expect was the white Christian media's reservations concerning the film.

Christianity Today was offended by the movie's ending,[10] which allowed the heroine to finalize a divorce that had already been granted by the court earlier in the plot and to marry the man she loved. She had never been intimate with him, incidentally, and he, from his Christian convictions, had never asked her to sleep with him. At the end of the film, after the heroine's former husband has been healed at a church service and is now ready to move forward after a vicious prior life, the heroine acknowledges the divorce that has now become final. *Christianity Today*'s critic disliked the ending. She thought it was un-Christian. The critic wanted the battered wife to go back to her husband and rescind the divorce.

10. *Christianity Today,* review by LaTonya Taylor, 25 February 2005.

Personally, I would have liked the script to go that way, too. But here was an outspokenly Christian movie with an outspokenly Christian "belief system" in play that was in radical contrast with the message of almost every other movie in the theaters. *Diary of a Mad Black Woman* was being seen by millions of people. Yet *Christianity Today*'s reviewer carped! She could not just say, Thank God for Tyler Perry. He is doing more for our cause than ten thousand other efforts out there. Thank God for Tyler Perry!

In *Christianity Today*'s inability to swallow *Diary of a Mad Black Woman,* I saw the vivid portrayal of an offense against grace. It is common among Christian people, this finger pointing. At the root of the finger pointing is the fear that if grace is given to a sinner, the sinner is going to take advantage of the amnesty and do a bad thing. This is the fear of antinomianism, the conviction that grace equals permissiveness. On this view, grace is against the law.

Is grace against the law? Are Christian critics of grace right about that? Are nonreligious critics of grace right about that?

The problem with the world's criticism of grace, that grace is unfair, lies in its worldview. The world wants to think that there are good people and bad people, good countries and bad countries. The world wants to think that innocence exists over against guilt. The world also wants to think that innocence and guilt can be established in the context of law. This is not how Christianity sees things. Christians see every person as guilty before God, subconsciously guilty at all times. External actions, as Jesus said, are not as important as internal motives. And internal motives are the most compromised of all data (Mark 7:20, 23).

The world's problem with grace is that it is unfair. But all you need to do is turn the tables and observe people on the defensive against law. If someone is pulled over by a patrol car and roughed up because the sheriff thinks the driver is carrying a gun or has drugs in the trunk, that driver will cry for grace with passionate intensity. My issue with the world's problem with grace is that it fails to have compassion when it is on the wrong side of the law. Jesus said he had not come to call "the righteous," by which he meant the people who seem to be on the "right" side of the law. Jesus added that he had come to call "sinners," by which he meant people who are on the wrong side of the law (Matthew 9:13). Implicit in Christ's statement is the idea that everyone is on the wrong side of the law. Therefore Christ came to call everyone.

When you are an accused person, you always turn in the direction of grace. You never think for a minute to turn in the direction of the law. The law will only spit at you. The human condition is forever on the wrong side of law, and therefore, in the "wee hours" (Frank Sinatra), it always tilts toward grace. The argument that grace is unfair — the notion that the definitive forgiveness of the criminal Henry Marshall, the forgiveness that took on his penalty and his bullet wound, is wrong — is pharisaical. It disappears, like spider webs before a broom, when the tables of life are turned and *you* become the accused. Is grace the refuge of scoundrels? Absolutely.

Why do religious people have a hard time with grace? People come to faith during times of trouble. Even if they grew up in church or had a religious experience as a teenager, they usually come to faith during a period of trouble. A specific problem in life leads them to question or to look at God in a new way. Sometimes it prompts them to read something or go to church or talk to somebody they respect. A time of trouble leads them toward the grace of God. But right after they receive this grace, they get punished with the law again. The church punishes them with the law. Here lies the problem, an unburied one.

You could put it this way: The law, the stress of life driving you to a breakdown, reduces you to a walking question mark. The question is answered, amazingly, by God's one-way love. Grace changes everything. You then enter some form of church or community. At this point, the iron curtain of the law comes down. You are told you need to be "discipled" or "mentored" or "coached": held "accountable." Sermons contain lists of things to do, "disciplines" to take up, a "Christian worldview" to embrace. The law is reimposed.

No wonder the hymn writer complained, "Where is the blessedness I knew/When first I saw the Lord?" People become semi-Pelagians the day (after) they become Christians. This is the heart of it. People in the world, including Christians, are Pelagians by nature. They want to do it for themselves. "Control" is the key word and concept. But control fails massively at some specific, vulnerable point of opening. When this happens, people are undone and they open up to grace. The grace of God makes its appearance, usually in the form of compassionate one-way love from another person. But the moment things are patched up a bit, life morphs back toward control, into semi-Pelagianism. Semi-Pelagianism is the compromise Christians force between the grace that saved them and the Pelagianism inherent in their human nature. It is the Achilles' heel that besets Christians and all the Christian churches.

Semi-Pelagianism, which acknowledges grace but insists upon an effort or response from the pained human side, defeats Christians just as wholly as Pelagianism defeats the world. Semi-Pelagianism dies hard. It is the old "control" theme in a new and sanctified form. It is not grace. This control hates grace. It explains why *Diary of a Mad Black Woman* received mixed notices from white Christian people. The movie seemed to be *against* the law. But did you see it? Everyone in the movie, I mean everyone, got better. Everyone was healed. Everyone was put back together by grace, and no one was left out in the cold. Mothers loved their children again, drugs were thrown away unneeded, physical abuse was forgiven, adultery was punished. How could anyone see this movie as anything but a victory for character and self-sacrifice? But the Christian world continues to swallow camels and bat against flies (Matthew 23:24).

I have emphasized that grace and law are opposite forces resolved in the crucifixion of Christ. Grace and law are separate in experience. There is either grace in love or law in judgment. But law always destroys love in its reception. No exception to this exists within human experience. Either grace is entirely grace or it possesses not a drop of creative worth. There are no double messages in grace. *Grace in this sense is against the law.*

The irony is that grace always produces the sterling character that the law intends. But that promise can never be stated within the initial offer of grace. It cannot even be thought. It cannot even be hoped. If we think this or hope for it, our grace has strings attached. Grace must be tied to nothing. This is the key to its being effective in practice in everyday life. Grace *is* against the law. Nevertheless, in the twilight zone of the "back story" that operates behind all human beings throughout all of time, grace fulfills the law.

A final note on grace in relation to law: grace is not finally against the law, because the qualities that grace births in people are the same qualities that the law sought but failed to birth. That idea, which is central to this theology of everyday life, is stated with unforgettable succinctness at the end of Paul's letter to the Galatians. Paul writes:

> The fruit of the Spirit is love, joy, peace, patience, kindness, generosity, faithfulness, gentleness, and self-control. *There is no law against such things.* (5:22-23)

That is the perfect thing for Paul to say. When grace produces its natural fruit, the law drops away. There is no need for it anymore, because its work is done. It did not do anything!

Is grace against the law? Let the Bible speak: "Against grace there is no law."

CHAPTER TWO

The Four Pillars of a Theology of Grace

The Human Condition: Anthropology

This theology of everyday life requires a one-way love because the human situation is in quarantine. There is no successful two-way love. That is because "our" part of it is always tainted. Our part of it is confined to a straitjacket. This second chapter now maps the anthropology of faith, faith's understanding of human nature. It is a "Mordor" sort of anthropology, dark rather than light, swampland rather than solid ground. But it is the building block of everything that happens later in systematic theology. When the anthropology of a system of thought, its picture of human nature, goes wrong, then everything else goes wrong. Theology does not start from the top; it begins from the bottom. If theology starts from the top and moves down, it is not earthed in everyday life. It is conceptual rather than real.

Christian theology that starts from the bottom up, however, has an everlasting "back story." The back story affirms a plan set in motion long before the human world was created and our ancestors first walked on two feet. The back story understands God making a way to us even before we were born. From *our* point of view, however, the story begins with us. The story begins here. It begins with our enmeshed and constricted need. To this theme, the theme of theological anthropology, we now turn.

Original Sin

Early in my ministry, I learned that there were three ways to empty a room if I were attending a social function. The first was to mention "original sin." The second was to refer to "total depravity." The third was to say that I do not believe in free will. Each of these expressions, especially the third, which is a negation, was sufficient to give me all the elbow room in the world. The discomfort that everyone has with these three ideas lies in direct proportion to their diagnostic depth. They had the same effect on my listeners as a diagnosis of cancer would from an oncologist. "Get me out of here!"

Original sin is the idea that every woman and every man who has ever been born is infected in their DNA with a tendency to think the wrong and do the wrong. Original sin is the universal tendency in people to look out solely for themselves to such an extent that when they are on the defensive they become violent and libidinal. A more palatable definition would be just to say that human nature is evenly distributed.

A classic definition of original sin is found in the Thirty-Nine Articles of Religion (1561) of the Church of England. Here is the Elizabethan declaration of the true condition of life:

> Original sin standeth not in the following of Adam, (as the Pelagians do vainly talk;) but it is the fault and corruption of the Nature of every man, that naturally is engendered of the offspring of Adam; whereby man is very far gone from original righteousness, and is of his own nature inclined to evil, so that the flesh lusteth always contrary to the Spirit; and therefore in every person born into this world, it deserveth God's wrath and damnation. And this infection of nature doth remain, yea in them that are regenerated, whereby the lust of the flesh . . . is not subject to the Law of God. And although there is no condemnation for them that believe and are baptized; yet the Apostle doth confess, that concupiscence and lust hath of itself the nature of sin.[1]

1. *The Book of Common Prayer and Administration of the Sacraments and other Rites and Ceremonies of the Church according to the Use of the Protestant Episcopal Church in the United States of America Together with the Psalter or Psalms of David* (Boston: Printed for the Commission, 1928), pp. 604-5.

Not only does Article IX assert the evenness of distribution of a very strong drive, "concupiscence," but Article IX also asserts the continuing power and presence of "concupiscence" in Christians. Original sin is so deep in persons that, even when they submit to the great change wrought by grace, it is still there. It is like the fetal implant in *Alien* (1979). The "face-hugger" falls away when grace swallows up the law, but the implant is still there, silently feeding on you and preparing to erupt again. The metaphor is strong because the teaching on original sin is strong.

St. Paul's description of original sin in Romans 3 is vivid, complete, and defeating. Here is Paul's view:

> We have already charged that all, both Jews and Greeks, are under
> the power of sin, as it is written:
> "There is no one who is righteous, not even one;
> there is no one who has understanding,
> there is no one who seeks God.
> All have turned aside, together they have become worthless;
> there is no one who shows kindness,
> there is not even one."
> "Their throats are opened graves;
> they use their tongues to deceive."
> "The venom of vipers is under their lips."
> "Their mouths are full of cursing and bitterness."
> "Their feet are swift to shed blood;
> ruin and misery are in their paths,
> and the way of peace they have not known."
> "There is no fear of God before their eyes." (Romans 3:9-18)

Christ declared his full acknowledgment of original sin on the human planet in his repeated descriptions of the human being as someone from whom evil proceeds, rather than someone who is the victimized object of outward influences. In Matthew, Mark, and Luke, Christ gave out bad news when he traced the problem of sin to the human inwardness he called the "heart." While everyone else in his culture was trying to tie a person's moral performance to the number of pollutants coming into him from the outside, Christ, a parasitologist of the human condition, traced the virus to the most hidden part of our being. The Pharisees then plotted against him (Matthew 22:15).

The two practical nouns that define original sin are *universality* — everyone is born with it — and *immunity* to a change of perspective or condition — even the most fervent Christians retain it. Original sin's immunity makes it especially perplexing and upsetting. Many religious people underestimate original sin, especially as they "grow in grace." This renders them vulnerable to its attacks, which grow from the id and the boiling unconscious. Millions of harassed and uncomprehending Christians have thought their faith was a lead shield against the radiation of original sin. The prime problem was that they forgot what Jesus taught: sin comes from the inside, not from the outside.

Sin is a disease that is never healed. It is forgiven. With the intervention of grace, sin is regarded and grappled with in such a way that it no longer surprises or takes over in quite the same way. It is shown grace and therefore robbed of its total power. But it is never healed until death, nor is it ever wiped out within the "human comedy." Original sin, which is the under-muscle of human personality, never diminishes in its strength and its grip.

Side Bar: Listening in the Light of Original Sin

A prime example of original sin is the way people listen, or rather do not listen, to each other. When you are on an airplane, a train, or a bus, don't you overhear conversations between two people, sometimes two friends even, when everything that is stated by the first person becomes the opportunity for the other to bring the conversation back to himself or herself? One person says, "I was sick last week," and the other replies, "You know, I was, too," or, "I've been pretty healthy this summer." "I had a summer cold. I couldn't believe how nasty it was." "I don't get summer colds," the other answers; "anyhow, colds don't bother me." "Well, at least I didn't have to lose any days at work," the first person says. The second counters, "I haven't lost any days at work this summer, either." What is happening in this conversation? The two people are taking turns talking. That's all there is to it. They are taking turns talking about themselves. This is routine in almost all human interchanges.

Here is another example: "I had a miscarriage." "Oh, that's terrible," says a friend; "I had a miscarriage once, too." "You did? So you understand why I feel so bad." "I sure do. Let me tell you what happened to me. . . ." Then, forty-five minutes later: "Yes, well, it feels like a death, and I just can't go into the room we painted for the baby's nursery." "That happened to me, too. I couldn't go in there for months."

Note that even here, where there is something heartfelt in common between the two speakers, there is no real listening. The second person took her friend's admission and used it as a chance to talk about her own experience. Once I actually had this conversation with a friend and decided to end it on a lighter note: "And to think, our miscarriage took place in East Hampton, a supposedly perfect place." To this my friend could not resist adding, "Really? I spent a weekend in East Hampton once."

Do you see the point about original sin? If you do not believe in original sin or find it uncomfortable or just plain morbid, listen to any conversation, not to mention your own. You will be amazed at the evidence. Listening to another person without hearing their words entirely in reference to yourself hardly ever happens. Everything I hear is just an excuse to bring the attention back to me. Wonderfully, if someone ever does really listen to you, if they really do evince interest in what you are saying that is more than just how it applies to them, it can be very powerful. You may end up telling them everything! You may end up loving them forever and thanking them forever.

Grace is listening to another person without bringing the conversation back to you. Original sin is listening to the other and compulsively, unconsciously bringing it back to you. You can't help yourself. Perhaps you have never even thought about it this way. This taking turns talking is an automatic-pilot response. The fact that it is unconscious makes it a prime example of original sin.

Total Depravity

The insight of this phrase has to do with both the reach of original sin and its quality. We say we want "total" commitment to our project from every member of the team. On the dark side, Goebbels, the Nazi propagandist, demanded "total" war from an exhausted people. Or your car gets "totaled" — totally destroyed — when it is rammed by a car that ran a stop sign. "Total" means complete, 100 percent.

Total depravity is a surcharge on the idea of original sin, which makes certain that we know it extends to every atom of a person. Its reach inside you has no borders. When I first heard these two heavy words, "total depravity," I thought it meant that a human being is totally bad, that people are so bad there is no room for any good. This is not what total depravity means. Total depravity means that the depravity of our makeup extends to every part of us. There is good and bad, in the usual mix, but there is some bad in every single part. Depravity's reach extends to every corner.

The second part of this is the concept of depravity itself. Depravity is behavior that is not softened or checked by any humaneness or conscience, any monitors linked to refinement and delicacy of feeling. Depravity is the behavior of animals that are not governed by human controls. Depravity is a strong word. It makes us think of lions fighting to the death over a piece of zebra meat, or gang rape in an abandoned subway car.

The reason why "depravity" is the right word for original sin–*plus* is that it relates to the human unconscious. The dream worlds of people are revealing. While there are all sorts of checks and balances in dreams, and sometimes conscience, too, you do things in dreams that you would not do in waking life. You do things and suffer things that are aggressive and criminal, things that have little tangible relationship with your everyday life. But the thought was there. You may wake up anxious and repelled by what the dream dramatized, but you did it, or it befell you. You say to yourself after a bad dream, "How could I possibly have had that on my mind? Where did it come from?" The fact is, nobody wrote the script but you.

Depravity is appropriate in theological anthropology because it relates to the inner unconscious man and woman. The totality of it suggests that depravity is an "infection of nature" (Article IX). "It's everywhere, it's everywhere!"

Historically, theology owes this emphasis, this courageous facing-up, to the Protestant Reformers. They were in touch, in a hugely fresh way in Europe at their time, with the whole person, especially the hurting, aggressive side of human beings. Søren Kierkegaard said that Martin Luther was a patient of great significance for Europe. He meant by this that Luther was in contact with a territory within people that many had neglected and of which many were unaware.

The Christian church of the medieval world was culpably unaware of people's depth. The church used its penitential system to skate superficially over the real thoughts and acts of its members, as if a few recited prayers in contrition could equal "what lurks in the hearts of men" *(The Shadow)*. The Reformers, on the other hand, understood that there are traces of the BTK killer in every man and woman. They were intent on understanding the true nature of the human condition, seeing it in its true colors. Once the grievous nuance and unplumbable depth of the psyche were named, the power of the absolution could rise to the occasion. Once the total depravity of original sin was out of the closet, then the magnificent response latent within the grace of God in the cross of Christ could be portrayed. It could be displayed for people to see. The majesty of the Reformers' views of Christ is in direct and prior connection with the heaviness of their vision of humankind. The same was true of the Jansenists, the Protestant Reformers' seventeenth-century "stepchildren" in France. The Jansenists thanked Christ in proportion to their appreciation of human introversion and self-absorption. The phrase "total depravity" paints the picture of original sin a little more darkly, a little more visibly, a little more helplessly.

Side Bar: The Devil and Total Depravity

"Sorcery and sanctity, these are the only realities. . . ."

St. Ambrose

Arthur Machen (1863-1947) was an orthodox Christian who wrote some of the best tales of the supernatural ever written. His stories, such as "The Great God Pan" and "The White People," are so chilling that they were considered scandalous in late Victorian England. He dealt especially with Satanism in relation to an oblique sexuality that only becomes clear to the reader after you have finished the story. "Oh," you say, "*that's* what it was all about." The back story, the mechanism of the plot, is veiled.

Machen, who was a convinced Anglo-Catholic and whose Anglo-Catholicism figures in everything he wrote (just as M. R. James's "low-church" Anglicanism breathes through every story he wrote), wished to add an extra dimension to original sin. He wrote powerfully about human sin, but he also envisaged a darker force at work behind the sin. He saw satanic worship "pulling the strings" behind human crimes and misdemeanors. There is always something worse going on, in Machen's stories, than the very bad thing that first appears to be going on.

In "The White People" you have a young girl's almost illiterate diary of summer afternoon outings with her governess. There is a pretty lake and bathing and a third figure who keeps "dancing with the lady." All is vernal and beautiful. What begins to emerge, however, is the fact that the governess is guiding her charge to some Roman ruins that lie in the woods. There, a bust of Attis, an earth deity from ancient times, is worshipped, and a goat-like male figure emerges. Supernatural evil is confronted (it takes at least forty pages before you have the slightest idea what is going on), and the girl kills herself to avoid a final, fateful meeting with the devil. The manipulation of the little girl by her nurse and her taking advantage of this little girl's innocence are bad enough. Worse, however, is the destination of it: her rape by the devil in the service of producing an heir.

"The White People" was written long before *Rosemary's Baby* (1967), which takes the same theme; and the standpoint of its author is a secure Christianity. But the point is powerful. Original sin is everywhere, but behind it is something worse. Behind original sin stands total depravity. And the cause of total depravity, this inhuman absence of conscience, is the great adversary, the circling vulture of biblical existence, the devil. "Like a roaring lion your adversary the devil prowls around, looking for someone to devour" (1 Peter 5:8).

In the anthropology of everyday life, this is an important point. Things are dire and very bad; but the truth is, things are worse than they appear.

Let's look at another familiar example. It also comes from popular art, a good place to look in penetrating to the heart of things. Robert Bloch wrote *Psycho* in 1959. In Bloch's novel, Marion Crane robs her employer in order to get enough money to run away with the man she loves. But she starts to feel guilty about her crime. She resolves to return home and give the money back. Having worked through a repentance, she is elated. She takes a shower in order to feel cleansed. But while she is in the shower, she is murdered by an unknown and scarcely seen assailant.

Marion has committed a sin and is honestly sorry for it. But she runs into a much bigger sin, which eclipses her own sin almost completely. She runs into a murderer who murdered his mother, and who now thinks that he has become his mother. Marion Crane moves from the real world of original sin to the even more real world of total depravity. Had Robert Bloch been Arthur Machen, Norman Bates would have been a worshiper of Satan.

Most Christians, faced with the repulsive "works of the flesh" executed by Norman Bates, will have no problem giving credit where credit is due. Those murders are committed by a man under demonic compulsion, call it what you will. My point is that original sin is blood-related to total depravity, which in turn is the creature of him who has the whole world under lock and key. As St. Paul said, "Our struggle is not against enemies of blood and flesh, but against the rulers, against the authorities, against the cosmic powers of this present darkness, against the spiritual forces of evil in the heavenly places" (Ephesians 6:12).

Who or what is the devil? We do not know exactly. He takes many forms, from the "satan" in the book of Job to the tempter who came to Jesus in Matthew's Gospel (4:1-11). We know the devil is personal and not a concept. He is stronger than any human being, and best avoided, not engaged. Moreover, he takes whatever he can — for instance, the law — and uses it not just to bind, but to torture.

The Un-Free Will

Essential to this systematic theology of everyday life is its doctrine of the human being. Everything hinges on how we understand the human being. If the question of everyday life boils down to "Help me!" then the answer will be one that looks up, or at least out. If the conditions of real life can be reduced to a defensive situation, beleaguered and completely surrounded, like Tolkien's outnumbered heroes at Helm's Deep, then the answer, if there is one, will have to be extreme. It will not be an answer generated from the situation itself, for the situation is irremediable. It will be an answer that involves rescue. Otherwise it will be no answer: deafening silence and extermination. This theology of everyday life takes its first breath from the irrepressible words, "Help me!"

It is crucial now to examine the human will. Can people "will" to save themselves? Is the human will an engine for self-help? To put it classically, is our will free or is it bound?

To preface this survey of the will, we have to admit that traditional Christian theology is swimming upstream against the surrounding culture. Traditional Christian theology, Catholic and Protestant, rooted as it is in the pessimism of Paul and the radical pessimism of Augustine, understands the will as bound, not free. Everyone else today understands the will to be free. For American people, this is almost a point of personal honor.

I have been talking about the un-free will for thirty years and have never had a single person agree with me on my first attempt. People instinctively rise up against the idea. I repeat, I have not experienced a single instance, in thirty years, of anyone immediately agreeing with me that the human will is not free. (In fact, the only people who display any receptivity at all to the idea are alcoholics and criminals. And even criminals behind bars want to go back to "free will" once they are settled into prison existence.) When I speak of the un-free will, most people wish to have a duel with me and leave me, like Alexander Hamilton at Weehawken, inert on the ground.

A theology of everyday life depends on the un-free will. If the will is free, then we do not need someone to save us. We may need a helper, but we do not need a savior. We may scan the horizon for "a little help from my friends" (Lennon/McCartney), but basically life is a matter of "God helps those who help themselves." This theology disagrees entirely with that concept of life. This theology of everyday life depends on the un-free will.

Yet there is something that can sweeten the pill. Often when the subject of the un-free will comes up, people jump ahead of my claim. They think I am talking about predestination. They think I mean Pavlov and little dogs with bells and shocks. They think I am trying to corner them into some kind of idea that makes people into puppets. To this I say, "You're ahead of the game. I am talking about one thing, and one thing only: how people actually act and whether they are under compulsion in certain situations. Please don't talk to me about puppets until you have answered me about addicts."

This is to say that the doctrine of the un-free will is a biblical and descriptive approach to everyday life, not the invocation of some overarching puppeteer. We are going to stick to one idea, a single observation: Human beings are not as free to act as they like to think they are. They are more hemmed in, more constrained by outward circumstance and forces within, than they wish to concede. We all want to do what we want to do. The fact is, we often do what we do not want to do, and do not do what we want to do. I am not the first person to have said this.

That the human will is born un-free is one of the plainest facts of the human world. It is also the most hidden. It is plain because it is plain from experience. It is hidden, in plain sight, because no one wishes to see it.

How can I say that we know that the will is un-free? It is an argument from experience. Think about anger. Anger can be triggered by a single word, a single contemptuous gesture. People have killed each other over a single contemptuous gesture. Anger is often compulsive. It takes you over. You get so angry you could scream. All it takes is two minutes in the room with a certain someone, and you want to explode. Only Machiavellian people can control their anger. But their control is in service of "another day." They may not lash out at you over drinks, but one day you are going to wake up and their vengeance has cost you your job.

Think about the obvious case, the obvious prison of the "free" will: addiction. You want to stop drinking. You insist that you can stop drinking. All you need is a little "strength" (these sorts of prayers for "strength" are always semi-Pelagian). If you could just get a little strength, you could stop drinking. But the fact is, you always go back to it. Addiction needs help, complete help. You have to start by putting yourself in the wrong and acknowledging that your life is out of control. Until you admit powerlessness in this one area, just this one area, you are hopeless. A defeating resentment, given the right outside circumstances, can impel you back to the bottle. It is evident that an alcoholic does not possess freedom of the will. Please concede this, concede that in this one forsaken area there is no free will.

It is the same case with addictions of other kinds. "Substance abusers" evince no control at all. The minute you begin to think they have control, the moment you fall for their protests that they have the power, they disappoint you. Until they put themselves in the wrong, the future is only one thing: repetitive compulsion. Can you think of an exception?

Extrapolate from addictions to the loaded question of weight. Can you control your weight? Have you read the statistics on weight loss? The pounds rarely stay off. Recidivism is the rule and not the exception. There is a *New Yorker* cartoon from a few years ago that depicts some droplets of fat having a discussion. They all have two legs and look a little confused. Then the leader pipes up and says, "OK, people, time to head home." You cannot keep the weight off, at least not by the means in your control.

This can sound to some as if it were an attack on human dignity. It is not an attack. Rather, it is the birth pangs of compassion. The moment you understand that people are not as free as they think they are, especially in the sectors of compulsion, you are able to have compassion for them. You begin to "try a little tenderness." Instead of judging them for doing wrong when they should be doing right, you start developing some sympathy.

There are many more examples of the un-free will. Mourning is a governing emotion. It is primally strong, and there is nothing "free" about it. People mourn in proportion to the loss they have suffered, which is to say they grieve to the degree that they have loved. When the loss is big, the mourning is big. It comes in great waves and actually overwhelms the mourner. You cannot tell it to go away or try to ride it out. Maybe you can do this for a little while, but it always and finally takes you away. Just when you thought you were alive again, and free to live, it hits you again and you're down. It shows no mercy. It haunts you.

Moreover, if mourning is not allowed to be felt, it never goes away. Its merciless power subsides only when you allow yourself to feel it. This is actually true and is not the jargon of a "grief counselor." There are many examples in literature of characters who try to get away from their grieving. But their grief only displaces itself onto another part of their life. Miss Havisham in *Great Expectations,* her life utterly halted because of the grief of being left at the altar, never recovers from the shock of that moment. It never has a chance to get out. It is turned into hatefulness and possessiveness. A kind of exorcism is required at the end of the book, an exorcism represented by Pip's tearing down the curtains of her house, for it to be finished.

A classic, poignant case of mourning as a rebuke to "free will" is Katherine Anne Porter's short story "The Jilting of Granny Weatherall." The old woman in the title is stuck, mired so deeply in mourning, that even at the moment of her death she is thinking about the rejection and humiliation that she suffered in her girlhood. It is a classic "Southern Gothic" theme, the same as in Tennessee Williams's *The Glass Menagerie,* the B-movie *Hush . . . Hush, Sweet Charlotte* (1964) and its several Hollywood descendants, and the moving short stories of Irwin S. Cobb. But it is not just a "Southern" story. It is a universal experience, the paralyzing effects of anesthetized grief. If the will were free, these people could "get over it" and "move on." But we do not get over it, and we cannot move on.

Take the further example of depression. Depression descends on you like "a wolf on the fold" (Lord Byron). For no "rational" cause at all, you find yourself taken over by sadness. You cannot look anyone in the face; you can barely put one foot in front of the other; the flowers have no smell and the leaves no color. You are a walking dead man. I was once so smothered by depression (which came, as far as I could tell then, from out of a clear blue sky) that I left my wife at the turnstile of a movie theater and shambled around a New York City block twenty-five times until the movie — it was *Kramer vs. Kramer* — was over. I could have slept for three days! What touched it off? What caused it? I do not know. But talking to me about "free will" at that time would have been cruel and inhuman. I had absolutely no control, no autonomy. It was a speechless subjection to a terrifying force. What are we doing when we speak of "free will" in cases like that? When a person commits suicide, is "free will" in play?

We can extend the point to any case of fretting or worry. Can you talk yourself out of fretting? Can someone else? People sometimes tell me to relax, especially when they feel a little uneasy with my unceasing activity. On the one hand, they are speaking out of their own discomfort, perhaps thinking, "If he's so busy, maybe I'm at fault for not being like him." More important for me, however, is the attack that the command "Relax!" conveys. If I were able to relax, don't you think I would? I can't relax! The more the other person tells me to relax, the more jumpy I become. If I had "free will," I would be able to switch from high-intensity to easygoing in a heartbeat. But I cannot. I cannot.

I have already quoted St. Paul on this fact. In the seventh chapter of Romans, Paul looks deeply into the un-free will. He explains that he wants to do right and knows what it is, but he experiences himself doing the opposite. If there is anything he desires for himself, it is free will. But free will is not for the asking. It is not just hard to get; it is impossible to get. That is why he is full of an inspired self-pity that cries, "Wretched man that I am! Who will rescue me from this body of death?" (7:24).

Paul's analysis of the un-free will, which made him a wise observer of the human impasse, corresponded to Jesus' approach to sufferers. Christ spoke to people as they really were: "publicans and sinners," the sick and the handicapped. He did not come to help the "free"; he came to save the bound. The prophets had understood the Messiah's unique work as that of giving sight to the blind and release to the prisoners. There was nothing semi-Pelagian about Isaiah's Suffering Servant who came to bring light to "those who sit in darkness" (Isaiah 42:7). The need of Israel, to which the Messiah would speak, was overwhelming. There was nothing free about the people who lay in Babylonian captivity. Jesus treated individuals the same way. His treatment of people defined the word "compassion" for all future time. Compassion is having mercy on people who cannot help themselves. This is the great benefit, in a theology for everyday life, of the doctrine of the un-free will.

The Relation of the Un-Free Will to Compassion

If you believe in people's free will, you will always judge them when they "choose" wrongly — or, as we say today, when they make "poor choices." If you understand, however, that these people are *not* free in their will, then you are able to summon some compassion in your dealings with them. One of the reasons we need to embrace the fact of the un-free will is for the sake of its effect on love. A benefit of the un-free will is that it increases mercy in daily relationships and decreases judgment. How is this so?

Perhaps the man you live with is smoldering with resentment. Most of his resentments are founded on half-facts and subjectivity. Most of them are not only falsely founded but damaging to those around him. They make him impossible to live with. They make him impossible to listen to. He is a cauldron of angry thoughts. The fact of the matter is that he cannot control himself. He is deeply wrong about many things, but he cannot control himself. He needs help. If you, as the person trying to love him, believe in free will, specifically if you think he has free will in this area, then you are going to fall out of love with him fast. You say to yourself, "Can't he see what he is doing, not only to us and to our children, but to himself?" You reason to yourself, "I have pointed out to him a thousand times how skewed his perceptions are. I have told him as plain as day that he is factually wrong about his grievances. But he doesn't seem to listen. He just goes on, railing against such-and-such and so-and-so. What is wrong with him that he cannot see what is painfully clear to everybody else?"

What is wrong with the man is that he does not have free will. He is operating out of *no freedom*. There is a deep uncontrollable anger in him, probably going way back in his life and genes, which is not about to succumb to rational argument. Something deeper and more powerful is required. The entry point for the person trying to love him is this: the poor man does not possess free will.

The relation of the un-free will to compassion is that the un-free will enables compassion. You can see this in the various sorts of Christianity encountered in the world. Forms of Christianity that stress free will create refugees. They get into the business of judging, and especially of judging Christians.

My wife and I could not begin to number the lapsed Roman Catholics and lapsed evangelicals we have known who have bailed out of Christianity on account of one word: "judgment." It always comes back to that two-syllable word. If you were to interview the millions of people who feel they have left Christianity although they were brought up in it, you would find that one two-syllable word, "judgment," tops the list of their objections to it. It tops it by a mile. Questions of doubt, dogmatics, and authority, which are often put forward as the principal objections to Christianity, are important. The big questions of theodicy, which is to ask, "Why did my son die?" "Why did my mother die?" "Why is my life a misery?" are hugely important. But the really heavy question, the one on everybody's lips, is this one: "How dare that Christian person or that Christian church sit in judgment on me?" It is judgment that drives people away from Christianity. Ironically, it is judgment — the absence of it — which drew people toward Christ.

The idea behind judgment, the driving idea of this species of Christianity that drives away, is the "free will." You see this in primary evangelism. The speaker gets up and makes a call to decision at the end of an affecting address. But he says that we all have a choice. If you decide in favor of faith, good for you. But if you decide, tonight, on this very spot, against faith, then, well, "poor choice." Such thinking, the concept that a hurt and hurting person has the full freedom to say Yes or No to love, is misconceived. It is simply not true. People "decide" for all kinds of reasons, some of which are hidden even from them. We have to smile when we see phrases on food packages such as "the heart-healthy choice" or "the smart cereal." Those are appeals to someone who does not exist. Just ask a person who likes to eat, or sadder, the person who eats to comfort himself or herself.

There is a *South Park* episode entitled "Weight Gain 4000," in which the Eric Cartman character gains so much weight that he has to be lifted out of bed by the end of the episode. National television interviews him at the end of the episode: "What is your advice to the young people of America, Mr. Cartman?" they inquire. "Stay . . ." (huff and puff) "true . . ." (gasping for air) "to . . ." (totally out of breath) "your dreams" (collapsing back on the bed). That is perfect. Cartman lives to eat, he cannot control himself, yet he tells others to "be all that they can be." The two writers of *South Park* see through the myth of "free will." That myth has been accepted by most Christians, and the result of it is thousands upon thousands of refugees.

"Free will" creates judgment creates rejection creates flight. The un-free will creates sympathy creates mercy creates comfort creates change. Actually, there is only despair and hatred in the concept of free will. There is hope and mercy in the concept of the un-free will. The un-free will is true biblically, it is true experientially, and it is true from the standpoint of its grace-filled fruit.

The Relation of the "Free Will" to Self-Righteousness

Not only does "free will" produce judgment in relation to paralyzed people, it also produces self-righteousness in relation to its own people. If the will is free, and I choose the right way but my benighted neighbor chooses the wrong way, then I have achieved something praiseworthy in choosing the right. Credit belongs to me if I made the "good choice." It does not belong to the other who made the "poor choice." You can see that the very word "choice" is bound to separate the sheep from the goats. There is nothing conciliatory or unifying in the word "choice." It makes a strict separation, a division so sharp that it is like the glass shards stuck along the top of a concrete wall. You cannot get over it.

Here is an everyday case of the self-righteousness inherent in the idea of the free will. My friend is a busy pastor who works long hours. He is completely, exhaustedly faithful to his calling. He goes out of town to make a speech and gets picked up at the airport by a jaunty former assistant. She takes one look at him, sits down in the driver's seat, and exclaims, "John, you look tired!" He replies, "Well, I guess I must be." She says, "Oh, you're always tired. How come you are *always* tired? I'm not tired." The "I'm not" is the giveaway to her gracelessness. She sees his fatigue as the confirmation that she takes better care of herself. Translation: "If you could only be like me! I'm not tired." This is the essence of self-righteousness.

Jesus told a story to illustrate the peril of the "free will" in relation to self-righteousness. You can call it either the parable of the self-righteous Pharisee or the parable of the penitent tax collector. It reads as follows:

> Two men went up to the temple to pray, one a Pharisee and the other a tax collector. The Pharisee, standing by himself, was praying thus: "God, I thank you that I am not like other people: thieves, rogues, adulterers, or even like this tax collector. I fast twice a week; I give a tenth of all my income." But the tax collector, standing far off, would not even look up to heaven, but was beating his breast and saying, "God, be merciful to me, a sinner!" I tell you, this man went down to his home justified rather than the other; for all who exalt themselves will be humbled, but all who humble themselves will be exalted. (Luke 18:10-14)

The Pharisee gave himself credit for the "smart choices" he had made in his life. The tax collector recognized his complete and necessary reliance on grace in the light of his overwhelming sins of being and doing. The tax collector was justified before God, not the Pharisee. For the tax collector, God's grace was one-way love, not a two-way operation that relied on his effort. For the Pharisee, it was semi-Pelagianism all the way. And there was no compassion on the part of the Pharisee, none at all. There was self-congratulation and contempt. This is the unpitying position of the free-will idea, yoked inextricably to the inflated self. There is no single more distancing character in life than the Pharisee.

You know many Pharisees. Part of you, maybe a lot of you, takes after one. They are the universal product of all religions, of all belief systems. They are the Frankenstein's Monster of the "free will."

The Un-Free Will as Object, not Subject

In this theology of everyday life, there is only one Subject. There are countless objects. The one Subject is God; the countless objects are us. This is because there is only one will that is free, God's will. The wills of all human beings are bound. This is good news for the human race — although we first hear it as bad news — because it puts us all on the same level. None of us is free; none of us can choose freely. We all make "poor choices." No one makes a "smart (heart-healthy) choice."

Decades ago, Dr. Frank Lake was talking to a group of theology students in a Church of England seminary at Lincoln. He had spent a painstaking morning describing the universal symptoms of neurosis in everyday people. He had made his listeners, every one of them, feel as if they were desperately neurotic individuals in a vast neurotic world. At the end of the morning, one bowed-down student raised his hand and asked: "Dr. Lake, is there anyone, according to your view, who has ever lived, who is not neurotic?" "No," he replied, "but I have heard that there was one once." That was a surprising answer. In one crisp and concessive clause, Frank Lake acknowledged the broad band of human neediness *and* the hope of deliverance.

We have to make the same statement about the human being in relation to God. The human will is un-free. It is determined and conditioned by forces outside itself, as well as by forces within. Our wills follow our hearts, the seat of our desires; and the mind, or reason, tags along behind, finding rationalizing reasons to justify what the heart has already decided. This is why people can almost never be talked out of an emotional course of action once they have "decided" to do it. Just try to convince someone involved in an extramarital affair to give it up. You can present all the good reasons in the world, past, present, and future, yet none of them will be sufficient to deter him or her. The will is tied to the heart, with the mind as a sort of "face-saving" caboose. The reasons the mind devises to justify the heart's needy desires are always pathetic.

Jesus of Nazareth, on the other hand, lived freely. As the alarming King Missile song "Jesus Was Way Cool" (1990) puts it: "Jesus was way cool. Everything he wanted to do, he did." That is a terse statement of the thesis of this chapter. Jesus had no original sin. He did not possess total depravity. He possessed a free will.

I do not think that the free will of Jesus Christ has to be demonstrated. It is evident from his childhood freedom from his parents; it is evident within his teaching solo in the temple; it is evident in his famous sleep in the stern of a boat during a violent storm on the Sea of Galilee; and it is evident in his freedom of action at the end of his days, the uniform discretion of his personal sacrifice. What usually has to be demonstrated is not Christ's free will, but rather *our* un-free will. I hope this discussion has helped to do that.

The point for theology is that we are not subjects; we are objects. We do not live; we are lived. To put it another way, our archaeology is our teleology. We are typically operating from drives and aspirations generated by our past. What ought to be free decisions in relation to love and service become un-free decisions anchored in retrospective deficits and grievances. This is the message of tragic literature. It is the message of diagnosis that sees into the animating engine of the unconscious. It is the scene in *The Exorcist,* when the possessed girl is spitting foul words at her mother, yet her mother and the nurse detect on her chest, dug into the little girl's skin, the words "Help me." That is it. We think the child is free, but she is under the thumb of a demon and there is someone there inside, crying to be heard and dying to be saved. She is an object in the only real sense of her destroyed humanity, but she is a subject to the degree that she is pleading. Her subjectivity lies in her need.

Free entities are subjects. Un-free entities are objects. Christ Jesus, the body of God on earth, was free. The world to which he came was un-free. It is un-free still. There is therefore only one Subject in the world today, and he is surrounded by countless beleaguered objects. St. Paul famously wrote, "Faith, hope, and love abide, these three; and the greatest of these is love" (1 Corinthians 13:13). I would describe an obverse trio this way: original sin, total depravity, and the un-free will abide, these three; and the root of the thing is the un-free will.

The Old, Old Story: Soteriology

The problem of human nature is the problem of history and of everyday life. It resists correction. It resists aid from outside itself because it wants to solve things on its own terms. This quality is sometimes referred to as "pride," but there is a reason for this pride. The cause of pride is original sin, which touches every life; total depravity, which takes "normal" sin one step further into the realm of sadism and vengeance; and the un-free will, which is the most discomforting of all conditions because the will insists and thinks that it is free. The un-free will is like the drunk who protests, "I'll quit tomorrow."

Soteriology is the formal word in theology for the province of rescue. Soteriology, which comes from the Greek word for "saving," has to do with rescue. It is the "hope of deliverance" of which Paul McCartney sang touchingly in 1993. For this theology of everyday life, soteriology is the keystone. Everything depends on the saving. The problem, our human nature that requires rescue if it is not to become suicidal, exists whether rescue comes or not. The problem never goes away from the point of view of our observing it and acknowledging its devastating effects. But everything changes if there is this hope of deliverance. It changes concretely if the hope of deliverance is more than a hope, if it is an accomplished fact. Soteriology is the study of that accomplished fact.

We begin with the crucifixion of Christ, which is the starting point for all talk of rescue. The teaching on soteriology begins with the atonement.

The Atonement of Christ

The atonement of Christ is the mechanism of grace. Without the atonement, the grace of God is a beautiful dream. It is a dream, like Pollyanna's "Glad Game" in the 1960 Walt Disney movie, that can even have impact in real life. But without the actual atonement of Christ, grace would not be strong enough to defeat the powers that be. The mercilessness of the world would finally walk right over grace — pitilessness is that endemic — if there were not this "secret weapon" that carries the power to overwhelm anything that is sent against it.

Atonement is also a kind of deep-buried treasure because people develop amnesia in relation to it. The Christian movement in general develops amnesia in relation to the atonement. It has to be drawn out for every person in every generation, over and over again. The atonement has to be revisited in every new life and day.

What is this truth? It is the principle of guilt absorbed by substitution. The atonement of Christ is the sacrifice of the one man by which the sin of the world is taken from the shoulders of the guilty and placed completely on the shoulders of an innocent. God the Judge, the unswervingly fair judge, accepts the substitution. Someone had to bear the just sentence of his judgment. That had to happen for justice to be done because justice is a part of God. But in the atonement, the direction of the thunderbolt of judgment swerved. It struck away from the guilty and hit the innocent one.

The background of atonement is "cultic." This is the word theologians use to describe the operation. It is a negative word because it sounds primitive, like a hidden sect of people who do bad and narrow things in out-of-the-way places. I want to say that atonement's background is *ethical* rather than cultic, but it is ethical on a big canvas.

Something must be done about guilt. Everyone knows this from their own experience. There has to be some relief for remorse, whether personal or collective. You have to "get the monkey off your back," you have to remove the tarantula that fixed itself to your neck when it dropped down off the trees. Atonement provides this relief. To quote Stephen King, it offers "the lock on the door you closed against the past."[2]

There are four parts to atonement. These parts are the judge, the of-

2. Stephen King, *The Green Mile* (New York and London: Pocket Books, 1996), p. 71.

fender, the guilt of the offender, and the offering. God the Judge has passed a just sentence. Justice must be done or there is no meaning to it. The turning of the earth depends on the fact of justice. If there is injustice or partiality on the part of this Judge, he stops being just, and the world spins off its axis.

The offender is the man or woman who did the criminal thing. She was caught; it was confirmed through overwhelming evidence that she was the one who "pulled the trigger," and there is no doubt that somebody else might have done it. The guilt of the offender is the thing that she did.

In *Woman Thou Art Loosed* (2004) the heroine admits to Bishop Jakes, who plays himself in the movie, that she shot her mother's boyfriend. All the extenuating circumstances aside, she is the one who shot him. But she admits something else. She admits that her act took away the only man her mother ever loved. "I didn't have the right to do that to my mother," she says. The guilt of the offender is always worse than it first appears. Somebody else was affected. The wife of a husband, the mother of a child, the dependent brother of a sister — a crime is never "done in a corner." Adultery involves more than two people. It involves four, or even six or seven, not to mention in-laws and future grandparents' rights of visitation, your children's weddings, and the dying months of a long cast-aside wife or husband. The guilt attached to a sin is always greater than we first wish to think.

So atonement involves the judge, one single offender, and the magnitude of the offense itself. It is the offering, however, that creates the atonement. The offering is the valued thing that satisfies the judge. What can the offender offer? His house in Boca, maybe; the other side's legal costs, of course; calibrated damages in terms of compensation, payback for the pain he caused; a verdict of "guilty" on the offender, so everybody knows who was wrong; maybe a scarlet letter on his chest, or a noisy beeper that lets the whole world know he is under house arrest for wrecking someone's life; and the "collateral" damage that the offender's wife divorces him, his children abjure him, and he has only his tag-along mother with him for the rest of his life in order for all to see how pathetic he really is.

But is that good enough? Does it really do anything except give the victim a little satisfaction for a short time? Does the punishment that takes something fairly important away from the offender — for example, his freedom for the rest of his life — bring back a daughter whom he killed? Does it bring back a son, who will never walk again as the result of one man's drunken carelessness? And how is justice served by that punishment in the *big* picture anyway? All we have done is make an example of one pathetic sinner.

The atonement of Christ puts all human crime and punishment on a bigger stage. The Judge is the same, God. The offender is everybody, for everybody is capable of a crime that destroys other lives. Most people, at least once in their life, have hurt another person in a ripping, incising way. There is a big condition of the earth to be engaged here. The guilt is widespread. It extends from the outward acts of the self to the inward thoughts of the self. The guilt is so omnipresent that only a vast event could absorb it. The atonement of Christ is the death of an innocent man in the place of every guilty man and woman. It is representative, as his death "represents" the death of every single guilty human person. It is vicarious because it is in their place. He dies *vicariously* so each of them will not have to die for the sin they inherently and historically bear. It is substitutionary because he actually takes on their identity. He is an "identity-thief" in the fructifying sense that their old identity, as a sinner, transfers to him; and his identity, as the perfect man for others, goes to them. It is an exchange. It is a one-way exchange because, as God, he alone can make this happen. I could wish for it, but I could never bring it off. It is the one-way love of grace.

The atonement of Christ satisfies the just demand written into the universe that guilt must be punished wholly. The atonement of Christ gives the one-way initiative in the matter to God alone. The atonement of Christ frees the recipient without a hitch. There are no hidden clauses in the contract. There is no contract! The entire cost of the arrangement is born by Christ Jesus, who is not me, nor is he you. That cost is the cost of death and a one-way trip to hell. Thankfully, the Father of Christ rescued him from hell.

The atonement of Christ on the cross is the mechanism by which

God's grace can be offered freely and without condition to strugglers in the battle of life. Grace is not offered by God as a fiat. We all wish that the innocent had not had to die for the guilty. We wish that a different road, a road less traveled in scars, had been taken. But we have been told that this was the necessary way by which God's law and God's grace would be resolved. It had to be resolved through a guilt-transfer, making it "possible" — the idea is almost beyond maintaining — for God to give the full scholarship to the candidate least qualified to receive it.

Ladies and gentlemen, I give you God's least deserving creature, whom he has made a little lower than the angels. Ladies and gentlemen, I give you the recipient of this aeon's award for being least endowed and hence the most endowed with perfections: I give you the Marquis de Sade and the Man of La Mancha. I give you the Countess Lucrezia Borgia and the "wench" Dulcinea. I give you man and woman!

The Imputation of God

The progress of soteriology, the old, old story that is the beginning point for the Christian drama in personal experience, is like a pencil that narrows to a fine point. The pencil narrows from its widest point, which is the atonement. The narrowing or refining of the idea comes within the operation of imputation. The final point of the pencil, the place where the writing actually takes place, is *simul iustus et peccator* ("at once righteous and sinful").

The atonement is the first fact. It reconciles law and grace and constitutes the "back story" that enables the grace of God to be spoken and heard as one pure word. In theology, the one word of grace depends on the two words of God, law and grace, being related to each other and reconciled through the crucifixion of Christ. Without the atonement, law would reign and grace would have no foundation. Without the atonement, grace would be Don Quixote's "impossible dream." With the atonement, grace is firmly grounded on a rock, and the rock is the finished law. The atonement makes it possible to speak grace to sufferers and criminals and really mean it.

Imputation is the dealing with people by which grace makes its impact. Imputation, which is a new kind of naming, is the format of grace that is the word as heard. It is the agency of grace that disarms.

Grace imputes. Grace sees the image of God in men and women when the reality is the twisted image of fallen people implicated in original sin, people who have unsavory associations in the form of total depravity and are prevented by their un-free will from helping themselves. Grace looks on all that failure and imputes. To impute means to ascribe qualities to someone that are not there intrinsically, to regard somebody as a person that he or she is not. Imputation calls bad things by a good name, and this is what grace does. On the basis of the atonement, grace imputes Christ the substitute to someone like Dorian Gray, who is in critical need. Grace calls the Selfish Giant, in Oscar Wilde's children's story of that name, a friend to be trusted, a friend to the end; and he becomes one. Imputing grace looks on a pathetic person, all bound up and dependent on the opinion of others, and calls her confident. Imputing grace is how my sixth-grade teacher treated me during an exam when I was afraid I had misunderstood a question and sat jittering and waving my hand and biting my nails like a sawtooth tiger. The teacher came over to this impossible little boy, put his hand on his shoulder, answered his question softly and kindly, and added, "I think you're going to do fine." I have never forgotten that. He treated me other than I was. All the jitters went out of me at once. Such is the force of imputation.

Imputation is one-way love made concrete. It is mentioned in the Bible in the book of Romans, when Paul remembers how God treated the faith of Abraham by reckoning it "to him as righteousness" (4:3-5; Genesis 15:6). This means that Abraham's faith that God would provide him with an heir, even though he and his wife were beyond childbearing years, was applied to Abraham's "credit" before God as if it were equivalent to moral righteousness. God substituted faith and trust for moral good standing. The mechanism is the taking of one attribute, faith (which is scarcely an attribute), and saying that it is something other than it is — that is, good moral standing. God calls faith by a different name: righteousness.

From this "chance" quote from Genesis 15, Paul takes a further step with imputation. He remembers the word as it occurs in Psalm 32:2, where David writes: "Happy are those to whom the LORD imputes no iniquity." Paul sees the non-imputation of sin as the blessing devoutly to be wished. Yes, you are a sinner, but God does not impute it to you. He imputes to you sinlessness where there has been actual sin. In other words, God calls sin by a different name: sinlessness. God names sin out of existence.

We have to go back now for a moment to Psalm 32. The full quote is as follows:

> Happy are those to whom the LORD imputes no iniquity,
>   and in whose spirit there is no deceit.
> While I kept silence, my body wasted away
>   through my groaning all day long.
> For day and night your hand was heavy upon me;
>   my strength was dried up as by the heat of summer.
> Then I acknowledged my sin to you,
>   and I did not hide my iniquity;
> I said, "I will confess my transgressions to the LORD,"
>   and you forgave the guilt of my sin. (32:2-5)

Blessedness, or a happy life, consists of forgiveness. The sin is not done away with; it is covered. The release of a man or woman by means of divine grace is the imputing of no iniquity to that person even as it is there. All that is required of the individual is to be frank about his or her sin. Faith in New Testament terms is transparency about the true state of affairs concerning sin and need. God covers over this sin and need. He does not destroy it but calls it by a different name. He calls the damned blessed; the weak, strong; the impotent, fruitful; the pathetic, confident; the ugly, beautiful. In the one-way love that anchors this theology of everyday life, the imputation of God is the heavy lifting. It is the big effect that no one but God is able to pull off. It is creative naming, which has the power of changing.

Imputation is the heavy lifting of grace that occurs in daily life. It does not occur often enough, unfortunately, but when it does occur, it changes everything. It probably happened to you once. Remember when you were a high school boy, cowering and gangly, the last stop on the train of teenaged "I-wish-I-hadn't-been-born"? You would go reluctantly to dances and hug the wall, and every second was torture. Or remember when you were a young woman, a college freshman. You were invited to fraternity parties but no one danced with you. Again, every second was torture. (It permanently ruined "Louie, Louie" for you — not to mention "Shout"!) Then one day, somebody noticed you. You had a little pixie smile and a kind of demure mischievousness. He asked you to dance. He obviously liked you. That was the day things changed. "Mom, I think I'm beginning to like college now."

It is sometimes a teacher who imputes. There is a fidgety new boy in school this fall. He *hates* being here. He does not have a single friend and cannot seem to find one. But his teacher sees something in him. The teacher imputes substance to the child. Maybe the child gets a role in the class play or is selected for a special classroom job. The teacher imputes, and the child changes. It is like the chrysalis that turns into the butterfly. With people, the transformation never takes place unless it is from imputation. Unlike the butterfly, the transformation in human beings does not take place because of a natural process. The transformation with people takes place because of the species of one-way love that is called imputation.

Imputation rarely fails to connect. As the receiver of it, I am touched and thrilled and converted. As the giver of it, I watch its transmuting power. Imputation is the mechanism of grace in everyday life. It is the "back story" of which I have written and which causes grace to be true in divine fact and not simply in human metaphor. God has imputed Christ's perfection to me and has transferred my twisted and confused "qualities" to Christ. Paul says this in 2 Corinthians: "For our sake he made him to be sin who knew no sin, so that in him we might become the righteousness of God" (5:21). The one-way love of grace could not be more apparent or concrete than in this one-way granting of love to another that theology calls imputation. It is the saving grace of soteriology.

There is one more thing to say about the way imputation writes its new name onto the old writhing thing that is human identity without imputation. This is the new description of identity called *simul iustus et peccator* — justified and also a sinner, loved and also fully human, at the same time.

Simul iustus et peccator: *The Key to Living*

Imputation is an either-or action. It is the substitution of a name, "good," for a reality, "bad." When the imputation is done, nothing more of the bad covered-over reality can be seen. It is like the line spoken by the Anna Lee character toward the end of John Ford's *Fort Apache* (1948), as she watches the Seventh Cavalry disappear into the distance: "All I can see is the flags." Her men are all going to their deaths. She and we know this. But all we can see is the flags. In imputation, nothing is left of the sallow thing that has now been imputed to be healthy and fit. Imputation covers the thing to which it attends. Thus the woman taken in adultery was imputed sinless by the Lord: "Neither do I condemn you" (John 8:11). "All I can see is the flags"! In the same way, what has taken the place of Mary Magdalene, the adulteress, is St. Mary Magdalene, the repentant, who will be the first to see the Lord on Easter Day.

However, in its reception, in its being received by us, imputation produces a paradoxical *both-and*. I referred to this when I compared the wide angle of soteriology to the narrowing of a pencil point. The wide part of the pencil is the atonement of Christ's crucifixion. The narrowing part is God's imputation. The imputation justifies; it makes right what is twisted by naming it right. The imputation is creative, for it creates what it evokes. We see this in life when a "geek," imputed to be attractive and winsome, actually becomes attractive and winsome. One imputing overture toward a person who is pathologically shy, and she starts to become outgoing. One imputing overture toward a person who sees himself as unattractive to women, and he gains confidence and begins to date. Imputation brings into being what it evokes.

But the fine point of the pen, the razor edge, the part that inscribes grace visibly on "tablets of human hearts" (2 Corinthians 3:3), is the reality of imputation as experienced by its object, the imputed being. This is the miracle that I am regarded by another as perfectly sufficient while *at the same time* being in my own person quite insufficient. The result of imputation, which is fully either-or, is *simul iustus et peccator,* which is thoroughly both-and.

"Ain't that peculiar?" (Marvin Gaye). My status from God's side is unassailable and indefectible. My substance from my side, from the analysis of anyone who knows me, is good and bad at the same time, or rather, mostly the same old, same old that I have always been, though now covered over by the thin red line, the imputing blood of Christ. We could say that this position of the *simul-iustus-et-peccator* self is the last word in what the world wants to call "maturity." That is, the *simul-iustus-et-peccator* self is secure in the love of another, and at the same time cognizant of its limitations, faults, and insufficiencies — its sins, in other words. The world's "maturity" would leave out the divine stamp on the *iustus* ("righteousness") and talk instead about our inherent goodness, the spark of humanity that is always inside.

This is the place where Christianity becomes a matchless definition of human maturity. It is the key to living, because it lives in hope and belovedness *(iustus),* while at the same time accepting the limitations of a fallen, tripped-up character *(peccator).* This is integration. *Simul iustus et peccator* integrates the human object. It combines imputation, the fact that God brings everything to the table as far as my identity is concerned, and the fact that I bring nothing to the table whatsoever. The No pronounced on my sin, which I shall carry in my body and person for the rest of my life, is united with the Yes pronounced upon that sin. Imputation makes it all right for me to live as I am and also in the light of what I ought and want to be. Human identity works best under the sun of *simul iustus et peccator.* It works fruitfully on no other lines.

Soteriology, in its progress from atonement to imputation and finally to *simul iustus et peccator,* creates the ideal man and woman in this life. They are what the New Testament calls "a new creation" (2 Corinthians 5:17; Galatians 6:15; Ephesians 2:15).

"What If God Was One of Us?": Christology

The title of this section comes from a popular song written by Eric Bazilian, sung famously by Joan Osborne, then by Prince, then again by Cheryl "Pepsi" Riley in *Diary of a Mad Black Woman*. The song title drives purists mad with its emphatic rejection of the subjunctive, but it is still a great song! With its strong refrain and open, searching spirit, it pleads for divine intervention, for one-way love. It takes the next step in this theology of everyday life. This is the step from soteriology to Christology.

I have said that the starting point for grace in practice is the human condition. It is a condition denatured by original sin, total depravity, and the un-free will. The denaturedness of human beings requires saving, but the conditions for the saving do not lie within the situation that requires saving. The soteriology required must be an operation of grace, which is one-way love. Human beings bring nothing to the table.

The divine saving, under these truly hopeless circumstances, is a dazzling performance. It forces you to ask, Who can this be?

> "Who is this that comes from Edom,
> from Bozrah in garments stained crimson?
> Who is this so splendidly robed,
> marching in his great might?" (Isaiah 63:1)

The idea is that something very important has transpired, an intervention that involves a delivering from paralysis to full walking, from effectual death to "walking and leaping" (Acts 3:8). The required and fully normal human question then becomes, Who is he? He has served me unasked and with success. I want to know who he is.

It is the same in romantic love. Once you are hooked, once you are drawn powerfully to your beloved, you desire to find out all about her. Where did she come from? What are her parents like? How did she come to be the engrossing person she has become for you? What did she look like as a little girl? Has she ever liked another guy? Who are her friends? You just want to know everything you can possibly find out about her. (P.S. Don't ever read her journal.)

The point is this: what she has done *for* me makes her interesting *to* me. This is why soteriology, the science of what Christ has done for me, leads directly to Christology, the science of who Christ is.

The assertion that Christ is God is not provable in a strict sense. The identity of a historic individual with the unseen God is not provable. It is a compelling thing to say based on the evidence of the kind of life he lived and the things he did. But the identity of Christ with God, formally called the mystery of the incarnation, remains a mysterious thing simply because God himself is invisible.

Thus, while I am convinced of the divinity of Jesus, I cannot prove it in a scientific, unassailable way. What I can demonstrate is that the divinity of Christ is essential to the religion of Christianity having impact on our daily lives. The divinity of *God,* a first principle of Christianity, has little to say about the situations of everyday living. Just ask a European! Most Europeans like to say that they have "finished with God." That is the expression in northern Europe. It captures the feelings of most northern Europeans in relation to Christianity. The indifference of most Spanish people and now many Italians to religious faith as they understand it asserts the same resigned thing. They wish to see belief in God as childish, at best adolescent. A Danish man told me that disillusionment with the Christian church was in direct proportion to the degree of education of the populace. I asked him to be more specific. He said that what he meant was that education dispels the need of people to worship something that does not exist.

My point is that human nature's original sin, total depravity, and the un-free will are empirically verifiable ideas, but not the idea of God. The anthropology of everyday life is provable. You could say it is a scientific fact. This fact elicits either suicide or an urgent search for deliverance. That is the main reason why Christianity should be taken seriously. The need represented by its obvious but often denied diagnosis of reality calls for urgent solution: either some form of suicide (alcohol, the Hemlock Society, physician-assisted suicide, or the kind of desperateness portrayed in Neville Shute's novel of nuclear holocaust, *On the Beach*), or total consecration to the search for a solution.

This systematic theology of daily life recognizes a solution in the atonement of Christ's crucifixion. It understands soteriology to be the only possible alternative to ending it all by one's own hand, and it sees one necessary consequence of soteriology to be an extreme importance attached to the person of Christ himself.

What is essential to say about the person of Christ? It is expressed with perfect logic in the healing of the paralyzed man (Matthew 9:2-8; Mark 2:1-12). A man is healed by Christ through his pronouncing of forgiveness in relation to the man's sins. The Pharisees grumble, the usual response to grace from the anachronized direction of the law. They say, "Who can forgive sins but God alone?" (Mark 2:7). A syllogism is at work: Jesus forgave the man's sins and the result was that he was released from paralysis; only God can forgive sins; therefore Jesus must be God.

In theology, yet also in experience, Christ has to be divine in order for soteriology to work. On the cross, only a perfectly innocent subject could substitute for me in my corruption and lack of innocence. In the old cult, the lamb to be put forward on behalf of sins had to be "without blemish" (Exodus 12:5; Leviticus 4:28). "New lamps for old!" (Aladdin). For the operation of the substitution to work, the quality of the subject substituted has to be the opposite of me. The subject has to be perfect. Thus we say without skipping a beat: "Truly this man was God's Son!" (Matthew 27:54).

On the one hand, I need to know and be assured that Christ was fully human to such an extent that he took on the whole business of the human vale of tears. But he was without sin (Hebrews 4:15). While he did not see around corners — he was human — he did not partake of original sin, total depravity, and the un-free will. He was God as well as sinless man.

For the sake of soteriology, Christology requires the assertion that Christ was fully God and fully man. This assertion is sufficient to equip his person to accomplish the needed act: full atonement for the sins of the whole world.

To sum up, soteriology is the only solution proper to a human nature properly diagnosed. Soteriology draws its only full effect from the Christology of the man who was God and the God who was man. It is only now, after the saving act and the saving person have been placed within the environment of the otherwise unending nightmare of existence in this world, that we can move forward to say something about God in himself.

The Being of God: Holy Spirit and Holy Trinity

In a systematic theology of everyday life, metaphysics is beside the point. Ontology, which is the study of being, the study of the nature of things in themselves, is beside the point. God's *being* is beside the point. This is because "no one has ever seen God" (John 1:18; 1 John 4:12). It is a simple but undeniable fact that God is invisible. Even when God made his invisibility visible in the Bible, no one could look at him without holding a veil over his face (Exodus 34:33, 35; 2 Corinthians 3:13), or, in the very best case, seeing him only from behind (Exodus 33:20-23). The Bible, unlike many believers, gave up long ago on seeing God, in himself, with the eyes.

The best we can do, and for Christians it is enough, is to look at "the Father's only Son" who "has made him known" (John 1:18). All other concepts of God are beside the point. They are interesting, but they are speculation. Speculation concerning God produced the doctrine of the Trinity. I myself believe this doctrine. It artfully and subtly allows for the unseen-ness of God (the Father) to relate to his seen-ness at a point and time of history (in Jesus Christ), and for both the unseen-ness and the seen-ness to relate equally to his presence in the now (the Holy Spirit). The conceptual brilliance and wholeness of the doctrine of the Trinity gives it an intellectual and hence a theological appropriateness in giving verbal expression to the "big picture" of God's relation to the world. I accept the doctrine of the Trinity and believe in it.

What is less impressive about the doctrine of the Trinity is the various interpretations offered by theologians to its supposed "portrait" of the *inner* life of God. It is proposed, for example, in some contemporary Western theology and in some branches of Eastern Orthodoxy, that the Trinity mirrors an inner "family life" within the Deity. The many-ness within the oneness of the triune God is supposed to "exemplify" or idealize human relationships within human families. *Perichoresis* is the Greek word that theologians import to describe the sort of weaving-back-in-upon-itself of the divine Trinity, an interpenetrating sort of cosmic loving that approximates some sort of human loving. I find this "family life" idea of the Trinity to be anthropomorphic, in just the way Muslims fear Christian theology really is.

Trinitarian theology can become vulnerable to Islam's critique, for trinitarian theology posits the existence of humanity within the Deity itself. Whenever I say this, whenever I critique emphases on the Trinity that display "God in relationship," some Christians want to say that my critique is unorthodox. I disagree. The doctrine of the Trinity is powerful, evocative, and satisfying; and it honors the majesty of the divine Father who came to the world in Christ and acts in the world now through the Holy Spirit. It is an important and safeguarding conception. But we should not press the point! To employ the doctrine of the Trinity as the starting block for anthropomorphic speculation and extreme metaphor is to cut away from real life. It also ignores the burning critique from Islam, which must be answered if Christianity is to be a partner in the pursuit of world peace after September 11, 2001. Christianity *must* parry the centuries-old Islamic criticism of the doctrine of the Trinity, which is the Muslim world's enduring objection to the religion of Christ, if we are to live in the real world.

From the side of plain human experience, it is necessary to affirm that theological anthropology, soteriology, and Christology override in importance *from our side* any doctrines — intellectually satisfying as they may be — which concern the being of God in himself.

One partner in the Trinity, however, is extremely important from the side of human experience. This partner is the Holy Spirit. The Holy Spirit is the presence of God active in the world in the absence of Jesus Christ and in the absence of the Father. The Holy Spirit was promised by Christ in the Gospel of John (14:26; 20:22), and then encountered electrically in the book of Acts (chapter 2), which tells the story of how the Christian church began. The Holy Spirit acted as the inspiring presence of Christ after Christ himself had left. The Spirit's guidance, as the first Christians experienced it in the absence of Christ, and the Spirit's comfort, as they felt it in the absence of his firsthand consolation, were real to them. The Spirit was an active, specific force. It took them out of prison cells and pushed them toward the Gentiles. It told them what to say when silence was necessary. It convicted them of their sins and made them soar in the light of their forgiveness.

It is easy to have too low a view of the Holy Spirit. It comes naturally to settle for a sort of "Christianity-as-great-idea" view of religion. Jesus as the teacher, Jesus as the master, Jesus as the way-shower: these are ideas with which I grew up myself. You can admire Christ and be touched sincerely by the example of his compassion, yet still be on the outside of anything objectively real in respect to him.

It is the Holy Spirit who brings Christ to life. He takes the "old, old story" and applies it to your point of need. The Spirit takes the general and applies it to the specific, which is to say to you and me. In a theology of grace in practice, the Holy Spirit plays an indispensable part.

Have you ever heard the saying, "Nobody is indispensable"? It is not true. Say that to a man who has just lost his wife of fifty years. Say that to a mother who has just attended the funeral of her child. For that matter, say that to the producers of performance art. Somebody once asked Michael Mann, the producer of the television show *Miami Vice,* whether the actor Don Johnson was indispensable to the show. The interviewer added, "After all, Mr. Mann, is one actor ever really indispensable?" He answered, "Yes! Don Johnson is indispensable. There would be no *Miami Vice* without Don Johnson."

The Holy Spirit is indispensable to a theology of grace. Why is that? It is because a theology of grace blows up the engine of human control. A theology of grace says, "Hands off!" to the human being and gives God a chance. When you love someone from grace, there is no result for which you are looking. It is one-way love. Grace neither expects anything in return nor "tweaks" the object of its concern. It is not action-consequence love. It hopes all things but expects nothing. Certainly it expects nothing back. It is prayerful, in the extreme, but has no plan for the future. A theology of grace in practice depends on the Holy Spirit of God. The heavy lifting in all human relationships comes from grace, which is block-and-tackle like no other. The results of this heavy lifting, however, depend on the Holy Spirit. This is why a theology of grace always involves prayer. Having offered to someone the one-way love of grace, the only thing you can do is pray to the Holy Spirit to take it from there.

I have written nine other books about Christianity, but I have underemphasized until now the role of the Holy Spirit in practical Christianity. The main reason I believe in the Three-in-Oneness of God is the Holy Spirit. The Spirit represents the ever-absent Father and the presently absent Son. Without the Holy Spirit, we have nothing in the now. With the Holy Spirit, we can love in the one-way direction of grace and trust the result.

CHAPTER THREE

Grace in Families

A systematic theology of everyday life has to be focused on relationships. Immense factors of grace and law operate in every relationship possible to human beings. Not only does the relation of grace and law determine the outcome of any relationship you can name, but each misfire and also each reunion form an analogy to divine law and divine grace.

We have to look for a moment now at the idea of *analogy* in theology. It is evident that "no one has ever seen God" (John 1:18) and that our knowledge of God, in Christian thinking, is dependent on Jesus of Nazareth. This information is not slim pickings, but it does go back to a very long time ago. It is easy to invoke Christ's example and easy to be moved by the compassion he lived. But to ground it now, this way of God in the life of the long-ago Christ, demands analogy.

Analogy occurs when you answer the questions "Where is God now?" and "How do his law and his grace function now?" by referring to illustrations from life. A preacher does well when he or she inserts illustrations or analogies drawn from life in order to illustrate what the Bible is saying about the unseen God. The preacher's illustrations have to be consistent with the biblical picture of life, but that is not hard. The biblical forces of law and grace are obvious in life when you begin to look for them. Every marriage, every romantic misfire, every point of trouble you have with a growing child, every resentment you store up against a parent, every argument you get into at work, every single possible site of tension in the relating to other people — these are all factors of law and grace in tension.

I need to demonstrate this. The demonstration will take place in an inventory of "all the usual suspects" *(Casablanca)*. First, singleness will become a field of analogy in observing law and grace in human terms. Then romantic love and marriage will become the very richest field of analogy. Then, too, the relation of parents to children and children to parents, and the relation of siblings to one another — each of these freighted and vulnerable theaters of everyday life is a fruitful field of analogy.

If you understand what is going on with your spouse in terms of grace and law, almost every problem you can name in your marriage will become comprehensible. If you observe what is happening with your children and also with your aging parents in terms of law and grace, the perspective will deepen. It could lead to some creative new hope in the situation. Much of what follows in these chapters on everyday life comes under the rubric of analogy. It is what Jesus did when he taught in parables. The parables were analogies drawn from everyday experience, in which the law and the grace of the unknown invisible God became dramatized. Jesus would tell a little story and then say, this is how God is. In the many analogies that follow now, the idea is to be able to say, This is how law works stuntingly in daily life, and this is how grace works creatively in real life.

Grace in Singleness

Singleness is the first state of a man or a woman. How does law drive the single being, and how is he or she driven by grace? There is an aloneness to the relation of God and human beings that is unavoidable. There is an aloneness to the human being that is within the nature of things and that is at times denied. The poet's assertion that "no man is an island" (John Donne) is not true. While it is fair to say that everyone shares certain experiences with everyone else (birth and death, for example), it is untrue to say that we share these experiences together or in community. In fact, everyone is born alone and everyone dies alone. To say differently is to live in your head.

I have been with many people in their dying. No matter how much love surrounds the person, no matter how many encouraging and stroking words he or she receives from devoted family, it is up to the dying person alone to "let go" and slip away from human life. When you die, neither your child nor your spouse dies with you. You die alone. This is not a concession to dereliction, for Christians believe that God makes you never alone. But from *your* point of view, you die alone. The act of dying is solitary, just as the act of being born is solitary.

Like many fathers today, I was able to be present at the birth of each of our three children. They were completely surrounded by marvelous doctors and nurses, and two ready parents. But as I watched each of our three newborns looking around, chewing on their ID bracelet and resting after the total effort of battling their way out of their mother's womb, I saw a single child in full sensory openness. There were not two children there, or three. There was one.

It is an abstract concept and not a report from life to say that we exist in community. We may *wish* to exist in community. It may be possible to *become* community. But in the demanding givens of the struggle of life, we are, in our human nature, single.

A man I know lost his wife of fifty-five years. He says he changed drastically after her death: he was no longer the person he had been. I asked what he meant by this. He said that he and his wife after almost six decades of happy marriage had become so much of a unit that he was a *broken* object now, a half-man. This was testimony to the fact that individuals over time can merge. But my friend's grief also reminded me that, before he had bonded so affectingly with his wife, he had been "an island." Now that she was gone, he was an island all over again. This is to say that singleness is the initial case of being human, and it is tangibly so in relation to death. Singleness is the first state of a human being. It is also the last.

What is the law in relation to singleness, which at bottom is the real condition of any man, woman, or child? What is grace in relation to the hard core of a man or a woman, the being alone? Singleness is an enigma because it goes back to the origin and also to the end of bodily existence. Why did I come into the world?

On each occasion when I looked into the faces of our three newborn sons in the delivery room, I saw a question mark. The question was more along the lines of "Where is love?" than "What is this place and why am I here?" But they were all the same question intensely felt: To what end am I here? When their mother's eyes met the newborn child's, the question was answered — for the time being. It is an overwhelming question, articulated within eyes and arms: Why am I here? For each new life, that question must be answered.

Similarly but more disconsolately, the question is asked at death. In intensive care, there is often a look of terror on the face of an extremely ill person. Once I was with a woman in her early forties who had suffered a grievous injury. The doctors had put a football helmet over her head to prevent her from injuring herself. Her arms were bound to the side of the bed. She was in the most acute distress one could imagine. She was also alert and conscious, although without speech. The look with which she fixed me, who knew her well, was of such communicating terror that I have not been able to shake it to this day.

Another time, I was with a considerably older woman who had entered the hospital for a "routine" coronary bypass. There was a valve leak, however, and she had to be rushed into surgery a second time the same day. After the second surgery, I visited her as she was strapped to a table that was tipped at a 75-degree angle. The look of terror with which she fixed me was, again, completely arresting and unforgettable.

The second woman in my story recovered. The first woman did not. The first woman's ashes were scattered over a pond a few weeks later, and because the water was shallow and the pond was still, they sank to the bottom and we could see them there in a kind of gray gash. We die alone.

We are born in singleness, with high hopes. We die in singleness, with terror and mixed hopes. Even "Christian" in *The Pilgrim's Progress,* the hero and man of faith, cries out in despair as the waters of death come over him. When the moment comes, he is required to die alone. The purpose of this brief meditation on singleness is to root the sad case of human existence in its true state. We are not born in community, nor do we die in community. We are single, alone. It is the first fact of human existence. Grace must speak to this.

A theology of everyday life must address the single life. Before it addresses the social relationships of life, grace must address the single life. I am thinking of the life of a "Bridget Jones," a sort of icon of unfulfilled singleness, someone who is simply living to be not alone. Every step she takes is a cry to be not alone. She makes "poor choice" after "poor choice" in her quest to be not alone. Only the intervention of a Mr. Darcy figure, walking right in from a Jane Austen novel, is able to save.

There is sad singleness beyond Bridget Jones. There is the singleness of the widow or widower, happily married for fifty-five years and now disoriented and puzzled. There is the singleness of the single mother, another iconic figure, who works all day, mothers all evening, and has no one to support and comfort her. There are many millions of single mothers. There are many millions of widows and widowers. There are many millions of single people and divorced people. Every one of them is looking for love. How does grace address the single life? What is the meaning of grace in relation to everyday singleness?

Singleness, as the natural state of a human being, requires the grace of God in an urgent, one-dimensional way. Some people like to speak of singleness as a gift. We have to take their word for it. But for most single people, young and old, divorced or never married, widowed or simply life-longingly alone, singleness is not a happy state. They tell me this. They have told me this over and over through thirty plus years of parish ministry. And when those who protested they were comfortable with being single got the chance to be married, they seemed almost to jump at it. This is a demographic fact demonstrated in the hundreds of thousands of "Internet marriages" that now take place.

Just as there is a desperateness to the solitary nature of death and dying, there is a chronic desperateness to the state of being single with no end in sight. This means that the connection of grace to singleness must be an intimate one. Nothing but that which comes from outside is able to help the solitary human being who craves an end to his or her solitariness. The grace of God exists in its pure state in relation to singleness. Only God can step in, we might say, when no one else is there.

An accurate and agonizing illustration of singleness as loneliness occurs in a 1953 short story by Theodore Sturgeon entitled "Saucer of Loneliness." In the story, a plain-looking single woman is terrorized and then strangely exalted by a beam of light that comes down from the sky and buzzes around her as she is standing in a very public place. She says she has been given a message but will not tell anyone what it is. She stands by her silence. Utterly eschewed by the world (which had eschewed her long before the event of the "saucer" ever happened), the woman becomes even more lonely than she was before. At the end of the story, a man approaches her, quite alone and also lacking confidence himself. He is a walking instance of pure emotional neediness and is obviously the one for her. To him, this kind and empathic man, she reveals what the "saucer of loneliness" told her:

> There is in certain living souls
> A quality of loneliness unspeakable,
> So great it must be shared
> As company is shared by lesser beings.
> Such a loneliness is mine; so know by this
> That in immensity
> There is one lonelier than you.[1]

As sentimental as the ending is, you can't help brushing away a tear.

I think of the more than 10,000 elderly citizens of France who died in Paris in 2003 during a severe heat wave. They were mostly elderly women who lived alone. The lonely deaths of 10,000 people, most of them elderly women, from heat prostration should have been sufficient to start a collective nervous breakdown in France. It almost did. But now it is beginning to be forgotten.

What hope of relief is there for the terminally lonely, but a loud cry of complaint to God! In the absence of relationship — in the presence of singleness, in other words — grace has to function in pure verticality. I

1. Theodore Sturgeon, "A Saucer of Loneliness," in *The Complete Stories of Theodore Sturgeon,* ed. Paul Williams, vol. 7 (Berkeley, CA: North Atlantic Books, 2000), p. 13.

am alone; I seem to be able to do nothing to amend my state; and the only help must come from the God who is outside of me.

In a way, then, singleness is an enviable point of need. It suffers the "total war" of the law, for it is a total state of accusation in the face of what the single person would wish for herself. Singleness cries out for solution: the intervention of one-way love.

Thus singleness, in the "unmarried" sense as well as in the helplessness of dying alone, is both the worst that can happen and the most obvious place for God to speak. God spoke to the desolated Elijah in the cave, in God's "still small voice" (1 Kings 19:9-18, Revised Standard Version). And to Christ in Gethsemane came ministering angels (Luke 22:43). In this sense, married and related people could wish that they were single again.

Grace in Marriage

Grace and the Origin of Marriage

The feelings leading to marriage are aroused by the physical and romantic ecstasy resulting from being discovered, in one's true hidden existence, by another person. This is the thesis concerning grace in relation to marriage: Being known in weakness is the origin of marriage. Marriage, in other words, depends on a theology of the cross rather than a theology of glory.

If you are married or were married, remember the origin of your marriage. The root and fountain of the relationship was the discovery by another of your true but hidden self. You disclosed yourself. The disclosure lit a fire that gave off a lot of heat. A "purely" sexual relationship did not have this fire. But the sexual relationship that accompanied the disclosure did. It led to your desire to be married.

I first noticed this almost coincidentally while seeing the movie *Tom Jones* (1963) as a child. It was clear that Tom Jones, the lusty "Alfie" of the eighteenth-century novel, was conquered by Sophie Western because she nursed him back to health after he broke his leg. This being nursed, this being dependent on Sophie in almost every sense, led to his having ardent feelings for her. For Tom Jones, there was no going back.

At the other end of life, I saw this fact again in my early years of parish ministry. A very old man was being nursed back to health after a serious illness. His wife of many years had died recently. All that time she had lied to him concerning her age, and only when she succumbed to Alzheimer's disease did he find out that she was ten years older than he. He was just a little bitter about this when I met him, although he was bitter in an ironic and rather gentle way.

But when he became ill himself, he found himself in a town far away from his normal life, in a completely unfamiliar hospital. A middle-aged unmarried woman was his nurse in the hospital. She nursed him well and gently. The man happened to be rich, in the world's terms, and was also living under a microscope, as it happened, from some distant relatives who stood to inherit his money. But he outfoxed them. He proposed marriage to his nurse, and she accepted. I asked him, as his Episcopal rector, why he had decided after so many decades of marriage to marry once again. He cried. He said that his nurse was the only person who ever loved him without wanting anything back. She had cleaned him and been boundlessly tender to him. He wanted nothing more in life than to be with her. This was grace. It was one-way love, and it evoked a fantastic response. I have seen the origin of marriage at the point of youth and at the point of something like dissolution. It is always the same. Grace evokes a love that creates the desire to be married.

The concrete interplay of grace and law came violently into focus during a funeral I once conducted. The man who had died, another wealthy man by the standards of the world, had been looked after for almost ten years by a devoted housekeeper. It was obvious that they were indispensable to one another. I used to visit them during their happy years together. He was blind, and she led him around and looked after him right up to the period of his last illness. He wanted to leave his money to her. He felt married to her in everything but name. His nephews and nieces, however, who represented law in this case, were focused sharply and actively on seeing that his legacy went to them, the "next of kin," and not to this grace-full interloper. They deliberately did not invite this woman to the funeral. The next of kin were lined up at the bier. They looked like something out of Edgar Allen Poe. As the officiant, I asked a nephew why a uniformed guard with a revolver was also posted by the bier. He said that he and the other "family" members feared the presence of the housekeeper. They feared she might make a scene. In truth, she did not appear. I believe she was a devout Christian and did not in fact have designs on the man's money.

That was the slimiest and least Christian funeral I have ever conducted! Whatever grace had existed between an old blind man and his nurse was obliterated by the law. How upset the dead man would have been to see a holstered guard posted by his coffin, poised to keep away with deadly force the only person who had loved him at the point of need.

Grace at the origin of romantic love, which is the entry point for hopes of marriage, is related to the concept of intimacy. "Intimacy" is a word that can make you wince. It is used in sentimental settings, and it is sometimes deployed to describe relationships that are unworthy of the word. But it actually means something important. Intimacy is when I know somebody else as they really are. It is when I know someone inwardly and not just outwardly.

Christ was uninterested, for example, in human beings from the outside in. He was only interested in people from the inside out. He pulled away from people who looked like "whitewashed tombs" but whose insides were filled with "the bones of the dead" (Matthew 23:27). Intimacy is the opposite of a whitewashed tomb. It is seeing into the core of a person while not being repelled by what you see.

Grace in everyday life operates at the origin of every marriage. It is the spark that got it going. I was human with this person, and instead of turning away from me, which would have been an act of the law, this person turned toward me. It was one-way love. It had nothing to do with my worthiness. It was love in my direction from the eye of the beholder. It all happened in a sodium flash, like the exploding lights of the old newspaper photographers. The grace that came to you from this woman or man begot the fruit of grace, and the connection was sealed.

It is the origin, the grace-origin of every marriage, on which the future of the marriage depends. In trouble, you have to retreat to first principles. What was it like at the beginning? What created the spark that led to the promise? It was not sex per se or physical attraction in a vacuum. It was the underlying moment of truth coupled with belovedness that dazzled your life. The light of being loved, and loved in your humanity as opposed to ideality, was the inaugurating sun of this particular system. God help you if you were married in a deception. God help you if you loved one another but there was failure in the truth-telling.

Whenever the clouds of crisis, not to mention resentment, begin to come down on our marriage, my wife and I go back to first principles. What got it started? What was the octane sufficient to bring together two such different people from two such different lives? What was sufficient to overcome the differences? What formed a unity, when there had existed only disunity and difference? *Whatever formed the unity is the only agency that can re-create the unity.* This is the analogy to Christianity. When you are beaten by the law, which is so bound up with stress, you have no safe place to go but the grace of absolution and the newness that changed your life in its initial situation. Grace in experience is what made you a Christian. It is the same with marriage as it is with God.

The Protestant Reformers discovered this as their first principle of the Christian church. The way forward in healing a distressed church was the way backward, *ad fontes,* "to the fountain," the source. To reheat an old love, always go back to the heat of your first love.

Law in the Mythology of the Marriage

While the origin of most marriages lies in a situation and moment of grace, there is also a law accompanying that origin that must be fought off forever after. While grace illuminates and forms the one-to-one relationship of the couple, the law weighs in with the baggage they bring to the relationship. The law comes down with the givens, the insistent archaeology on which each person's previous life stands.

Let us say the wife comes from a "socially prominent" family and the husband grew up "down in the boondocks" (Billy Joe Royal). The mythology pregnant in that fact will always shadow the footsteps of this couple. The mythology is that she married below herself and thus did him a favor. No matter what degree of chemistry he brought to the relationship, it will inevitably decrease over time. But the myth will remain. It will be passed along to the children, either in the form of good-humored detachment or in the form of taunts and rebukes hurled in anger.

Let us say a husband considers himself an intellectual, someone who is interested in ideas, and his wife sees herself as a person of feeling, someone who focuses primarily on relationships. This will make for either a very successful partnership or a stormy and accusatory truce that is at times open warfare. "Why do you always hide behind a book?" she asks. "Because," he replies, "you always want something from me." The differing givens that each partner brought into the marriage become a mythology in every day of their lives. Grace birthed the love between them, but law is at the door, working on the "paradigm," the "metanarrative," of two people as they struggle to be one.

Perhaps the couple has a good marriage and two happy children. But he loses his job in a down market and suddenly finds himself at home during the day. He never knew that depression ran in his family; it had been pretty well covered up. But now he finds himself overcome with listlessness. He can barely get out of bed in the morning, not to mention look for a new job. Soon his wife realizes that she is going to have to go back to work to make ends meet. Before you know it, this man has become a depressed house-husband, ferrying the children to their activities and feeling like a failure in his career. Worse than that, however, the relationship of wife and husband starts to go bad. She is exhausted and blames him for his inaction. He is a deflated balloon and is angry at the world. Accusations and criticisms fly: "If I had only known about your family's history of depression, I might have thought twice before marrying you"; or "You are utterly lacking in sympathy for me"; or "You're just like your mother"; and so on.

The mythology of the marriage lies in the earlier lives of husband and wife. This is their original sin, which each person in the world carries within himself or herself. The law enters the "paradigm" (i.e., she married beneath herself; his family was always depressed; "you are heartless and remote, an egghead like your dad was," and so forth). The law increases the sin (Romans 5:20), sin rears its ugly head, and married love turns into married and then unmarried recrimination.

From the point of view of grace, the law of marital mythology can be parried only by the complete and undiscriminating acceptance of the human givens of the other person. Grace knows that human nature is evenly distributed. Grace also understands that Kennebunkport, Maine, is more heavily laden with certain associations than Warren, Ohio. But the details of each person's archaeology are unimportant so far as the readiness to be loved is concerned. Everyone needs the same amount of love, which is 100 percent unconditional love, the one-way love of God.

The quintessential antidote to the law in the mythology of marriage is found in 2 Corinthians 3. There Paul contrasts the mythology of law, which he calls "the ministry of condemnation" (v. 9), with the deeper magic of grace, which he calls "the ministry of the Spirit" (v. 8). Comparing the first with the greater splendor of the second, Paul writes, "If there was splendor in the ministry of condemnation, much more does the ministry of justification abound in glory! Indeed, what once had glory has lost its glory because of the greater glory" (vv. 9-10).

This is to say that paradigms of judgment, heightened by the law in any atmosphere of blame and accusation, are overridden in every case by the greater fact of grace. Grace is infinitely stronger than law.

Married couples are faced with big odds in the form of myths and mythology. But the point of origin of their love, the grace that made the first magic happen, is bigger. Charles Spurgeon, a famous preacher in England more than a hundred years ago, used to say that when ministers begin to write a sermon, they should always "make a bee line to the Cross." Apply this to marriage and it goes as follows: When you get all rolled up in the tar baby of criticism and attack, retreat to first principles. How did the relationship start? What first fired the love?

Law and Grace in the Competition of Marriage

Men and women encounter a serpent-ridden wilderness of Eden when they enter into marriage. Competition for need-fulfillment and attention squanders huge amounts of energy in resentment and suppressed antagonism. The nature of the law is to place every single marriage under the Damocles' sword of needs to be met. The word "negotiation" comes to the fore: wife and husband have to negotiate who is responsible for what and when. The negotiation model for marriage seems even more important with the arrival of children. Add to that the care of aging parents, and who is going to handle the finances of the family, and who gets what rest and recreation and when, and the whole life of the family becomes an economic system of barter and exchange.

The law excels in dividing married couples on the basis of power and influence. Many marriages become long-term struggles for power. "You men are all alike," lashes out Michelle in *Diary of a Mad Black Woman*. "You only think about yourselves." Her good man retorts, "Yes, and you women are so angry. No wonder that husband of yours left you." These are law-driven accusations. They destroy relationships every time. They imply a model of marriage as alternating need-fulfillment.

Grace demolishes the idea of need-fulfillment. Need-fulfillment is a law that has no possible final satisfaction. Human need is limitless on its own terms. It is a bottomless well, a pail with a hole in the bottom. Grace nullifies this. The need for personal fulfillment is not met in Christianity. It is destroyed.

In Christianity, grace assumes a bottomless need on the part of every single man and woman. It is the self-serving expression of original sin or selfishness. This unfulfillable need is worse than it sounds, for there is a scorpion at the bottom of the bucket. The original sin of the unattainable need is made worse by a sadism that bonds with it in practice.

We have already seen that the un-free will is unable to put up much of a struggle against original inward sins. If I had the person alone who has hurt me and left my own needs far back in the dust, I might break his legs with a mallet like Annie Wilkes in *Misery* (1987). I could rationalize my cruelty on the basis of the injustices he did to me, but I might not be able to rationalize myself out of my cruelty.

Grace nullifies competition in marriage. Grace says you are both equally at fault in everything, because the fault is in your chemistry and in your head. All men and women are "under the power of sin" (Romans 3:9).

Grace also states the answer to psychic and actual competition between men and women, in grace's one-way love that asks nothing in return yet "believes all things" (1 Corinthians 13:7). Grace forms love in return.

The characteristic form of competition in marriage is competition over identity. The man thinks, maybe without giving it much thought, that his job, his difficult and demanding job, deserves more credit than his wife's needlepoint shop, or her raising of their children day after day while he is at work. On the other hand, the woman may believe that only if she is chairing the board of Goldman Sachs can she bring credible equality to the marriage. Unless she is bouncing up and down against the glass ceiling, her "weight" in the partnership is not equal. The wife, in her stereotyped views of what is important and "identity affirming," is just as enslaved as the husband is in his own stereotyped views. *From the standpoint of grace, both partners are equally mistaken.* The best thing that could happen to them is if they both fell down from these stupendously misconceived ideas of human prize-winning and landed together on the same hill of sand, like pole-vaulters who have failed to clear the bar. Then they could observe their common failure.

Grace demolishes the human idea of success. It laughs about it. Do you remember the popular song from the 1970s entitled "The Piña Colada Song"? The singer wanted out of his marriage so badly that he answered a want ad in the newspaper: for someone who liked piña coladas and "getting caught in the rain." What happened when the two finally arranged to meet? What a surprise! It was his wife; it was her husband. The lyric, by Rupert Holmes, finished this way: "It was my own lovely lady and she said, 'Oh, it's you'/And we laughed for a moment, and I said, 'I never knew.'" The song is charming. The two unsatisfied partners are both looking for the same thing. They just don't know it. So they "fall down" from an Olympian height of marked judgment, laugh for a minute, and begin again. They begin again from self-knowledge, humility, and, in new fact, high hopes.

Grace does not satisfy the search for a safe, human identity. Grace destroys the search. Humor helps to universalize the pathos of people's compulsive attempts to shore up their "identity" with some sort of external predicate. Life deconstructs such attempts. Grace puts the competition on the same level and gives the same to every single person. For this reason, St. Paul says that in grace there is "no longer Jew or Greek, there is no longer slave or free, there is no longer male and female; for all of you are one in Christ Jesus" (Galatians 3:28; Colossians 3:11). This is the only satisfying news for ending the marital competition that drives men and women away from each other in the heat of the day. No presentation of symptoms of identity one-upmanship will ever "win" the war between the sexes. Each person will only "put down" the other. Only God has the will and power to put down "the powerful from their thrones, and [lift] up the lowly" (Luke 1:52). Grace ends competition in marriage. It demolishes self-righteousness and increases, past the Richter scale, the level of compassion required for love to exist, thrive, and continue. No more "Vive la différence."

Boundaries

Grace has no space for boundaries. It has space for everything, except for boundaries. This is because "boundaries," as that term is sometimes used to describe a safe relationship, do not exist in love. We all realize there is a smothering kind of love that causes its receiver to run in the opposite direction. Smothering can take place within maternal love. It can also take place in romantic love. Sheldon Vanauken's book *A Severe Mercy* (1977) paints a picture of romantic love in which he and his wife become possessed of such a fixation on each other and on their love as pure romance that they erect a "shining barrier" to keep all other loves and all other loyalties and interests out. This arbitrary "boundary" exists to prevent any other boundaries from coming between them. Today, readers of *A Severe Mercy,* which was a big success in the 1970s, become nauseated before this hermetic love fashioned by the Vanaukens. Fortunately for truth and also for the readers, their vacuum-sealed relationship was pierced in later years by envy, resentment, and mortal illness. Their "shining barrier," their boundary, came down.

We recognize smothering love both in romance and between parents and children. In *Les Miserables,* Jean Valjean has to detach himself intentionally and courageously from a "no boundaries"–type love between his stepdaughter Cosette and himself, in order to free Cosette to be able to marry. Valjean forces a kind of boundary to come between him and her, so that another boundary can be brought down between her and the man who truly loves her. Yes, some relationships that have no boundaries need them, like the overwhelmed daughter in relation to her possessive mother. But in marriage, *in principle,* there can be no boundaries.

Why do I insist on this? I insist on it because grace goes everywhere in pursuit of the beloved and especially to the places where the "boundaries" of guilt and humiliation say "Keep out!" Grace must pursue the loved person to the end of his or her being in order for this love to be married to the truth. The boundary-less character of grace is expressed in the children's story "The Runaway Bunny." There is no destination to which the bunny can flee or be taken to which his mother will not follow in love. The boundary-less character of grace, one-way love, is expressed in the "all points bulletin" of divine love from Psalm 139:

> Where can I go from your spirit?
>   Or where can I flee from your presence?
> If I ascend to heaven, you are there;
>   if I make my bed in Sheol, you are there.
> If I take the wings of the morning
>   and settle at the farthest limits of the sea,
> even there your hand shall lead me,
>   and your right hand shall hold me fast.
> If I say, "Surely the darkness shall cover me,
>   and the light around me become night,"
> even the darkness is not dark to you;
>   the night is as bright as the day,
> for darkness is as light to you. (139:7-12)

I learned that love knows no boundaries when another's love shrunk at nothing in me. I saw this in my own marriage. The demolition of boundaries was a moral act. There was no boundary sufficient to repel the grace of God in the love of my wife.

Conversely, I learned something about "boundaries" in the popular or therapeutic sense when I began to counsel a husband and wife, the latter of whom was a psychiatrist. She was evidently not attracted to her husband physically. She was always talking about the importance of establishing boundaries in their marriage. I think the boundaries were intended to keep him away from her in the bedroom. I thought to myself, "This sounds a little overstated, this 'boundaries' concept. She doth protest too much." Then it came out that she was involved in an extramarital affair with another man. No boundaries there! "Boundaries" in service of the self: this is where the language of boundaries leads.

Let's concede that the "Whatever Happened to Baby Jane?" kind of love needs a few boundaries. Let's concede the sort of boundaries that the man in an old *Twilight Zone* episode needed. When, by means of a love potion, he finally got the beautiful girl he thought he wanted, she fell so hard for him that he was hemmed in on every side like being in a prison. He then realized how much he preferred his old "boundaries."

In principle, however, within lasting romantic love that drops the walls between persons in their fully unclothed selves and premarital givens, grace knows only exploration and absolution, fascination and infatuation. Grace is looking into another person's eyes and achieving recognition.

The Word of the Cross in Marriage

The bond of marriage is forever unraveling and forever being rewoven. Because original sin is distributed evenly within wife and husband, every marriage is affected doubly. Without help from outside, marriages go bad. A man and a woman are in a constant process of withdrawal from one another. Part of you is longing to love and be loved; part of you is dying to pull back and be alone. These two dimensions, the marital form of *simul iustus et peccator,* are in chronic conflict. The *peccator* has the upper hand and always wins unless "the word of the cross" (1 Corinthians 1:18, Revised Standard Version) is heard and received.

What is this word of the cross that marriages require to remain in a state of grace? The word of the cross for marriage is the word of perpetual absolution. It is the word that forgives the *existence* of the other. Sin is such that I believe myself to be an overriding god. Everything comes back to me, as in Bette Midler's line, "Okay, enough about me. What do *you* think about me?" I am the man in another *Twilight Zone* episode (an episode later parodied on *South Park* and *The Simpsons*), in which the hero discovers a world in a sandbox, the inhabitants of which worship him. He is the object of worship on the part of a miniature, self-contained world. He receives the worship and believes in it until — needless to say — he is destroyed by it. But the picture is powerful: "O king, live forever!" (Daniel 6:21).

Marriage is not made for the good of a single person. It is not designed for the good of one man or one woman. Marriage requires an end to selfishness. Marriage fails if selfishness is not diminished. Marriage is, despite its inherent design to create children, *un*natural — unnatural, that is, from the vantage point of original sin.

A man has to forgive a woman for being a woman. This is not too strong a statement. A woman has to forgive a man for being a man. The differences between the sexes are vast, in terms of outlook, timing, attitude, and body. We can try to legislate away the differences, take the line of Soviet Russia in the 1930s in which sexual differences were supposedly swept under the rug. But it never works, even in the service of our highest aspirations for equality in idea-driven social engineering. This is because men and women will always be wary of one another. In the bedroom, differences of speech and drive are brightly lit. They require more than social engineering.

For Christians, the male-female divide requires the word of the cross. I refer to the word of absolution, which forgives a man for not being a woman and releases a woman from the law that she be a man. Do you remember Professor Higgins's musical outburst in *My Fair Lady*?

> Why can't a woman be more like a man?
> Men are so decent, such regular chaps.
> Ready to help you through any mishaps.
> Ready to buck you up whenever you are glum.

Why can't a woman be a chum?
Why is thinking something women never do?
Why is logic never even tried?
Straight'ning up their hair is all they ever do.
Why don't they straighten up the mess that's inside?
Why can't a woman behave like a man?[2]

Higgins's concluding line gives it away, however:

Why can't a woman . . . be like me?!

The word of the cross is the forgiveness offered by a man to a woman for the crime of being not him, and vice versa.

In this theology of everyday life, the word of the cross in marriage can take a simple form. It is a plan so simple that it sounds lightweight. The word of the cross in marriage consists of daily exposure, very early in the morning, to the Bible. They read a verse or two of the Bible, not more than a few sentences; the husband asks the wife what her prayer request is for the day; the wife asks her husband what his prayer request is for the day; and they pray out loud, briefly and extemporaneously. It takes about ten minutes. It makes all the difference.

What is happening within this simple plan? Two people are gathering their unvarnished, early-morning energies before a word that comes from outside of them. They are placing themselves under this word. They are therefore placing themselves on level ground. They are listening for a word that is not derived from within their natural givens. Then they are being asked to express their honest hopes and deficits in relation to the coming day. Provided they have not yet read a newspaper, checked their e-mail, or turned on the radio or TV, their honest hope and deficit for the day may well surface. They may actually talk about real things, which are usually real needs, and talking about them vertically. No advice from the other, no comments or sublime interpretation from a human avatar, but a personal, intimate expression to God of their actual need.

2. Alan Jay Lerner, *My Fair Lady* (Milwaukee: Chappell, 1969).

This simple plan gives the word from the cross something like a real hearing in a concrete relationship. It detaches the marriage from the purely horizontal and conditional and attaches it to the vertical and unconditional. This condensed time of supplication, this "quiet time" that sounds almost quaint, is countercultural in every sense of the word. Yet, it is a moment of liftoff for almost every marriage. Because it places man and woman on a level plain, each listening for a pulse outside themselves, it demolishes for a quarter-hour the innate difference between them. This is its profundity in concept and in practice. Before God, the male-female dimension is eradicated. Male and female identities are not affirmed before God; they are eradicated. Better, they are wholly subsumed under the banner of original sin, atonement, and imputation.

The short "quiet time" of this simple plan becomes the forum in marriage for God's word of the cross, a countercultural eradication of difference from which marriages can live and thrive. Without this quiet time early in the morning rooted in the Bible, a period insistent on non-denied disclosure in the presence of another, a time requiring spontaneous words of asking to the one truly Other, marriages are left to their own devices.

Grace in the Procreation of Children

Not everyone believes that a primary reason to be married is to have children. I myself do, and I take that as part of God's law to humanity to "be fruitful and multiply" (Genesis 1:28). This comes under the signature of what theologians call "natural law," the law written into the nature of things. Everything functions according to natural law, or things fall apart. Natural law is not the same thing as the law about which I have been talking, which is in direct antithesis to grace. What Roman Catholics call "natural law" is closer to what Protestant theologians call the "first use of the law." For Protestants, the "first use of the law" is God's protection of the earth and our world through his use of stop signs, traffic lights, patent laws, lighthouses, air traffic control, and school crossing guards. It is the "no brainer" function of the law, and it is neutral. No judgment attaches to it in the sense of moral evaluation of performance and infraction. Without the "first use of the law," the world would spiral off its axis.

The procreation of children is written into the nature of things. It is, you might say, an unconditional nonnegotiable. If children are not born, the world will die. We see this today in large sections of Europe. While America becomes overcrowded and teeming, while Dallas expands and Orlando explodes, Schwabia in Germany is empty, and those parts of France that are not overrun by English holidaymakers are so underpopulated that you can barely find an elementary school within fifty kilometers. While the coast of Morocco is sinking into the sea because of overpopulation, large parts of Italy have become a ghost town.

But here, in this chapter on grace and marriage, I am not thinking about whether children are a required part of married life or not, or whether having them is a matter of choice. I am assuming, on the basis of the "first use of the law," that their being born is a requirement of the sort of life that is in a different category from the neurotic interplay of grace and law that poisons the world. This theology of grace in practice takes for granted the conception, birth, and rearing of children.

The question at issue here is how the procreation of children affects the law/grace dynamic in marriage. I am thinking of husband and wife as father and mother.

> The union of husband and wife in heart, body, and mind is intended by God for their mutual joy; for the help and comfort given one another in prosperity and adversity; and, when it is God's will, for the procreation of children and their nurture in the knowledge and love of the Lord. (*Book of Common Prayer,* 1979)

The assumption of this theology of everyday life is that the procreation of children is an indispensable part of the marriage promise, even if God does not always fulfill a couple's hopes. In practice as a minister, I will not officiate at the marriage of couples of child-bearing age who tell me they do not wish to have children. The possibility of children has to lie within the intention of any married couple if they are of child-bearing age.

It is odd that this view of marriage in which the hope of children is a given, even if it be unfulfilled, needs defense. But in our contemporary context, it requires a defense. Here, it is a premise.

The "problem" of children from the perspective of grace and law is not the having of them, but the effect of their coming on the couple's engagement with grace and law in the intimacy of the man-woman relationship. The problem is this: the new child becomes for the mother the number-one priority of her loving, rather than her husband, at least in the first stages. The father is relegated to number two. The mother now has two competitors for her best and deepest self. Who will win?

The grace-law problem in the procreation of children is the redefinition, for a time, of one-way love. The child is the embodiment of the human being to whom love is entirely one-way. There is no relation more redolent of grace than the love for the child that emanates from the mother. The baby gives nothing back.

Similarly, the mother requires one-way loving from the father as she seeks to love from one direction this needy person who is able only to receive. The mother understands that she "has no choice" in her mothering. It is a complete commitment, and the father needs to offer his complete commitment to her. Her resource of love emanating from her husband issues in the resource required to envelop the child in grace. The father, however, may not understand things that way at all. He is perhaps more likely to be frustrated with the mother. He may find himself becoming unconsciously jealous of the child. Who is this whose every need gets met?

The struggle of grace to repel the law within marriage is acute in the early years of child rearing. The father may feel "out in the cold" as the child starts life in "the sunshine of your love" (Cream). The jealousy of the father is suppressed. The poor man hardly knows where these militant feelings are coming from, except that they are somehow related to feelings of sexual frustration. The mother knows she is doing right by the child, and she may become oblivious to the pressure cooker who used to be her husband. She may sense there is something wrong, but she barely has the time or physical energy to pick up on it. The incessant needs of the child are powerful. They are urgent and unending. All she wants is her husband's physical help to do the job, as well as his listening ear. He, on the other hand, begins to regard her as obtuse, as well as unavailable physically.

The pattern is familiar, and it continues. This little child can pry husband and wife apart. It is the observed order of things. The wife resents the man, especially if he ploughs all that male energy into his job. The man resents the wife because he is no longer number one.

My wife and I have worked alongside hundreds and hundreds of married couples with young children and have watched the judgments form, like gathering clouds of ash. She blames him for focusing his energies, really his love, outside the family. He blames her for focusing her love lopsidedly on the children, by which he means not thoroughly enough on himself. She sees him as selfish. He sees her as ignorant of what he knows are his obvious needs. My wife and I have seen countless marriages-with-little-children existing under threat.

The result is that the children can become mother's first love, and career can be more and more the father's first love. Sometimes he finds someone, almost always at work, who is interested in him, someone who "understands" him and listens to him. Adultery follows, and divorce follows that. I remember a wise and beloved parish clergyman telling me that in his forty years of ministry he had never encountered one single case of divorce in which there was not a third party involved. "That can't possibly be true," I protested. "There must be other causes." Now, after thirty years of ministry myself, I agree with that wise man. There are many things that *lead* to the existence of the third party, but there are few dead marriages that have not involved a triangle of some form.

The cause, theologically understood, is always the same: some form of judgment, some accusation from the law. In the case of little children, the man judges the woman for putting him second, and the woman judges the man for being unsympathetic and un-self-controlled. These judgments are widespread and cause those crazed tables of young couples with small children that you see at popular restaurants between 5:30 and 7:00 on Friday and Sunday nights. The parents are not saying a word to each other, and the mother is focused on the children. The man is nursing a beer and looking ten years older than he ever imagined he would at age 34.

Where is grace in marriage during the lengthy but not everlasting phase of the procreation of children? I can describe it rather than prescribe for it. Grace is the man stepping back from his self-absorption and focusing his entire loving on aiding his wife. He comprehends the importance of what she is doing. He also understands that it will not last forever and that she will come back to him. He also derives some pleasure from knowing that soon his little children will actually become fun for him. Not so much at first, when they are babies, but not long after. His children will become a joy to him.

She, on the other hand, has not forgotten that her husband is a physical being. This is what he thinks about a lot of the time, although he would deny it if you asked him. When they get away, very occasionally, for a little trip together, she realizes that for him it is all about sex. For her, it is all about time to read quietly and debrief him on her life, with him as that attentive listener for whom she longs. But if she focuses on sex, initially at least, he will be happy very quickly. *Then* she can detach and read her book, or whatever she is longing to do. The wife will never forget how the marriage began — her understanding of this real man as he really is combined with warm affection that was the moment of grace for them both. (And yes, it had a physical component.) When she acknowledges what is going on with him, it gives him such a lift. Her grace will serve to calm him down. And his law against her will immediately lower its demands.

That is the empirical description of grace in practice for married couples struggling to stay married in their child-rearing years. How does it actually happen? What is the bridge from law to grace in this exceptionally demanding time? On the surface, there is no substitute for the early morning quiet time. But the real engine, the operation that goes on beneath the quiet time, is one-way love. He forgives her for being a mother, and she forgives him for being a man.

There is one more thing about grace as it applies to the everyday life of marriage in the phase of child-rearing. It is this: the struggle continues. When the husband and wife are not intimate, when the law has fashioned its veil and the veil has hardened into a wall, human love still has to go somewhere. The devotion of husband or wife might be poured into careers, but it could also be misdirected toward the children: for mothers it could be the siren of the son, and for fathers it could be the siren of the daughter. This is the origin of *Psycho* (1959), and it is also the origin of most sexual abuse of daughters. When I say this in sermons and addresses, I am accused of overstatement. People say, "It is not that bad. You are portraying human beings as if they could become monsters at any point." But that is what I am saying. Original sin lacks only a few steps to travel to the place of total depravity. We see this in court case after court case, in child abuse testimony after testimony, and in the mental cruelty involved in divorce deposition after divorce deposition — the cruel things people commonly say and do!

The conflict of grace with law in child-rearing as it relates to the marriage of the parents is unending. D. H. Lawrence wrote *Sons and Lovers* in 1913, and part of that somber book is a description of the invisible emotional force holding back a man. The force has to do with his mother's love, which has been "turned" in the wrong direction. Love is never the problem in relationships that fail. It is the direction of the love and the angle of the love. In short, within marriage, the prior claim of loving is between the wife and the husband. When that is working grace-fully, then love of the children flows grace-fully. If the prior claim of the husband and the wife for each other is working grace-fully, the love to the children will be in the right proportion.

The Resurrection of Marriage

Original sin applied means that every marriage of two human beings is subject to divorce in every moment of its existence. This fact is in theological opposition to idealism, but it is borne out in daily life. Moreover, the divorce of married people is very often sealed with the reverse sacrament of infidelity. If grace applies to marriage, which is ever vulnerable to the influence of original sin, then grace can address the death of marriage in the interest of its rebirth.

The key idea here is resurrection in the light of God's creation of life. St. Paul invoked the creation by God of things that did not previously exist, to explain the miracle of new life. He wrote in Romans:

> [We] share the faith of Abraham (for he is the father of all of us, as it is written, "I have made you the father of many nations") — in the presence of the God in whom he believed, who gives life to the dead and calls into existence the things that do not exist. . . . [Abraham] did not weaken in faith when he considered his own body, which was already as good as dead (for he was about a hundred years old), or when he considered the barrenness of Sarah's womb. . . . [God] raised Jesus our Lord from the dead, who was handed over to death for our trespasses and raised for our justification. (4:16-25)

For Christianity, the only way to approach the death of a marriage, which is often embodied in acts of unfaithfulness, is to affirm the resurrection of Christ. That in itself is an awesome leap, but there is no hope otherwise for a dead marriage, except to "cut your losses" and try to "move on." Grace in the death of a marriage comes to concrete shape in the resurrection of the marriage.

Paul applied this work of grace as follows: God created the earth from nothing and performed a similar action in raising the dead Jesus back to life. This unique creativity allowed the patriarch Abraham to hope "against hope" that his wife and he could conceive a child even though they were way past child-bearing age. Paul then applied this unique creativity of God to the new life of absolution: "Jesus our Lord . . . was handed over to death for our trespasses and raised for our justification" (verses 24-25). Justification here is shorthand for absolution. The rebirth of Christians is an act of resurrection.

We can apply this logic to the logic of marriages that require resurrection. For injured parties in marriage, forgiveness is much more easily invoked than enacted. People sometimes say, "Yes, I have forgiven him [or her]. I just want to get back to where we were before it all happened." But this is not true. The layers of bitterness are too deep. Even when forgiveness is spoken in words, the train of it is lifelong accusation, as in, "I forgave you then, so you owe me for the rest of our life together." I sometimes encounter couples dealing with this inward scenario.

More often, however, I encounter a pervasive lack of forgiveness. Even if the word is spoken, it is spoken too soon or in a facile way. It is neither understood nor meant. Lasting forgiveness is an act of grace so rich as to be enduring in its effects. Love "keeps no record of wrongs" (1 Corinthians 13:5, New International Version). Who can forgive betrayal on their own? Such forgiveness is performative in that it creates new life. I see this pastorally. I read it biblically. I learn it theologically.

What a contrast to read the account of marital death in John Updike's short novel of 1976 entitled *Marry Me.* A marriage is gored and murdered through infidelity, and at the end, the husband has an extended poetic daydream of reconciliation: what it would look like and feel like if he and his wife and their small children were reconciled and able to love and live again. But it's all a dream. The man is in fact alone, on a Caribbean island where they were once, long ago, happy together. Updike's picture of marital death is bleak. It is not a Christian vision, perceptive as the novelist is about original sin. A Christian vision is a vision of death and resurrection, not of hurt and hard work. The resurrection of a dead marriage is a divine act. Only a miracle will save it.

I like Gene Pitney. As a picture of a sudden fall into extramarital adventuring, his song "Twenty-Four Hours to Tulsa" (1964) has no peer. The pity of it is that its hero is happily married when "lightning" strikes. But there is no hope for him once the lightning has struck. He sings, "I can never, never, never go home again." That is the truth. But the truth lies also in Pitney's other, less alarming classic, "Only Love Can Break a Heart." There, the closing refrain is more hopeful — sentimental but hopeful: "Only love can break a heart, / Only love can mend it again." I suspect the lyricist was thinking of a new love affair rather than the old broken one. For us, however, the old one is the object of grace as grace was demonstrated on Easter Day.

Grace When Children Leave Home

The cliché about the "empty nest" syndrome is that when the children leave home, mother goes into mourning and father realizes how shallow his relationship with his wife has become. He realizes the marriage has been on "automatic pilot," and she begins to feel some negative effects from the one-sided emotional investment she has placed on the children. Looking at each other now, in the absence of their children, the husband and the wife start to fail. They fail to stand on their own, in their horizontal relationship, because they have failed, for several years, to love one another face to face. The children became the mediator between man and wife. When the mediator was removed, they had to look at each other directly. What they see now is not very likeable. What they see now is no longer buffered by the children. What they see now is no longer buffered against the law. At this point, law comes massively into play. Unless grace is present, the marriage may well slide into a phase of increasing emotional disengagement.

The theological concept in play within this sector of everyday life, as it is in every other, is original sin. The wife and husband whose children have left home are just as susceptible to the continuing effects of original sin as they were when the children were small and they fell out of touch. To the degree that they possess original sin, people do not change. The consequence of this is that every phase of life is equally implicated in the anthropology of failure. The scorpion's tail of the phase when children leave home is a surprising lash. No one expects it. Just as you do not expect that elderly people can be as cruel and self-willed as younger people can be, just as you are taken by surprise when you see radical sinfulness among "seniors," you do not expect marital sin in the third and fourth decade of the relationship.

The grace in marriage as children leave home requires the low anthropology of the New Testament as well as a devout prayer for deliverance. Here the *sameness* of the Christian response to everyday need comes to the fore once more. The word of grace to this period in a marriage is repetitive. It is the same word to each marriage at every other point of need. The word has two parts: (1) admission from the woman and the man that they are now in a new kind of glare that reveals the cracks in the foundation; and (2) admission of the forlornness they may be experiencing because of an improperly weighted love for the children and of their failure to respond lovingly to each other's grief.

You could criticize this systematic theology of everyday life by saying that its diagnosis is too dire. You could say that by no means every couple experiences the absence of their children to this dark degree. You could add that many marriages do not contain the deep cracks that are revealed when the mediating factor of the children is pulled away. You could say my theology is too negative.

But the disengagement of couples who have to face one another across the table after years of relating through third parties is actually very common. The binding theme, the core of my argument, is the anthropology of lifelong original sin, which is always one potential half-step from total depravity. Always look for the Achilles' heel in the situation. It is the point of entry through which the devilish temptation to fall apart will enter. Although the point of entry is individual, there is a point of entry in every life and every phase of life. Like the Death Star in *Star Wars* (1977), there is always a specific place that is vulnerable to attack. For married persons whose children have grown up and departed, the point of attack is typically a lack of "practice" in facing each other in the non-mediated equality of their new situation.

Grace at this stage means the completion of maternal (or paternal) mourning, on the one hand; and some forbearing understanding, with tangible comfort, on the part of the spouse. Neither of these moments will occur until the grief inherent in the situation is labeled and bewailed. The song remains the same: repentance and the cry for help.

Grace "Until We Are Parted by Death"

The great surprise of human existence is the persistence of original sin. It catches everyone unawares at some point in the life cycle. It usually surfaces, the strength of sin's presence in the human world, when you think you have finally achieved something for which you have worked and longed.

My own eyes were opened in a disillusioning way when I began to visit a woman who understood herself to be a patrician. She was suffering from breast cancer, and her husband had proven to be a loyal and sacrificial support. He spent most nights in the hospital on a cot in the same room with her. He seemed to me unfailingly sincere in his attentiveness to his wife of thirty-five years. He never flagged during her long illness. I attributed her recovery, her survival in fact, to her husband's tireless and practical loving. When she was well enough to go home on his dear arm to an apartment on Central Park West, we all thanked God for it.

Two weeks later, when this woman was beginning to enter back into her old life with confidence and sincere joy, her husband broke the news. He had been in love with his secretary for two years and was leaving his wife for his secretary. He had felt so guilty and conflicted about his wife's unexpected cancer that he had both rallied and also "covered" for himself by giving himself totally to her care during the crisis. Now that the crisis was over, however, he could break the news to her, wish her well with a "clear conscience," and divorce her to marry a much younger woman. This happened after thirty-five years of marriage and the rearing of four children, all of whom had left home.

When the woman told me this, she was still in shock. Although she had been a "liberal" Episcopalian her whole life, nothing had prepared her for this. She said that her cancer was not as bad as her husband's rejection. She told me she wanted to die. This incident, which happened early in my ministry, forced me to go back to first principles, specifically to the theological anthropology of original sin.

Only a full-field, or comprehensive, theory of human captivity to the forces of sin and the law can account for facts such as these from everyday life. Only a full-field theory is sufficient to account for the behavior of that husband to his wife of thirty-five years, caring for her in her illness while waiting guiltily for his moment. Only a full-field theory is sufficient to account for the pettiness and jealousies of older people whom our cultural myths like to exempt from the venalities of younger life. Only a full-field theory is sufficient to enable the cry for help, which is the cry for grace, to be uttered in later life as well as in all the phases of younger life.

Grace in the final period of marriage is letting your wife or your husband grow old. Men may resent their wife's aging, even as they themselves age. And women may have to watch their men die, as it is a fact that the vast majority of women live longer than their men.

I am interested here in aging married couples, both of whom are still alive. For some elderly couples, their marriage becomes a hell. If the man develops senile dementia, he may have violent episodes or begin to use obscene language that he has never before been heard to use. What is his loving wife to do with him? Or there is the woman in her mid-80s, whom I had known for fifteen years, who suddenly accused her husband, himself in his late 80s, of sleeping with their daughter-in-law. This came out of nowhere. What was her husband to do?

In the last phases of a long life, married couples in nursing homes often have to be separated from one another. They often have to be moved to separate rooms in different wings, because of accusations and delusions. This does not happen in every case, but it happens more often than is reported. How many puzzled and hurt adult children in their 50s and 60s I have had to hear out when their elderly parents began to act irrationally. Once, in a very up-scale "assisted living" community in Florida, I had to act to protect an elderly wife from her husband of more than fifty years, who was savagely swearing and accusing her of unspeakable things. I had known this man in his prime: a brilliant man, a good man, a giving man.

It is not just violence and obscenity that can haunt old age. A specialist in Westchester County, New York, tried to explain to me the symptoms of depression among older people. He said that 80 percent of the people I would visit over the age of 75 suffered from clinical depression. No one had told me this, and the "liberal" theology I had been taught, with its governing assumptions about human freedom, had spoken otherwise.

A profound anthropology is crucial to grace in the last phase of marriage. Reliance on the continuing grace of the eternal God is the only response to the enduring fact of human recidivism. The cry of "Save me!" is the only engagement I find possible in the face of the march of old age against all human beings, as it is coupled with original sin and heightened by total depravity. The bad news of this is that there is no preserve allowed for the elderly that might protect them from themselves, let alone from their husband or wife. The good news is that there is no jail so maximum-secure that it can withstand the God who answers the prayer for deliverance. Even in one's oldest age, God can cancel the death of marriage by means of resurrection.

To conclude this section on grace in relation to marriage, we can resort to Stephen Sondheim, with one addition. *A Little Night Music* (1973), the libretto of which was written by Hugh Wheeler, is not a seriocomic or simply ironic portrait of marriage. This Sondheim musical is bleak. It is realistic and therefore bleak. An early song in the show titled "Every Day a Little Death" portrays the slow, cumulative end to a superficial marriage. "Every day a little sting/In the heart and in the head./Every move and every breath,/And you hardly feel a thing,/Brings a perfect little death." I would say that the dimension of original sin within all relationships confirms the song!

Empirically speaking, every relationship carries the possibility of dissolution. This is no surprise from a Christian point of view. *No marriage is immune.* No marriage is magically protected from tragedy. When a happily married woman reflected on her friend's divorce, which had taken place on account of infidelity, she told me, "My husband and I are just so happily connected. What happened to her makes my heart break, but it is all so foreign to my husband and me. This could never happen to us." I believed the woman: nothing could harm *that* marriage. But when her husband was killed in a plane crash shortly afterward, I wondered at the universal outbreak of original sin, which is to say the in-reaching hand of the universal fact of loss and limitation. By that middle phase in my ministry, I had finally been given the anthropology to deal with loss and limitation. "Every day a little death." It is a dry run for the big hurt, physical death itself.

What this theology of everyday life adds to Sondheim's devastating view of life in *A Little Night Music* is the hope of deliverance. It is the *a priori* claim of this theology: God saves the helpless. The identity of God, which is an immense mystery, has a single point of clarity. God is merciful. We know this for only one reason, which is the life and death of Jesus Christ. But that knowledge is something. As a result, we lean on the everlasting arms. This is the grace of saving, which is the plea, month to month, and day to day, of every marriage, at every point of sin's entry.

Grace with Children

In a systematic theology of grace in relation to everyday life, the relation of parents to children plays the most important role of all. I place it third, after singleness and marriage, simply because children proceed, in a Christian worldview and in time, from marriage. They certainly proceed from a relationship. So although this section about grace with children comes third after singleness and marriage, it is really first in importance. This is the most important section in this chapter about relationships because the relation of parents to child is dominant in the mediation of law, hence alternatively it is dominant in the mediation of grace.

"The child is father to the man." That is an ancient maxim. The idea is represented symbolically in a hundred famous paintings. My personal favorite among paintings that portray the primacy of the child in the formation of the adult is Caspar David Friedrich's *Stages of Life* (1835). In the painting, a child is crawling and playing in the foreground, crawling forward actually toward his "second stage," a young adult man who is looking toward a woman. Further into the scene, which is in forced perspective, there is an old man dressed in the costume of an honored sage standing on the edge of a dock. He is looking out of the picture and back at us, the observers of this scene. What impresses me about Friedrich's painting is the prior, foregrounded activity of the crawling child. The child comes first. He is father to the man.

What happens when you are a child, between your parents and you, is critically important to your whole world-picture. Most of the time, law is ingested by the child from his parents, and with law, the resistance to that relationship in later life. If the child absorbs law along with the "mother's milk," then the mother will lose the child. The child will end up running away the other way. If law is the father's "song that remains the same" (Led Zeppelin), the child will end up running the other way. Alternatively, if grace is in the mother's milk, then the child will return gladly to the mother. If grace is the father's "unchained melody" (Righteous Brothers), the child will always return.

The purpose of this section is to survey grace and law in the rearing of children. Law mars and destroys this relationship, even when it is offered in the name of love. Grace, on the other hand, creates a lifelong response of love. Every parent I know who has "lost" his or her children sees the effects of the law. If only you could go back and reorder the relationship from the top down, to instantiate one-way love. Every parent I know who still has the attentive love of his or her children is watching the effects of grace. Although there is neither a perfect correlation between grace-full parenting and the flourishing of adult children nor a one-to-one correlation between parents as law-bearers and adult children as fleeing hippies, there is still a close link between accepting love and its fruit, which is freed love in response, and stinting "love" and its result, which is half-love, or quarter-love, back the other way.

Grace with Little Children

People who believe in grace are stumped at first by the rearing of little children. They are stumped over the question of how it is possible to rear little children from grace rather than from law. They reason that little children require limits. Little children have to be told over and over again *not* to do things that will injure them. Parents have to place blockers into electrical sockets so that toddlers will not stick their fingers into them. They have to lock up their household medicines and anything with poison in it, so their children will not kill themselves. They have to watch their small child around the swimming pool or at the lake or by the seashore every single second of the time. They have to teach their children not to do innumerable things that would harm them. It looks to me, parents will say, as if the law is our best bet — the only bet — with our little ones. Then they add, even if we accept the premise that grace works in every other case, the case of small children is different. Small children require the law!

Is the care and nurture of little children the exception to this theology of everyday life? Is law rather than grace required during the "growing years"? Descriptively and empirically, is there any way one can get out of the obvious demand that parental law and order are key requirements for keeping children safe and well?

The task of this section is to demonstrate otherwise. It should demonstrate the premise that grace is just as important in the instance of little children as it is with everybody else. Children are not an exception to the universal good that is wrought by grace in opposition to the resentful stuntedness that comes from law. If children were the exception, then grace would not be a universal principle. Grace would prove useless in one foundational area of human shaping. That is unacceptable for a consistent view of grace as the source of human flourishing.

Grace works with little children in three ways. To begin with, it is the first use of the law, and not its second use, that children require. The distinction is important. The first use of the law is the use of the law that requires stop signs and traffic lights. It requires patent laws to protect inventions, and police cars to stop speeding drivers. It requires food inspectors to prevent infected meals from being served. This is the "no brainer" function of the law. It has nothing to do with condemnation or the birth of neurotic feelings of beholdenness and guilt. It is simply the regular and natural building blocks of a social world that wishes to avoid spinning out of orbit into Malthusian chaos. The first use of the law has nothing to do with the judgment and imposed neuroticism of the second or theological use of the law. Therefore all the proper protective devices and systems with which little children must be surrounded by their parents come under the heading of the first use of the law. These produce no fruit of flight or splitting because of guilt. The expressions of the first use of the law are written into the nature of things.

It is true that children require this first use of the law, but it is not the use that bares fangs. We know this because children as they grow up do not evince bad feelings about this first use of law. I have never heard a sufferer in my study complain that her mother was too protective of her as a toddler around electricity. I have never heard someone complain that his father washed unclean vegetables too much or was nosy watching him as a small child when he was at the lake. Yes, a parent can become overzealous in the first use of the law, but it rarely becomes the origin of fundamental resentment. Just ask grown children: What do you hold against your mother or your father? The answer never includes over-protectiveness, unless it got out of proportion during the teenage years. Even in the delightful children's movie *Finding Nemo* (2003), the "nervous Nellie" father is forgiven for his over-protectiveness because his wife and all their other children were eaten by a barracuda and because little Nemo really does swim away from his dad and get captured by a diver. There is not much neurosis in Nemo himself to which his slightly over-concerned father's efforts have contributed. The first use of the law is the instrument of choice in preventing little children from being physically harmed.

Second, grace in the raising of small children is utterly alive (or barrenly dead) in relation to the father and mother's marriage. As we have seen, if the father and mother are themselves living out of one-way love in their own relationship, then the rearing of children becomes grace-full. This is because neither parent is trying to force a response from the child. If the husband is content with his wife and the wife with her husband, then the law that squeezes love improperly out of the child as compensation and consolation is inactive. Grace in the marriage produces grace with the children.

When you interview children who have grown up and ask them to talk about their childhood, you often receive two kinds of feedback: a parent was too involved, almost suffocating at times, and I had to pull away; or a parent was not involved enough, not involved at all, never at my recitals or my games. One was too involved; the other was too little involved. Why do you believe that was? It happened because they were not involved enough with each other!

The law involved in rearing little children is the *first* use — so that the earth, as it were, will continue to orbit the sun — not the second use, which involves judgments, humiliations, rejections, and desertions. It is the *second* use, not the first use, which creates disturbances in the confidence of human beings. Moreover, grace is the thing in marriage without which the mother and the father are almost definitely going to ill-proportion their love to their child. The result of this for the child will be defeatedness or a hurried departure at age 18.

There is a third thing to say about grace in relation to small children. Mercy, as opposed to judging, is still the change agent even in the lives of little children. The child who fouled himself and then wrote with it on the bathroom wall could have been harshly punished or gently held. The difference can mean a lifetime of trust. The mere issue of toilet training can be a wrestling match between parent and child, a *quid pro quo* of significance; or it can be a waiting for nature to take its course, even amid a toddler's stubbornness. The spanking that a child receives for playing out in the road without asking his father's permission can be given in the context of a rueful protecting love, or it can be a staccato note of sadism that is never quite forgotten.

My father, the son of a pastor, told me that when he was a little boy in the small town where his dad was serving, he and a friend found a drum one day and started walking up and down the street banging it. It happened to be Good Friday, and they were German immigrants to America before the First World War. My father told me that his father whipped him with a belt as punishment, punishment for playing around on a most holy day. From that day and forever after that day, my father had no love for the church, none at all. Clearly the law given from Sinai on *that* Good Friday was not the first use, but a form of the second. It was received as a level of cruelty by its recipient. Even with small children, it is possible to invoke the second use of the law in a memorable way. This produces early resentment among many who have not only left their parents forever but have left God.

You can see this in the second scene of *Citizen Kane* (1941). It is one thing for Charles Foster Kane's mother to protect him from too zealously sledding down a sharp incline. It is another thing for her to basically sell her child to her Chicago relatives. In her mind, Kane's mother, played by Agnes Moorhead, is trying to get her son away from his alcoholic, abusive father. But the boy knows nothing of that. For him, it is all rejection, gross and inexplicable. That is the second use of the law, and it is felt even by a small child. It can be felt forever by a small child.

Grace for small children is possible. The killing law is possible, too. When grace lives within the marriage, the force of law is much diminished for the children. Grace sets the tone of one-way love by which even a babe in arms can be irradiated.

Grace with Teenagers

With teenagers, parents live their lives imprisoned within the kingdom of the law. This is because the identity of the child is formed by rebellion *against* rather than acquiescence *to* the law. Yet this is a *soft* reaction-formation. By this I mean that the child is still young and in formation. The edges of his or her reactivity are softer than they appear, especially from the angry and petulant words that accompany the reactivity. Because the edges are still soft at this stage, the grace of one-way love has a way in to the child that is crucial. In other words, there is grace-hope for teenagers and not simply law-reaction.

Let me offer two examples of the crisis that the teenage years present in the vital flow of grace and law. I worked with a family whose son was angry all the time. He was a pure example of adolescent male rage. His black clothing, his haircut, and his sullen expression were Esperanto for "I hate everyone and everything — especially everyone and everything related to my parents." This was the 1970s, and there was not yet a "Goth" subculture or a body-piercing subculture or even a "Guns n' Roses" subculture. It was also after the 1960s, so it was no longer an option to express rebellion in the form of being a hippie. This boy was born in an in-between time, culturally speaking, but was nevertheless completely taken over by a common thing, total and volcanic rage. One night he took his father's hunting rifle out of the closet and threatened his mother with it. That was the turning point. What took place next is for another book, but this instance of male teenage rage showed me what a powerful force parents are dealing with when they deal with an angry son. In pastoral experience, many cases like this are children of a recent divorce. This has to be said, although it is often rationalized away by divorced and divorcing couples. In practice, many of these young men become angry to the highest point of volatility after their father has left the home.

A second example is eating disorders, most of which occur among young women. The subject is touchy because many families are affected by it, and many families find it impossible to talk about it or let others in on it. But any experience of youth ministry in churches in this country, especially in middle- and upper-middle-class white suburbs, will instantaneously convert you to the wide and deep extent of this problem. I am no diagnostician, but there is a cry for help here in relation to "the way I look" as a form of the law. It is a shriek in the highest pitch. When my wife and I became personally involved with eating disorders in young teenage girls within our parishes and witnessed lives in the balance, when we saw girls' bodies resembling those of hunger strikers, we came face to face with a force identical to the law. There it was the law of thinness, the law of what other girls (let alone boys) think of me. It is an irresistible impasse between law and self-acceptance, and it can result in hospitalization and even death.

The first thing to say about grace and law in the life of teenagers is a familiar point: original sin hangs heavy on all phases of life. In the extent or reach of the problem, there is no difference between children, teens, and elderly parents. It is only the symptoms that differ, symptoms that are based on bodily strength, personality formation, experience of life, and so forth. The "vessel" of the teenage child is as full of original sin and total depravity as the "vessel" of the Alzheimer's patient. The sixteen-year-old who threatened his mother with his father's rifle is similar in aggression to the 82-year-old man in Vero Beach who chased his wife of five decades around the kitchen table with a butcher knife, crying out that she was two-timing him. Original sin is planted in the soul of man and woman, and there are no exceptions. We can teach this to parents.

The second thing to say about grace in the life of teenagers is that there is no substitute for it. What the teenage boy is saying is often one thing: I want my father. What the teenage girl is saying is often one thing: I want my father to hold me in a physically affectionate fatherly way. That is not all there is to it, but a linking theme in much teenage distress that is often acted out rather than fully sublimated is the emotional or physical absence of the father, hence the absence of grace in that relation.

I often say to parents that the mother is all-important for the grace-full lives of little children, and the father's role during that period is grace-fully to support the mother. My wife and I say, in turn, to the parents of teenagers, that the father is all-important for the grace-full lives of their stormy adolescents, both boys and girls, and the mother's role is to help keep the father present to their children. Saying it more concretely, the role of the father for teenagers is to embody grace by simply *not leaving*. The father must stay involved, emotionally and not detachedly, in the tempestuous emotions of his teenage children. They are begging you to leave so that you will stay!

The situation is of a deeper magic superseding the deep magic. The deep magic says, "Tough love! Hold them responsible for their actions. Do not attempt to bail them out or go out after them like the mother of the runaway bunny. They must be held accountable!" That particular expression of the deep magic, which got Aslan killed as well as Christ crucified, is the law. The "deeper magic still" speaks grace. Forget words like "responsibility" and "accountability." They only create an "equal and opposite reaction," as the law inevitably does. Instead, love the child through the worst. Go to the court appearance even the fourth and fifth times. Jesus said, "Not just seven times, but seventy times seven." One-way love is one-way love. Only grace will tame the wild beast of adolescence.

On the surface, adolescents are asking for the law precisely so they can break it. At a deeper level, adolescents are asking for grace, again and again, so they can return to the love that always gives thanks. If you do not understand this as a parent, you will start to sink below the waves of the tempest.

The third dimension of grace with teenagers is the dimension of retrospection. Parents frequently fail with their teenage children. The mercurial nature of the response to law within teenagers, its physical and emotional volatility, makes the situation "touch and go." I remember a very grace-full father at a moment during dinner when his daughter called her mother by an extremely vulgar name. Such a thing had never, ever happened in the life of this committed Christian family. The whole dining room went silent as night, white as a ghost. The mother ran out of the room, the siblings were uniquely silenced and shocked, and the father was left alone with his daughter. What happened then was grace-full, but it is important to see that the moment "came out of nowhere." In the context of that particular family, what happened at the dinner table was new territory. It took what I would call an action of the Holy Spirit to give the father what he needed to say and do in that particular moment. What he did say was, "You know, your mother has a lot on her these days and she's stretched pretty thin. Did you realize that?" Even in the most serene circumstances, the grace of God in relation to teenagers is "touch and go."

The rewards of grace are best appreciated retrospectively. You love your drug-addicted child through recovery program after recovery program. You do *not* listen to the voice of the law, which forever speaks of "tough love" and "accountability"; but you extend the hand of one-way love and extend it again. Your hand is bitten. It may be bitten off. But grace knows no limits, for words like "limits" and "boundaries" are the culture of the law. Christ spoke of the man who went after the lost sheep while leaving ninety-nine others safe in their fold (Luke 15:3-7). People will tell you that you are rewarding irresponsibility. But you know better. You know that, in the long run, grace draws its own back home.

This is what your child says to you later, when she herself is raising children of her own in her thirties: "Mom, you hung in there with me. Now I *like* to go to church, and I sure want to help you and Dad." Your son says to you, his tattoos still bright from shoulder to palm, "Dad, I get it now. I went way out there, but you were always ready to take me home. This is Martha, I met her in rehab, and we want to get married. And I think we'd like Dr. Duncan to tie the knot for us. Is that all right?"

The bottom line of grace for teenagers is this: they think they want law, but you have to know they want grace. Better they act out in their teens than in their thirties. (I encourage you to have your nervous breakdown as young as possible.) Retrospectively, grace proves to be the strongest approach.

Grace with Adult Children

In relations between people, the principles and activity of grace do not vary. I have argued that this is true even in the one potentially exceptional case, the case of little children. In the case of adult children, grace is the father in the parable of the prodigal son (Luke 15:11-32). Grace keeps the lamps lit and the door open.

The child is now grown and on his or her own course. But that phone call may still come that will bring about a reversal of your hopes. Inevitably, problems will come up, big or small, because your adult children, like all of us, are still made from original sin. We have to backtrack to total depravity.

It may come up in the form of drunk driving, or white-collar crime, or divorce and a child-custody case. Maybe your son committed a felony, or your drug-addicted daughter let her second husband beat up your grandson. Perhaps your thirty-five-year-old son has not yet found himself. He drifts from job to job and scheme to scheme, and now he is living at home in order to save money. Or your thirty-two-year-old daughter married the wrong man, and not only is she unhappy in her life with him, but you fear that your three grandchildren may soon have no father. Your daughter is on the way to becoming a single mother.

Perhaps your forty-five-year-old son is a misfire with women. The one thing you want for him is to be loved by a woman who will really care for him. You fear that if you die any time soon, he will be terribly lonely in his older years. You are also aware that he does not get along at all with his sister and brother, and that they will not be much good. You are only as happy as your neediest child.

There are some principles here tied again to grace, that enabling word to paralyzed lives. The first principle is always the unlimited reach of original sin. Just because your children are "settled" in ostensibly happy marriages and have produced lovely grandchildren for you to love and visit does not mean they are safe home. Every parent hopes it means that, and you pray for them every morning. But the visitation of sin is just a block away. Tragedy can be right around the corner. I once saw a man's hair turn white in eighteen hours. He was grandfather, in his mid-fifties, to a beautiful little boy. He was asked by his daughter and son-in-law and wife to keep an eye on the child while they went into town to do a few errands. He turned away for exactly 45 seconds. The child drank some cleaning fluid in the garage and died in minutes. The grandfather's hair turned from dark brown to snow white in eighteen hours. Guilt is coming down the block. No, it's here!

Original sin is present in all relationships and is therefore present in this relationship, the relation of parents to their adult children. This relation, like all others, "needs watching." I use that expression because it is the last words of Alfred Hitchcock's *Shadow of a Doubt* (1943), a movie in which a police captain says of the capture of a suspect whom they had never once suspected of terrible crimes, "I guess the world just needs watching." As the father of adult children, I wish this were not so. I wish my children's problems would always be insignificant. I wish that they, and my wife and I, would live happily ever after. But it is seldom so. The role of the father in the parable of the prodigal son has to be filled, even at the very end.

There is a moving close to another film by a director as famous as Hitchcock. This time the director is John Ford, and the movie is *The Last Hurrah* (1958). At the end of the film, the old mayor of Boston has suffered a stroke on the night of his defeat at the polls, and he lies dying upstairs. His son, a completely self-absorbed and self-styled "playboy," gets the word but arrives late. His dad is close to death. The boy, now in his late 30s, throws himself across his father's bed, shaking with grief and guilt. His father has just enough physical strength to pat the boy's head, saying very clearly, at the end of his life, "I forgive you, son." This scene is among Ford's most memorable vignettes, and his movies are full of them. It illustrates that your job as a parent is never over. Why? Because the needs of your children are never finished.

Two further points apply, and they are not new ones. First, grace is never mistaken in the case of adult children. When they return home in the wake of a divorce, love them and require of them no explanation. When they return home in the aftermath of their first twenty-eight days of rehab, no lectures, please. They will probably make it to the nearest "Big Book" meeting of Alcoholics Anonymous that night. When they return from time spent overseas in search of themselves, the trip you knew was sheer escape and not anything like the therapy that was called for, you do not need to ask them questions. In any event, something good may have happened.

I remember when the actor Burt Reynolds had his second divorce. He went back home to the small town in Florida where his parents lived, and his father did not say a critical word. Everyone knew what had happened. But his father and his mother did not say a word. Their grace-full "see no evil, hear no evil" reticence was the ticket. Reynolds says that everything in his future hinged on their grace at that moment. I take the story literally.

This brings me to the second and last point about grace in relation to adult children. You have heard this point before. It is a grace of repetition, which is the grace of retrospection. The fruits of grace are always in the future, yet they are marked out in the memory of your past. You say, "My mom didn't ask me any hard questions. My dad acted as if nothing had happened, although the whole world knew *exactly* what had happened." Grace imputes no crime. Its fallout is everlasting. Adult children who are treated along the lines of grace and imputation do not "look back in anger." It is the children of the law who look back in anger.

Grace and Grandchildren

In 1877 Victor Hugo published a book of poems titled *L'art d'être grand-père,* or *The Art of Being a Grandfather.* It is a sweet book and lighter than anything else he ever wrote. Its theme is grace. What Hugo brings out, in short impressionistic pictures, is the way the grace of being a grandparent is different from the law involved in being a parent. It is a meditation along the lines of the familiar end-of-family-vacation refrain that you hear on Sunday nights: "We loved having them, but it sure is nice to give them back!" This is coupled with another refrain: "I love being a grandparent. I get all the joys of a little child's love, without the responsibility. I especially don't have to worry about disciplining them."

It is commonly thought that the case of grandparents in relation to their grandchildren is an instance of pure grace, that there is no law in the equation. But this is a superficial statement. The ones who need grace the most from the grandparents is not their grandchildren; it is their children. It is the children, now raising children of their own, who draw down upon themselves judgment from their own parents. You judge your son-in-law for putting in too many hours at the office. You judge your daughter-in-law for going back to work too soon after the birth of her second child. You judge your son for being too permissive with his children because he is under the influence of his wife, who has no standards and keeps the house a mess. You judge your daughter for being too pliant when her husband wants her to accompany him on business trips and leave the children at home.

It is easy to fall into judgments concerning your son or daughter. The grandchildren become a footnote to that. Grace in the case of grandchildren should be grace in the care of your adult children who have demanding lives. Grace means running to offer your services as babysitter, not for your grandchildren's sake, but for your overworked children's sake. Grace means putting yourself in the place of that plagued thirty-five-year-old son of yours who is simply desperate as he tries to juggle conflicting commitments. Do you think he *wants* to spend all that time in airports for the sake of a job he hates?

What can happen with grandparents is that they become a kind of emotional dark cloud hanging in accusation over their children. The grandchildren are just a diversion from that judgment.

You see this enacted every five minutes on the other side of airport security, where grandparents stand to welcome their children and grandchildren for a visit home. Watch the scene before you. It goes like this: grandmother tries to crouch down and hold her arms out for her little granddaughter or grandson, who runs through the barrier first. She tosses the child up in her arms. Then she shows off the child to her husband, the grandfather, who is standing slightly behind her. Then the mother comes through, the daughter of these embracing grandparents. All she receives is a peck on the cheek or maybe a touch on the elbow. All attention, I mean all of it, is on the grandchild, being held zealously now by the grandfather.

Finally, about fifty feet back, struggling down the concourse, is the dad. *He* scarcely exists. He comes upon the complex greeting-in-operation, and sort of stands behind it and apart from it. He does get a handshake from his father-in-law; and later, in the car, a nod from his mother-in-law. But he has lost himself anyway, carrying the baby chair and all the baby food and diaper bags that are his lot to carry. Maybe he can hide behind them, thank God.

Just spend an afternoon by the exit door at airport security, where arriving passengers emerge to meet their families, and you won't have to wait long before you witness a similar scene. The grace is for the grandchildren. For the sons and daughters, the sons-in-law and daughters-in-law of the grandparents, it is less gracious. The whole scene will be replayed later that night in the little guest bedroom where the exhausted adult parents are now quartered.

The big mistake made by grandparents is that they fail to see the one place where grace is needed most. It is needed by their flailing children, who are tired and frustrated in their love-life and need just the tiniest open space and unspoken-for time. Forget the grandchildren. They are being well served. Serve your children! This is the real grace in the case of grandchildren.

Grace with Parents

The focus now turns to the operation of grace in the relation of adult children to aging parents. Grace with aging parents demands a death, the death of the child in relation to the mother and father. Grace also performs a necessary birth following that death, the birth of an adult in relation to two much older adults. What is this about?

In order to take care of your parents in their old age, at least with any joy, it is necessary to be freed from the law in your relation to them. The neurotic strain within the relation must be cut out. What this entails is the conclusion of the relation as natural child to natural mother and father, and its replacement by the relation of adult to adult.

Older parents often say to me something like, "I feel my daughter is a friend to me now, not my daughter really. I can tell her anything, and ask her views about anything that is on my mind. I feel like we have graduated." In my own case, I knew that I was an adult to my adult son when I opened up to him about problems with a job I had taken and asked for his wise counsel. It was not just adult to adult, in fact. It was student (me) to teacher (him). The parent had died, in that context, and the child had, too. We were so "adult" together that it bordered on role reversal.

Jesus said that you have to die in order to be born. He said that anyone who wants to gain his life will have to lose it. Dying precedes the being born again. This is how it is with aging parents.

If the relation is still determined by judgment and the law, it can be a doleful terminus to which the train of life finally pulls up. There can be, for example, a certain joy in your father's suffering, a terrible "I told you so" in your mother's incapacity. Did you ever read a short story by Roald Dahl entitled "William and Mary" (*Kiss Kiss,* 1959)? It was made into the first episode of a television show entitled *Way Out* (1961) and caused consternation among the millions who saw it. It involved a dying man whose brain the doctors are able to cut out of his body and place in a tank. In the tank, the man's brain can see and hear everything that takes place around him. But instead of offering kindness and tender greeting, his wife — who hated him, it turns out — blows cigarette smoke into the tank and plays the music he hated on a raucous record player right next to his brain. She says horrible things to him and at him, as his sensate brain just sits there in solution. Mary gets her vengeance on William.

This is not just a story. I have witnessed parallel, somewhat more veiled, cruelty toward elderly and dying parents on the part of their adult children. Such cruelty is original sin "upgraded" to total depravity. You can feel the temperature go up a hundred degrees in the hospital room when a particular son or daughter enters it. This kind of relationship, the "William and Mary" phenomenon, is the relation of law to the older parent who injured you long ago. There is no forgiveness.

That is a description and not a prescription. All that hard law has to die, in full, for grace to be able to flow toward elderly parents. Through absolution and the grace of God as received by the adult child, absolution and grace can become the angle of approach to forgiven parents. This is grace, the direction of one-way love.

There is a further element in this. There is a further stretching of the person, in order for the grace of God to access its sure vector toward the older parent who may well have been the origin of many of your problems. I am talking about identity. What is required to die, in order to help in any graceful way your elderly father or your elderly mother, is your identity as their child.

The child sits under the law. By definition, the child "eats and drinks judgment" (1 Corinthians 11:29). Even when parents and surrogate parents pour on the grace, there is always a part of you, the child, who hears the law. The classic example we already saw is when your twelve-year-old sister asks her nine-year-old brother how she looks. Brother says, "I think you look fine." Sister throws a hairbrush at him and cries, "Don't tell me how bad I look!" What? Yet that is what actually happens. He meant a compliment and she heard criticism. The receiver of a judgment always hears *critical* judgment. Thus, too, if your bishop is on the phone and your assistant calls in, "Bishop Smith wants to talk to you," you immediately assume that you have done something wrong and he is calling to criticize you.

That child in me must die. That particular antenna that is designed only to register condemnation must die. Like Christ's grain of wheat that "falls into the earth and dies" (John 12:24), my identity as the receiver of law must die. When that identity dies, the new being who emerges is an adult. (God help you if you are an ailing aging parent and your child has not died in this sense and become an adult.) The new adult will be able to depersonalize you, and that is excellent. He or she will love you better and more wisely and more sacrificially, but he or she will be able to depersonalize you. Only if you are depersonalized in this sense does the child belong in your hospital room, especially if "end-of-life" issues are in play. You do not want your child who is under the sway of law to be anywhere near when the time comes to "pull the plug." You want your detached child to be in charge at that point, fully in the saddle. Then the decision will be the right decision.

To conclude, the grace of God in relation to elderly parents involves the death of the child as child and the birth of the adult who is no longer the child. That "child" can love you from love, and not from need.

Grace with Siblings

I once buried a man who had three sons. He was a first-generation immigrant from Europe. One of his sons had become extremely successful in the real estate business. Another had become an alcoholic at an early age and was in bad shape. The third seemed moderately happy; he had a wife and two small children and an okay job. At the gravesite the troubled son became very anxious and had to be restrained by his brothers from jumping into the open burial plot with his father's casket. Was it sorrow? Was it guilt? Was it drink? The incident left a bad taste in everyone's mouth.

Another time I heard a preacher at a memorial service tell a light but loving anecdote about the dead woman. Her five adult children were in the church, and nearly everyone laughed with recognition and affection. One of the sons, however, was upset by the story, took offense, and came one step away from taking a punch at the minister. That son drove away right after the service and skipped the interment. Everyone else said it was only to be expected, since that brother had been scarce throughout his mother's long illness and was feeling judged by his siblings, guilty and angry. The fissure between the siblings was acted out in relation to the funeral of their mother.

The relation between siblings can be very touchy. The incident that most opened my eyes to this took place in connection with a parent's last illness and funeral. The father was sick for a long time and was cared for very well by his son and daughter-in-law, with whom he had been living. The other brother was far away, living out a hippie phase in the Southwest. He failed to come home during the illness of his dad. When the man died, that son not only failed to come home, but he *would not* come home. He did not attend the funeral and was harsh to his dutiful brother over the telephone.

Things got worse. When their mother died about a year later, the brother in Arizona again would not come to the funeral. Later, I spoke to the brother who had buried both of his parents alone. He told me he never wanted to see his brother again, and that if he ever did see his brother again, he would not be responsible for what he did. This is an extreme case, but not so unusual. Any minister or priest can tell you stories like it. Problems between siblings often come out in their final form at funerals.

This section could be more accurately titled "Law with Siblings." It is law that is operating whenever there is judgment between brothers and sisters. The parable of the prodigal son (Luke 15:11-32), with the self-righteous elder brother, is the classic case of this in the New Testament. But the category of law is solely diagnostic. It is not healing. Only the factor of grace in the relation between siblings is able to heal these lifelong infectious diseases that overtake families. How does grace operate between brothers and sisters in families?

Grace has to do with the unmeasured plenitude of affection for all, without regard for deserving. One-way love is equal by definition because it has nothing to do with the qualities or "merits" of the person to whom it is directed. One-way love is therefore *wholly in the eye of the beholder.* Because it stands apart from the receiver, grace makes no distinctions between receivers. Therefore, grace is an even distribution of affection.

Almost all sibling problems have to do with a child's feeling that the affection of his parents was unevenly distributed. The middle child thinks the eldest is favored, but the youngest is really the favored one. The youngest basks in the affection of his less-uptight parents, who have become wiser in their child-rearing. The eldest child feels she was imposed upon. Not only was she the guinea pig for first-time parents, but she had to look after the children who came after her. She had to be responsible too early. The mantra of "birth order" has something to contribute here, but each child always takes it in his or her own way. Ask adult children and they will let you know exactly how they think the affection was distributed: who was favored and who was slighted. The answer to the question might be expressed in where the adult child is now living. Children with resentments often tend to move away. Children who love their parents tend to live closer. Children who feel guilty in relation to their parents might either move far away or stay close. This is an effect of the law and has to do with the deeply felt conviction that the love from mother and father was proportional.

Grace demolishes the idea of proportional loving. It demolishes it, first, from the standpoint of God. People who suffer from the bitterness of proportional loving, which is the law, are able to find an immediate alternative in the evenness of the love of Christ. He loved everyone unconditionally, and the result was that there is no male and female, no high-class and trailer-trash, no black and white, no "Sunni and Shiite" in the family of God (Galatians 3:28; Colossians 3:11). There are no sisters and brothers in the sibling sense within his love. Because his love is one-way, removed from any relation with the receiver, there is no "rivalry." I am not reticent to say that the grace of Christ is the first stage of healing for siblings who are furious at one another.

Grace also puts an emphasis on the metaphor of adoption. Christians are all "adopted" (Romans 8:23; Galatians 4:5) rather than born. We are born into the psychogenetic legacy of original sin on the way to total depravity. Anything Christians have beyond this is the result of their adoption. The Bible image is significant. You can see it in extreme cases of rivalry between naturally born and adopted siblings within one family. I have visited homes in which adopted children and natural children grew up together, and the adopted child has now disappeared, fallen off the map. In some cases, an adopted child feels a deep rejection from the birth mother that cuts to the heart. Such a fundamental feeling of rejection can affect the adopted child's understanding of himself or herself. Despite the love of the adoptive parents, the feeling of rejection may remain. To use *Star Wars* language, in these cases there is a "disturbance in the Force."

For this reason the scriptural metaphor of adoption is a fitting one. God "adopted" the Gentiles, who were not of his "family of origin" (they were not Jews), by grace. He grafted them unto his organic or "natural" vine. But the natural vine had a life of its own. It was uncomfortable with grace. The natural children became as "difficult" as the adopted children. As always in biblical religion, everyone, from the standpoint of God's one-way love or grace, is on the same level, the level of empty-handedness. There is no difference between the adopted and the natural. Grace makes all siblings stand on even ground.

In human terms — that is, without explicit reliance on the grace that comes from God — sibling problems are difficult to heal. This is because they begin so early. The origin of the jealousies and competitions among brothers and sisters goes back to the earliest, most formative days of their lives. Will you ever forget the way your oldest child reacted when you brought home his first sister or brother from the hospital? Your family photographs reveal what happened. Serious and unique double-mindedness appears on his or her face in every picture you took. That big question mark came up again when you had to make sure not to leave the baby with his "adoring" brother. First he scratched him, then he pulled his hair, then he almost broke his arm. No one wants to be supplanted.

The origin of sibling rivalry is early and hard-wired. Good intentions and even conscious efforts later on to redistribute parental affection and time (even possessions) are insufficient to rewrite the script. I have never seen a reconciliation effected between siblings through hard work and mediation alone. I have seen reconciliation effected only when one or the other of the injured has become a Christian.

That is a strong statement, but it is necessary to make. In some sectors of human brokenness, grace as metaphor, grace as mediated expression of the grace of Christ, is the same thing as the grace of Christ. But not in this sector. In cases of sibling hatred, the only solution is for one of the bitter parties, whether victim or sinned against, to be so undone by the word of the cross that the reaching out becomes natural and unforced. I have seen this happen. When there is not such an interposition of a regenerated life, there will just be one more lonely funeral with separated mourners and absent children.

Side Bar: Grace and the Nuclear Family

All religions are affected by their first story. Islam's story involves a "manifest success" during the Medinan period of the prophet Muhammad. Thereafter, God's blessing for the Muslim world has been thought to be present in the victory that takes place before the eyes of the world. Buddhism's story involves a renunciation at the very start, the oft-pictured farewell of the Prince Gautama to his sleeping wife and child. Christianity's story involves a manifest failure in the heart of its establishing story, the abandonment of the leader at Gethsemane and his lone death on the Roman cross.

Another beginning theme in Christianity relates directly to the question of grace in families. This theme is the transformation of the nuclear family. It is true to say that it involves the end of the traditional nuclear family. Jesus left his mother and his brothers and established a new family, the "family" of his students and followers. In leaving his nuclear family, Christ broke out of the ancient prescriptions involving blood kinship.

In the ancient world, and in most non-Western cultures today, blood kinship is the thickest bond. If you spend any time in a developing region, whether it be Arab, Asian, African, or Aleut, you quickly see that blood kinship is everything. Your friend's brother is always going to be more important to your friend than you are. No matter what. Your friend's mother or father is always going to be more important than you could ever be. This is true from China to Chile. It is a fact of life that you must see clearly in order to live any sort of conscious life in a non-Western context.

From the very beginning, Jesus of Nazareth destroyed this idea.

Jesus attracted to himself a group of students and followers. He left what we today call his "family of origin" in order to construct this new family. Not long into this boundary-breaking ministry, Christ's mother Mary approached him, accompanied by his natural brothers. They reproached him for spending his primary efforts with outsiders to the family rather than with them. Just like today, ethnic families spend "Sunday afternoons" together, every week, like the Greek-American family in *My Big Fat Greek Wedding* (2002) and the Italian-American family in *Moonstruck* (1987). Your first identity and your overwhelmingly prior obligation in ancient society, and in ethnic cultures today, was to your blood relatives. Jesus broke with this obligation and identity. What he did was very close to breaking a taboo. And in spending time with prostitutes and "unclean" persons, he did break taboos.

Here is what happened when Jesus Christ was approached by his mother and his brothers: "Pointing to his disciples, he said, 'Here are my mother and my brothers! For whoever does the will of my Father in heaven is my brother and sister and mother'" (Matthew 12:49-50). This episode reflects a breakthrough in Jesus' thinking that would later be expressed in his views concerning "Gentile sinners." He universalized family. He put the whole world on the same level of connection if you were one of his followers. Family consisted of all who do "the will of the Father." The implication was that the relation to God always overrides relations of blood.

St. John underlined Christ's breakthrough in the Prologue to his Gospel: "To all who received him, who believed in his name, he gave power to become children of God, who were born, not of blood or of the will of the flesh or of the will of man, but of God" (John 1:12-13). St. Paul conceptualized Christ's breakthrough when he spoke of the unity of the human race in relation to the absolution of Christ. Twice Paul universalized the bonds of kinship and declared the end of humanly established blood bonds (Galatians 3:28; Colossians 3:11).

Grace does not destroy the nuclear family. It does destroy the supremacy of the nuclear family. It reconstructs the bonds of affection between human beings on the basis of the prior grace of God to universally fallen people, rather than on the prior fact of blood relation. This is not to disobey the Fifth Commandment, which commands the world to honor our fathers and mothers in the natural sense; but it is to place this commandment in a context according to which your natural mother can be your "sister" in the bond of forgivenness and your natural father can be your "brother" in the same bond. The bond of absolution, which results in the fruitfulness of doing the will of God — the "natural" order of grace as well as its consequence — is thicker than blood, which was always thicker than water.

Grace sits in opposition to the natural. To ethnic cultures, it is thoroughly and unquestionably natural for blood kinship and "natural family" to outweigh all other claims. Thus in *Godfather II* (1974), the Mafia man who has turned government witness against "The Family" is intimidated from testifying at a congressional hearing against them by the sheer fact of the Mafia's putting his Sicilian brother into the audience. The simple but overwhelming fact of his brother's being at the hearing is sufficient to deter him absolutely from speaking out, for the most just of reasons, against his "Family."

Grace opposes this. The guard sitting next to the man in *Godfather II,* if he is a Christian believer, should have just as strong a claim on the Mafia man as his brother. That is the hermeneutic of Christ's Christianity. It is expressed plainly in the letters of St. Paul, and it affected the public image and also the rapid rise of the Christian movement in the ancient world.

Grace set the family on a much broader foundation than before. Jesus demolished the conventional ethnic family in practice, and Paul demolished it in theory. They replaced it with a universal family of original sinners saved by grace. This was one of the most revolutionary things about early Christianity. E. R. Dodds, the Ulsterman who became one of the twentieth century's leading scholars of late antiquity, concluded that one reason why Christianity was so attractive to people living near the Mediterranean during the first century was its creation of a new family. These are Dodds's words concerning the change in the concept of familial community that the life of Christ and the teaching of Paul introduced:

> Epictetus has described for us the dreadful loneliness that can beset a man in the midst of his fellows. Such loneliness must have been felt by millions — the urbanised tribesman, the peasant come to town in search of work, the demobilised soldier, the rentier ruined by inflation, and the manumitted slave. For people in that situation membership of a Christian community might be the only way of maintaining self-respect and giving their life some semblance of meaning. Within the community there was human warmth: some one was interested in them. . . . It is therefore not surprising that the earliest and the most striking advances of Christianity were made in the great cities — in Antioch, in Rome, in Alexandria. Christians were in a more than formal sense "members of one another": I think that was a major cause, perhaps the strongest single cause, of the spread of Christianity.[3]

Let me return for a moment to the nuclear family in its essence. What becomes of the human nuclear family, the ties of blood, when they have been superseded by the ties of God's Blood, a superior connection? Should we conclude the matter as the new confirmand in my New York City parish did the night before an Episcopal bishop confirmed her as a

3. E. R. Dodds, *Pagan and Christian in an Age of Anxiety,* The Wiles Lectures Given at the Queen's University, Belfast, 1963 (Cambridge: Cambridge University Press, 1965), pp. 137-38.

new Christian? She telephoned her father, from whom she had been estranged for several years, and said, "Dad, I just want you to know, you are not my father." Click. When she told me this, I thought, "Well, that's not exactly it."

The supersession of the nuclear family by the grace-adopted family of Christian brothers and sisters means, not the destruction of the nuclear family, but the right proportion and due worth given to the nuclear family. As always when an idol dies, the thing upon which the disproportionate worship had been projected begins to receive its proper due. You begin to see it in its true colors. In the case of the nuclear family, you begin to love them as they are meant to be loved. They are meant to be loved as human beings, not as non-negotiable absolutes.

The mother can begin to love her natural children, not as extensions of herself, which may be her usual experience, but as very rich gifts to be handled with extreme care and then handed back. The father can begin to love his natural children, not as extensions of himself and his own lack of success, or as compensations for what he himself did not receive and did not achieve, but as gifts to be handled with extreme care and then handed back. The daughter can begin to love her mother as flesh-and-blood rather than divine soul-friend; and the son can begin to love his father as the fallible man he really is. Grace's deconstruction of the nuclear family renders back the nuclear family. Children are properly loved, but with a little detachment. Parents are fittingly honored, but with less suppression and resentment. Sibling rivalry is deconstructed, although that may be the last wall of Jericho to come tumbling down.

The end of the absolute claim of the nuclear family, for which grace strictly calls, emancipates the nuclear family from the very nerve of neurosis, which is the projection upon human beings of what belongs only to God. The grace of God releases the possibility of non-demanding love among men and women who are united by human blood. This is the salvation of the famous nuclear family.

CHAPTER FOUR

Grace in Society

Grace in Politics

In the Christian tradition, theologians who stress grace have tended to be apolitical. This is because they have understood political action as a function of the law. Political action, in other words, seeks change that can be measured. Political action stems from the idea that political and social change can make a lasting difference in the world. Political action operates out of a higher anthropology than most theologians of one-way love have been able to support. Theologians of one-way love have always tended to be more passive and less hopeful regarding human agency than others who stress human participation in the improvement of the world. There is definitely a leaning toward passivity, and what is sometimes called "quietism," in the theology of grace that underwrites this systematic approach to everyday life.

Luther dealt with this tilt toward passivity by developing a theory of the "two kingdoms." On the one hand, he said that God and the human race relate from God's side only. God is the sole free agent, and his grace is the sole hope for a species hopelessly in flight from him. Nothing we do can make any difference in deterring his judgment or attracting his love. Every conceivable weight in the divine/human relation is placed upon the cross of Christ. This weight is heavy and unique.

On the other hand, Luther said that in political or social affairs the state has its own rules, and these rules must be honored. While one kingdom, the kingdom of God, operates entirely from grace, the other kingdom, the kingdom of the world in the here-and-now, operates from the first use of the law, by which order and equity can be measured and established. This means that Luther split reality into "two kingdoms": the kingdom of grace and the kingdom of law.

An illustration of this approach came during my time at Tübingen. A distinguished theologian and Luther scholar gave the following as a sort of epigram: "In life we believe in grace; in the examination room, law." That shocked me. It seemed dualistic and compartmentalized. The shock has not worn off.

This theology of everyday life, this understanding of grace applied, attempts not to split the kingdoms. The idea here is of a unity, a single approach to the entire reality of moral life and human relationship, a full-field theory that seeks to account for all the data using a single premise carried to its full consequence and effect.

Luther's "two kingdoms" theory is the least credible section of Luther's theology. It is a well-meaning attempt to keep to some idea of human distributive justice, even while the grace of God is offered pride of place in eternal or ultimate justice. It conveys the impression of a rationalization. It has the feel of a bowing of the knee, for some sort of short-term or utilitarian gain, to the powers that be. As a theologian of grace I have always felt uncomfortable with Luther's theory. It reads like a compromise.

It would be easy to criticize the "two kingdoms" idea in the light of institutional Lutheranism's failure, in the main, to resist the rise of Adolf Hitler. But as an Anglican, I am able to criticize the "two kingdoms" theory from a different context. I can criticize the "two kingdoms" theory from the way in which it has compromised the Anglican approach to Christianity.

I am referring to Archbishop Thomas Cranmer's similar "two kingdoms" approach to the monarchy during the first phase of the English Reformation. Cranmer was converted to a theology of grace in the 1520s, but he was also committed to consistent obedience, as a Christian believer, to the powers that be, and thus to his king, Henry VIII. He believed with his entire being in the Reformation of the Church of England. He also believed, however, in the role of the king as executor and enactor of the Reformation. This was partly because Cranmer, like Luther, was a child of his age. It would have been inconceivable for him not to see the hierarchy of the world as being a divine given. The problem was the inevitable conflict this would involve with Cranmer's theology. The invasive agent was not Cranmer's idea of monarchy or Luther's idea of the political kingdom. The invasive agent was their rediscovery of one-way love as the change agent of the universe. This grace part of their thinking caused the conflict. It always has.

The "two kingdoms" theory — grace in religion, but law in the state — boomeranged against Cranmer. When he was forced to serve a monarch who had a different idea about the gospel, Mary Tudor or "Bloody Mary," he entered a box canyon. It was a point with him that he must obey the queen. But in matters of salvation, he must obey God. He therefore swung back and forth in his loyalties. One day he recanted and left his Protestant views in order to bow to the ruler. The next day he recanted his recantation. He actually died in good conscience (1556), having resolved the duality in favor of the grace-relation. But he teeter-tottered right up to the last minute. You can still see the marks on a pillar in St. Mary's Church, Oxford, where the platform was anchored on which he recanted his recantation. It is a lasting monument to the perilous inadequacy of a compartmentalized view of religion and politics.

Luther, too, was caught, although less dangerously, between his sense of obligation to the grace of God in the gospel and his sense of obligation to the law of God in the person of the duke. Fortunately, in his own Saxony, the succession of gospel-believing dukes was safe, at least during Luther's lifetime. Much later, however, in the early 1930s, Lutheran Christians found themselves trapped in the duality, this time without resolution. They believed in placing the gospel over the law, as prior to and superior to the law. But they also believed in the second kingdom of this world, in which they must be obedient to the "secular" authority. How could they be loyal to the gospel in its freedom in the church *and* be loyal to the ruler when this ruler was Adolf Hitler?

Ernst Käsemann told me several times that the Nazis approached him when he was pastor in the town of Gelsenkirchen and said, "Pastor, you take care of the people's spiritual needs. Let us handle their temporal needs." Stick to your knitting, in other words. Fortunately Käsemann was beginning to break with the "two kingdoms" idea, especially with the traditional interpretation of Romans 13:1-7 from which the "two kingdoms" concept had in part been derived. Herr Käsemann could not buy the "split." He was no longer able to divide the political from the spiritual.

Käsemann was arrested after preaching down the "two kingdoms" idea in principle and denouncing Christians who wished to Nazify the church. Käsemann completed his powerful book *The Wandering People of God* (1939) in prison. I learned to criticize the "two kingdoms" as a dualistic interpretation, because I learned it directly from this man whose breakthrough had made him a "partisan." "Partisan" was Käsemann's word for himself. No neutrality for him: no splitting, no compartments. God's grace is true in the province of the political as well as in the province of the church. Separating the two will only get your fingers burned. Again and again, that was his phrase to me: Do not separate the spheres or you will get your fingers burned, as we did.

This systematic theology of everyday life cannot separate the spiritual and the temporal. Christianity is by its nature critical of all institutions — including government — in every case. This theology also rejects Erastianism, which is a technical term for state control of the church. Erastianism sometimes sounds good, especially if it suggests a kind of Christianization or baptism of secular society. This is the sort of idea that T. S. Eliot embraced for a time (as in his 1939 *The Idea of a Christian Society*). But it is never truly successful, because the trend of the world is too much against the church, which in its institutional form is always compromised, human, and bends with the wind. In Erastianism, or "established church-ness," the official church always ends up captured by the strongest voice of the surrounding world-culture.

An important instance of the failure of the "establishment" principle in religion was the inability of the bishops of the Church of England in the fall of 2005 to take a consistent, not to say a principled, stand against the imposition of the Labor Government's bill to legalize so-called "civil partnerships" of same-gender couples. The Church of England was tied to the government (unlike the Roman Catholic Church in England, which distanced itself from the bill) and had to decide what to do given this extraordinary legal assault on what most regarded as traditional church teaching. In response to this assault, the bishops came up with a casuistical *apparent* compromise that involved a distinction between what ordained people are able to promise and what lay people are able to promise, as well as a kind of fairytale distinction between civil partnerships that include sexual activity and civil partnerships that are chaste.

The Church of England became compromised by its ties to the state. Either it could knuckle under, which it did, or the bishops could have taken a principled stand and said No. This they did not do. No wonder traditional Christian people are now envisaging the Church of England's disestablishment.

We should remember what Konrad Adenauer, the chancellor of Germany, wrote on February 23, 1946, concerning the Roman Catholic Church's compromised situation in the Nazi period. Adenauer wrote: "I believe that if all the bishops had together made public statements from the pulpits on a particular day, they could have prevented a great deal. That did not happen, and there is no excuse for it. It would have been no bad thing if the bishops had all been put in prison or in concentration camp as a result. Quite the contrary. But none of that happened and therefore it is best to keep quiet."[1] These words are a precise dismantling of the "two kingdoms" theory. The theory will never fly again. It will never fly in England again either, after the historic failure of the Church of England bishops to be critical in the face of government pressure. The Christian community worldwide has every right to be skeptical concerning the official side of English Anglicanism.

Is there a concrete approach to politics that arises from the grace of God? Is there a political philosophy that is essentially Christian? If grace cannot be compartmentalized, then it must relate to every sphere of life. Grace must relate to politics. On the one hand, the Erastianism of the distant past, as well as its vestiges today, like the current establishment of

1. As quoted in Klaus Scholder, *A Requiem for Hitler and Other New Perspectives on the German Church Struggle,* trans. John Bowden (London: SCM Press, 1989), p. 139.

the Church of England, made Christianity captive to the propulsive issues of the world, which vary from decade to decade but are always victorious in the short term. On the other hand, pulling back entirely, which is the sectarian way, restrains the application of grace to a tiny sphere. Christian communities that have withdrawn from the world, such as the Amish or the Harmonists in nineteenth-century America, have had little impact on the world as a whole. They have hidden their light under a bushel (Matthew 5:15; Mark 4:21; Luke 11:33).

The political life of Christianity has gone in two directions. *Either* Christianity has been forced into conformity by the issues of the age, *or* it has withheld its pertinence and potential benefits that might make the world a more compassionate home. The alternative to the two positions is not a balance or a middle space. The alternative to the two separated positions is a positive political philosophy that is comprehensive and knows no exceptions or variances to the influence of grace on every aspect of life.

This systematic theology of everyday life is Kantian in that it affirms the aptness of grace *without exceptions* to all the situations of life. If grace is true in my inmost identity, if it is the confidence that makes me what I am, then it must also hold true in my outward identity and in all the extensions of that identity which comprise the life I practically lead. Grace is therefore true in politics.

What is the political philosophy of grace? Grace, as over and against law, describes a positive political philosophy. The political philosophy of grace is countercultural in the extreme. It has also never been put into practice. The novelist William Hale White, who wrote under the pen name "Mark Rutherford," expressed the pathos of its apparent impracticability in the concluding paragraph of his biography of John Bunyan:

> We cannot bring ourselves into a unity. The time is yet to come when we shall live by a faith which is a harmony of all our faculties. A glimpse was caught of such a gospel nineteen centuries ago in Galilee, but it has vanished.[2]

2. *John Bunyan* (London: Hodder & Stoughton, 1905), pp. 49-50.

The main features of a political philosophy of grace are equality versus fairness, gifts rather than entitlements, and personal acquiescence rather than the struggle for one's own rights. Consequently, these features of grace in politics actually produce fairness, the satisfaction of what caused the zeal for entitlement in the first place, and — this is important — the achievement of human rights. As before in this systematic theology of everyday life, grace performs the thing that law set out to achieve. What the law asserted to be good is in fact good. The question is not the what, but the how. We have observed through unending centuries that the fact that human life is political is not the problem in itself. Fairness has always been the right thing of which to dream. Entitlement feels like fairness, and fairness is righteous. Human rights are indeed what the world needs. The problem of political life has never been these goals in themselves. The problem in political philosophy has been the *means.* Grace forecasts the means.

First, consider equality versus fairness. The anthropology of grace, which is original sin, regards the whole human race as being on an equal footing with no exception. The problem is not that of distribution, the distribution of merit according to *performance.* The problem is that of shielding, shielding from equal and uniform *punishment.* The human race under law is not the object of a distribution of rewards based upon earning, but rather the object of an indiscriminate "carpet bombing" from the law, which speaks so that "every mouth may be silenced" (Romans 3:19). A theology of everyday life based on the principle of grace in opposition to law understands this. We cower under judgment. This is because our motives are flawed, even when our performance appears altruistic.

Here is a metaphor from history of the "equality" of God's judgment. When Berlin was being bombed during the last days of the Soviet siege in the spring of 1945, the one remaining hospital in the eastern sector of the city tried to distinguish itself from other targets. A huge white cross made out of sheets was created on the park outside the hospital so that enemy pilots could see it. The nurses also painted big red crosses on the roof so the bombardiers would not drop their bombs on the hospital. Whether it was spared or not I do not know, but one observer on the ground wrote in her diary: "'Carpet bombing' is woven so tightly that there are no holes for compassion."[3] Law exempts no one on the basis of compassion. Law is woven that tightly! Grace exempts everyone on the basis of compassion.

How does this work in practice? The fruits of grace, even in politics, are situational. They are situational in the sense that equality takes shape in differing ways in differing contexts. Equality is not ideological, but equality is uniform. What we can say about this first principle of a political philosophy based upon grace is that it protects all people — men, women, and children — as sufferers and as sinners. It never places people into ethnicities, genders, groups, types, or classes. It is highly protective of the individual and of all individuals. It cannot scapegoat. It cannot say, as one Israeli settler placarded on departure from his erstwhile home in the Gaza Strip: "No Arabs, no problem."

This philosophy of politics is protectionist of the individual and of all individuals. It includes criminals and abusers. It is not just protectionist of victims. Why? Because it understands everyone as a victim. Grace sees people existing under enormous and high-pressure "principalities and powers."

A political philosophy of grace is uniformly egalitarian and protective of all human beings on the principle of their humanity. There is room here for the first use of the law. We can envisage putting people away who are threatening to others. We do this from first-use grounds only, however, to keep chaos from spinning the world off its axis. But we do not harbor illusions about criminal behavior. Everyone is a potential criminal. The history of manslaughter and "crimes of passion" has taught us this. The worst criminal in the world may in fact be living next door to you. He may be living in your house. In this sense, incarceration is arbitrary, if the truth were known. Grace does not divide people up. Everyone, absolutely everyone, is made of the same material.

The second principle of a systematic theology of grace applied to political philosophy is that of gift versus entitlement. The word "gift" is sometimes invoked without much material content. I am using "gift" to

3. Anonymous, *A Woman in Berlin,* trans. Philip Boehm (New York: Henry Holt and Company, 2005), p. 29.

mean the dynamic principle of generosity that results from "the one, full, perfect sacrifice, satisfaction and oblation for the sins of the whole world" *(Book of Common Prayer),* which is the law-absorbing death of Christ.

Consider the slogan the United States Marine Corps uses in its recruitment practices. Recruiting officers drive huge vans into shopping centers, and the vans have these words emblazoned on all sides: "Earned Never Given." There is a large, ornate sword painted next to the phrase. In a way, this is a perfect evocation of the law: the sword of justice and the motto of justice. You have to earn it — the sword and the uniform, the name of honor — in order to get it. It is not just given to you. That slogan is a recruiting slogan for the whole human race because it seeks to achieve what the world promises. From the standpoint of the eternal law, the slogan is as true as brass. From the standpoint of grace in practice, it could not be more misleading.

In the grace-anchored philosophy of politics, all benefits accruing to the human being are gifts and not entitlements. The only entitlement we possess is that of "the damned sinner" (Luther on Psalm 51).[4] To quote the same Reformer, the only identity we bear as human beings is our shared need "to be justified by faith" (Luther's *Disputation on Man,* Thesis 32). We are entitled to nothing. If we are entitled to anything at all, it is a one-way ticket to the loss of all things, which is death, and to regret for most things, which parallels our death. Therefore, the aim of political life is to establish the benefits of life on the basis of gift, which, for Christian people, is the result of the gift of God's grace-full love in the redemption of the world. Simply put, everyone is entitled to death and judgment; therefore whatever we receive that is positive exists over and above that. It is gift.

What does this mean in practice? The answer is mostly situational. It could mean that everybody gets to drive a "New VW Beetle" with a CD-player. It could mean that everyone receives a "little pink house" (John Cougar Mellencamp). This philosophy of grace does tilt toward some general form of socialism. The early Christians discovered this when

4. Martin Luther, *Der 51. Psalm,* ed. Hermann Kleinknecht (Munich: Claudius Verlag, 1983), pp. 20-23.

they pooled their possessions in the immediate aftermath of Pentecost (Acts 2:44-45). But it is a knowing branch of socialism, for it understands the human stain as deeply soaked in. There is an Ananias and a Sapphira (5:1-11) in every community and family always, so the Christian tilt in the direction of socialism is always a little sly. We expect it will be used for "entitlement" on some fronts.

The direction of this political philosophy is generally leftwards, but within the context of a wise anthropology. Such a political philosophy envisions the distribution of human benefits as gifts to all and not as entitlements to some. It is therefore a philosophy of thanksgiving in every case, not an "Employee of the Month" approach. (Whenever I see those plaques — and they are almost everywhere — I can barely resist the temptation to draw on a moustache with my felt-tip pen and scribble the words: "Criminal of the Month." My anthropology makes me that skeptical.)

Let me try to explain the concept of "situation" as it applies to these principles that constitute a short and positive political philosophy. "Situation ethics" is a relatively contemporary phrase that says that moral decisions are contextual rather than universalizeable. Moral decisions depend on the givens of each individual situation in which we find ourselves. They vary from case to case. There are some general principles, such as "love one another" and "do no harm," that watch over the concrete practicalities of moral life. But any such high principles need to be applied in particular and differing ways depending on their contexts.

This idea of "situation ethics" is related to what I am saying, but it is not exactly the same thing. What I am saying is that there are broad principles, arising from the identity of grace, that create a general approach. There is also context, which can mean "little pink houses" in one setting and the sale of your designer lake house in another. What distinguishes the view affirmed here from the normal teaching of "situation ethics" is its theological anthropology. The view of human nature being offered here is simply so despondent that one can have little hope of really scoping out what is right and true in general. The best we can do will probably be in broken pieces. There is the Holy Spirit, however, to which this approach gives a high place. The Holy Spirit takes and makes concrete the principle and operation of grace. The principle of grace I have laid out is broad and radical, a more or less "hippie"-sounding view of the world's goods. But it is also permeated by a pessimism that is intrinsically Christian. I am sincerely skeptical of our situational engagement with big ideas, because the quotient of self-deception is always high. Therefore I go at the big theme, the political philosophy that arises from grace, with caution.

The third and final principle of this provisional, grace-based philosophy of politics is this: acquiescence rather than human rights. This is the most sensitive one, at least for me. It is sensitive because it seems at first to run counter to one of the richest fruits that was produced in the rediscovery of God's grace that took place through the Protestant Reformation: the fruit of human rights.

The concept of human rights, certainly in its Western political sense, is derived directly from the Reformation, and specifically from its Dutch and British branches. More specifically, the idea of human rights in which most Americans believe was the direct result of one solitary battle that took place in July 1690 at the Boyne River in Ireland. In the Battle of the Boyne, the Protestant idea of human rights won a surprising victory over the forces of the suppressive French "Sun King," Louis XIV. It was a consciously Protestant victory, a victory, as the people then and there understood it, of human rights over tyranny. To the victors, the Battle of the Boyne was a victory for grace over law.

How then can I state that the third big principle of a grace-philosophy of politics is the principle of acquiescence, or acceptance of what is, over against human rights? It is because acquiescence, which is the surrender to grace, is always the prelude to receiving again — actually for the first time — your identity. When you are forced, by life and law, to give up your ideas about control and autonomy, when you are forced to cede and concede these ideas because they have failed you over and over again in experience, it is grace that gives them back to you again. But this time they have a different motor. This we have already seen. Everything that the law requires is given back after it is given up. This is why St. Paul and Christ talked ever about the fruit of a changed life. "Love, joy, peace, patience, kindness, generosity, faithfulness" (Galatians 5:22) were never the prerequisites of a changed status; they were always the results of it. Thus, when you acquiesce to the loss of important things, God restores them. This is not *quid pro quo.* It is simply in the nature of loss. We lose, God restores. We acquiesce, God gives. We surrender, God waves the white flag of grace. On our side, the result looks very much like the thing of which we had dreamed: human rights.

I saw this, negatively, a few years ago at The High Museum in Atlanta. My wife and I went there in hopes of viewing a fine collection of African American paintings, several of which depict church scenes. What Mary and I found instead was an overwhelmingly assertive exhibition of contemporary photographs entitled "Here's Looking at You!" The exhibition consisted of room after room after room of "face shots" of everyday Americans. It screamed "identity," or rather, the search for identity. I compared what I saw in Atlanta to the snapshots taken in Cambodia of the hundreds of thousands of young people who were soon to be shot. Each of the Cambodian photographs depicts the true case of the human race. Each picture is a heartbreaker that engenders the highest pitch of compassion from the viewer. Each picture is also highly individual. You want to reach out and touch each one, and ask their subject, "What are you feeling? Why have they put you here? Can't I help you?"

Not so at The High Museum! The faces there all read, "I want you to want me" (Cheap Trick). They said, Affirm me, please! I do not like my job at Wendy's or my job at the Renaissance Hotel or my job owning the Renaissance Hotel. I am a pure lost soul. I want my MTV.

Let me put it a little more strongly. The pictures at The High were a monument to human rights when the idea of surrender is not on the table. They came across to me as arrogant and also pathetic. The Cambodian photographs are art because they are profound. The Atlanta series were "candles in the wind" (Elton John), shallow and pointless.

How does a political philosophy that emphasizes acquiescence rather than human rights work out in practice? Again, there is a situational factor to this philosophy, but the tilt affectively is always going to be toward the victims of power. The tilt is going to be in a "Cambodian," a "Rwandan," a "Post-War famished German" direction: these are the deadened people, the people who have been forced to lose their hope. Over and over again, perfectly consistent, this tilt toward those who have been forced to acquiesce will have the effect of restoring human rights. As with all movements of grace, the thing that was lost will be restored. Yet it can be restored only when it is utterly given up. Jesus said this emblematically, and he repeated it: "Those who want to save their life will lose it, and those who lose their life for my sake will find it" (Matthew 16:25; Mark 8:35; Luke 17:33). Up with the Cambodian victims of murder and the 100,000 victims of rape in Russian-occupied Berlin. Down with the "tell me a story about how you adore me" (Rolling Stones) face-shots at The High. In any case, the truth behind each of these face-shots is a down and driven-down character. Only acquiescence to that fact, which will always come in all lives finally and decisively, produces the openness to grace that alone achieves the fruit of human rights.

That is the political philosophy of grace.

Grace in War and Peace

In relation to the never-ending event of war, grace takes a consistent view. Grace rules out the idea of a "just war."

So-called "just war" theory says that Christians can approve of war provided certain conditions are met. These conditions include barring the destruction of "innocent" or civilian life, possessing a basically defensive origin, and being something like the last resort after every attempt at making peace has failed. According to the "just war" theory, certain great crimes, like genocide, are appropriately stopped by the action of war. War, on this line, should be undertaken for as short a period as possible and should be ended as soon as the cause that gave rise to it no longer exists. The theologian Thomas Aquinas is usually credited with having developed the contextual conditions that make it possible for Christians to take up arms.

Grace cannot make peace with the theory of a "just war." This is because we take Christ's principle, which is also Kantian, when he said, "Whoever is faithful in a very little is faithful also in much" (Luke 16:10). A moral principle, in order to be law, has to be good in every case. We cannot say, "You shall not kill," and then temporize it or compartmentalize it within a category. We cannot mute it to suit conflicting goods. When the law speaks, it speaks with the authority of no exceptions. This is what makes it law. If it speaks otherwise, it is casuistry. Casuistry is the idea that the law applies differently to differing cases. Casuistry says that the law needs to be interpreted situationally, within specific contexts. Christianity cannot hold with casuistry. Christianity understands the law in an absolute sense.

Moreover, Christianity understands original sin to be evenly distributed in *every* instance of human action. To posit a "safe" zone of human action in making war is to say that one zone of human activity, a "just war," for example, is less likely to be tainted with sin in practice than another zone of human activity, such as interventionist war. Our theological anthropology rules this out. The people who wage "just war" are the same people who wage "unjust war."

This theology of everyday life opposes the "just war" idea, therefore, on two grounds. The first is that it makes an exception to the universal law "You shall not kill" and thus overturns the principle of law as universal demand, which would in turn make Christ's substitutionary death on the cross unnecessary in *some* cases. Exceptions to the law overturn the atonement because they soften the law. Second, "just war" mutes original sin and conceptualizes a good, or at least a better, war. This cannot be so if human nature is always and everywhere the same. All murderousness is intrinsic in our DNA, and no one can be protected against the sin of the murderer, even if he or she be excused.

Take the example of the liberation of Auschwitz. We all know that Auschwitz was an extermination camp for Jews. We also know that the Soviet Army liberated the camp on January 27, 1945. This was a victory over genocide.

Not everyone knows, however, that many of these soldiers who liberated Auschwitz also raped over 100,000 women between the ages of 12 and 80 in Berlin a few months later. We could say that the German women, unprotected and defenseless, had it coming. After all, they were the women of the country that had perpetrated the genocide of Auschwitz. But no Christian can say that with a straight face.

What happened in Berlin, at the hands of the very same soldiers who had freed the prisoners at Auschwitz, was horrible. Horrible, too, was the English and American bombing of cities where only women and children lived, as "payback" for earlier atrocities. Is it possible, on the lines of a Christian anthropology, to speak of a "greatest generation"? We are required to remember, although we seldom do, that the same Soviet soldiers who freed the camps systematically raped every single unprotected woman they could find with such violence that thousands of these women died or committed suicide. A systematic theology of grace — focused on a systematic understanding of law, and noticing the even distribution of human nature — cannot sanction the theory of a "just war."

Where does this leave us? What is a theology of grace in relation to war and peace? A positive theology of grace in relation to war and peace is instinctually pacifist. This is unavoidable. A positive theology of grace is not ideologically pacifist, as if to say that the state of peace is an end in itself. Pacifism in human terms usually implies that peace is an irreducible good, as if to say that peace itself were not tainted by original sin. All human ideologies take insufficient note of the anthropology of grace, which is an anthropology of human bondage to original sin and total depravity. To have peace in a human or political sense alone is no *summum bonum*. You can have peace in a political sense but with just as much self-absorption, pitilessness, and judgment within the overall equation.

There were certainly times of peace in human history that were decadent and hostile to human flourishing. The Soviet Union was peaceful during the 1920s, but millions of people were deliberately starved to death by their government. England is peaceful today, but the absorbing materialism and high levels of alcoholism of the island are grossly apparent to anyone who visits Britain. People often say that the 1950s in the United States, the "Eisenhower years," were times of peace with hypocrisy and boundless social conformity. All of these generalizations may or may not be true. What is true is that peace is not an end in itself.

Moreover, Christians often see the hand of God in the conflicts of life. We do not cry down conflict as an answer to living, nor do we instigate it if we live from grace. But God exists in the midst of storms. That is a perspective on trouble that almost all Christians have always held.

God works through conflict, even through wars. The cross of Christ was an act of violence, an aggressive assault on an innocent person, a grinding up, within the wheels of temple and Roman politics, of one man who should never have been held for trial. We call it Good Friday.

Christians are not ideological pacifists, because they do not carry illusions about a "chicken in every pot" and also because they understand the Holy Spirit of God typically to work through desperate situations.

Christians are, however, consistent opponents of war. What does it mean to oppose war from the standpoint of grace? If grace cancels out war in all cases and with no exceptions, what is the state of grace in relation to peace? It is the state of trusting to the Holy Spirit in receptivity, within an entirely passive situation. Grace is not even self-defensive. It gives over to the one who overbears. Here is a controversial passivity, which creates the instrument of non-violence as the main dynamic of Christian resistance to oppression. This is also where Christianity receives its bad reputation for being a license to doormats. Lars von Trier, the Danish movie director who has expressed very mixed feelings about Christianity, made a movie called *The Idiots* (1998), in which he mimicked Christians who see every reversal of fortune and every instance of being put upon by others as an opportunity to bear their crosses as "gifts" of affliction. In the *Life of Brian* (1979), the Monty Python film, there is a character who is supposed to exemplify the Christian doormat. He actually gets snookered into being crucified, along with the title character, out of sheer passive goodwill.

Grace does work just this way in relation to peace. Grace, to use Christ's metaphor, turns the other cheek (Matthew 5:39; Luke 6:29). Grace submits to injustice and does not fire back. Admiral Gaspard de Coligny, the French Huguenot leader who was martyred in 1572, said that his Protestant people in Roman Catholic France were like an anvil being hammered and hit constantly by the mallet of the majority. Eventually, he said, the mallet would fissure or break from hitting the anvil so many times. Imagine being the anvil! The image of the anvil supported the hundreds of thousands of Protestants in France, most of whom were murdered, imprisoned for life, or sent to the galleys, while a few escaped to England, Ireland, and South Carolina.

I cannot evade the metaphor of grace in relation to peace. It is nonviolent (Matthew 5:39); it goes the extra mile with the oppressor (Matthew 5:41); and it appears to capitulate before the palpable injustice of the world (John 18:33-36), even when grace discerns it in deep focus. The only thing to add to this quite literal approach to what Jesus taught, with strong counter-cultural force, concerning nonresistance is the high place of the Holy Spirit within this theology of grace. Christians can be confident in the active and personalized power of God to *act*. This is contrary to human action, but it is the more active because it originates from a truly Free Will, the subjectivity of God.

The grace approach to peace is foolishness from a human or worldly point of view. But its passivity is tied to faith in God's Spirit to dispose of life. Without the confidence that there is a God who acts, this grace-based theology would be something out of Lars Von Trier's movie. But with such a confidence — which is foolishness on the face of it — the passivity of grace in respect to peace is sustained. It is surely in keeping with the spirit of God's being the sole animating agent of the world.

What is grace in relation to war and peace? *It is to support no war ever under any conceivable circumstances,* and it is peace in all things, the passive peace of Christ-like nonreactivity, bound to the never-passive operation of the Holy Spirit. This is a strong and consistent program. It has never gained much of a hearing, but as William Hale White (Mark Rutherford) wrote, "A glimpse was caught of such a gospel nineteen centuries ago in Galilee, but it has vanished."

Grace in Criminal Justice

The law is the essence of criminal justice and is also a total failure. That is to say, the law is a total failure in the redemption of the world from the effects of crime. Here is a list of the "proposals" that the law offers the world and to which grace is the alternative.

The Proposal of Deterrence

The first and most apparently impressive proposal that the law offers to the world is the proposal of deterrence. This is the idea that if criminals are punished publicly or within the public eye, and if the penalties for crime are sufficiently stringent, then prospective criminals will consider the possible consequences of the crimes they wish to commit and thus be deterred from committing them.

The classic example of deterrence is public execution. It was always thought that public hanging, in addition to its role in performing retribution, which is discussed below, would have an impact on future crime. It never did, and never has, at least in any fair statistic. Certain peculiar forms of execution did have some deterring value. For example, the public hanging, drawing, and quartering for crimes against the state, which was practiced in England for several centuries, did have huge symbolic impact. We know this from the accounts of observers, who described the "process." The condemned man was dragged to the place of torment; he had to climb up a ladder himself to his own rung for "swinging," that is, slow strangulation; then he was taken down before he had strangled to death and made to watch as he was first mutilated and then disemboweled. He died only at the end of the disemboweling, when the executioner cut out his heart. I describe this horror simply because it is "deterring" just to envision it. Thousands saw the thing take place in front of their own eyes. No wonder the Puritan preacher Hugh Peters, who was forced to watch several other "regicides" (i.e., men who had signed the death warrant of Charles I in 1649) hanged, drawn, and quartered before it was his own turn, lost his nerve and could barely speak when he was asked to give his "last words" before suffering in the same way. He had never been at a loss for words before! It was a terrible moment and should never have taken place.

Yes, brutal torture has a sobering effect. But punishment as deterrence has made little difference in deterring violent crime. This is primarily because so many violent crimes are crimes of passion. They are not premeditated but spring from surges of feeling. The law's punishment of criminals in order to deter further crime does not work, except, in a few cases, if it is grossly painful and very well publicized.

The Proposal of Retribution

The second and theoretically the main role of the law in executing criminal justice is that of retribution. Retribution is the idea that the punishment should fit the crime. Do you remember the song from *The Mikado* by Gilbert and Sullivan?

> My object all sublime
> I shall achieve in time —
> To let the punishment fit the crime —
> The punishment fit the crime;
> And make each prisoner pent
> Unwillingly represent
> A source of innocent merriment!
> Of innocent merriment![5]

If the man over there murdered your husband, then the state is entitled to take that man's life as retribution. This is sometimes called "an eye for an eye and a tooth for a tooth" (Exodus 21:24; Leviticus 24:20; Deuteronomy 19:21; Matthew 5:38). It is the concept of fairness applied to punishment. The distribution of punishment should be in direct proportion to the effect of the crime that was committed. Retribution does "God's work" in restoring fairness, equity, and right judgment to the world, when unfairness, inequity, and unjust judgment have been done. Retribution "satisfies" the demand of the victim for justice. Everyone understands this.

There are two problems with retribution as a principle of law within the system of criminal justice. The first problem is that it cannot restore or re-create the situation that was violated. Had every Soviet private been disciplined for his multiple rapes of German girls and elderly German women in the summer of 1945, their victims would not have been compensated for their lost innocence and extreme humiliation. Had every SS

5. W. S. Gilbert understood the relation between retribution and sadism. He understood that public retribution taps into public cruelty.

man who had killed Jewish men and women been executed for his crime during the same period, it would not have brought back those who had been murdered. Were every African American in the United States to be compensated financially for the crime that was committed in forcing him or her to be a slave in the American colonies and then the American Republic prior to 1863, would this restore "the years that the swarming locust has eaten" (Joel 2:25)? If every case of child abuse that has taken place within the last five days were clearly and publicly punished, the abuser in every instance being sentenced to a long prison term without parole, would this repair the breach and tear?

The second problem with retribution as a principle of law is that it is subject to error. It is possible to punish the wrong person! This is now more easily revealed through the testing of DNA samples. Several long-time prisoners have been released, because new DNA evidence revealed beyond a doubt that they did not commit the crimes for which they were imprisoned. Before this new era of medical information, the wrong people were imprisoned but the truth could not come out.

A classic instance of this wrong is the Alfred Hitchcock film of 1956 entitled *The Wrong Man*. Henry Fonda plays a New York City musician who is accused and found guilty of a robbery he did not commit. He is imprisoned, and his wife suffers a complete nervous breakdown. Later, through an act of God (in this movie, literally, an act of Christ!), the man is found to be not guilty and is released. His family never recovers, however, and the ending is one of the most downbeat of any of Hitchcock's classic films. Ironically, Henry Fonda also starred in a Western from 1943 in which several innocent men are hanged for a crime in which they took no part. It is called *The Ox-Bow Incident*. Human error enters into the sphere of retribution and makes it a very vulnerable expression of the law.

Grace in relation to criminal justice is skeptical about deterrence and worried about the operation of retribution. Moreover, grace rejects the principle of distributive justice on which retribution is founded. Grace is in fact the *opposite* of distributive, and by extension retributive, thinking. Before outlining the positive application of grace to criminal justice, we have to assess the whole idea of awards and punishments that is central to the idea of distributive justice.

Grace Opposes Distributive Justice

Grace opposes distributive justice because the only effective distribution of justice was the distribution of justice that occurred at Calvary, which was itself a complete *injustice.* "Behold, the Lamb of God, who takes away the sin of the world!" (John 1:29, Revised Standard Version). Grace understands justice in the divine and lasting sense to have been accomplished in the death of Christ, through the substitution of the one man's innocence in payment for the rest of the world's original sin and total depravity, compounded by the acts that they produce. For people who take grace seriously, there is only one act or performance of distributive justice. In the light of that one act, there is no justice possible of which it can be said that it was truly distributive. The alternative to a justice that cannot by nature ever be accurately distributive — for no human being could possibly judge the true state of things so as to distribute punishment and reward accurately without error — is grace.

Again, grace is the opposite of distributive justice, because it knows only one equitable distribution and because all human beings exist in a life of alienation from reasonable or fair equity. Any transparent picture of the world reflects the fact that the rich get richer and the poor get poorer, and the "sum of all human tears is always the same."[6] There is no way that you can repay or make right the painful wounds of the world. Grace opposes distributive justice on these two grounds.

Grace Opposes Rehabilitative Justice

Rehabilitative justice is the idea that the system for dealing with criminals can "rehabilitate" them and make them non-criminal and therefore productive members of society. The hope here is in a new praxis based on a new habit. The idea is to get criminals used to a non-criminal way of life through a benign and future-thinking time of imprisonment. Grace opposes rehabilitative justice because grace is skeptical of rehabilitation *in every case.* Grace exists from a theological anthropology that understands all humans to be

6. *A Woman in Berlin,* pp. 174-75.

caught up in prospective criminality, with no exceptions and no original sin/total depravity–free zones. We look for repair, we look for renewal, we look for redemption, but we do not envisage rehabilitation. To envisage rehabilitation would be to say that there was an earlier, pre-criminal "you" with whom you could connect and drive out the motives that prompted your crime. The pre-criminal "you" is purely conceptual. It does not exist.

A clergyman who has lived a truly sacrificial life of consecrated service over many decades once told me something apropos. He said that, as he celebrates the service of Holy Communion, a feeling sometimes comes over him that he should add a blasphemous obscenity to the prayer at the altar. He feels he is committing the sin "against the Holy Spirit" (Matthew 12:32; Mark 3:29; Luke 12:10) by even thinking this thought, and that doubles his anguish. The clear thought comes into his head sometimes, in a public act of worship, to say a phrase or two within the prayers that is obscene in the most shocking way. This man is a wonderful man and also in touch with these intrusive and surprising little compulsive thoughts. Everyone has experienced something similar.

How can he or I or anyone deal with such thoughts if we believe in a pre-criminal "me" or "you"? Such a person does not exist. If he or she did exist, we would only feel all the worse at the sudden impulses and cruel fantasies that we have at one time or another. Original sin and total depravity check the idea of "rehabilitation" and find it delusory. Thus this theology of grace of everyday life opposes retribution, deterrence, distribution, and rehabilitation in relation to punishments and rewards.

What Does Grace Affirm in Relation to Criminal Justice?

Grace affirms mercy, acquittal, and release. A positive system of grace in dispensing justice to criminals takes a line that deliberately blurs the distinction between the secular and the sacred. Opposing in principle all human efforts to dispense justice that are either deterrent, retributive, distributive, or rehabilitative, grace goes all the way in presenting an alternative to these efforts. Because this is a systematic theology of everyday life, it must be consistent. It cannot compartmentalize. It cannot be opposed to its own first principles. It is therefore controversial whenever it engages a concrete matter of life. Such a concrete matter is criminal justice. The controversy of grace is that it opposes what the world calls justice in its distribution of rewards and punishments.

Grace affirms mercy in the treatment of criminals. If it affirms mercy in the treatment of everyone in regular life, it must affirm mercy in the treatment of criminals. There is the principle of the first use of the law, which allows for some concessions to the law for the purpose of controlling chaos. But there must be no other concessions to the law beyond that very exploratory first use, for even deterrence is a weak idea. There is a stone carving on the outside nave wall of the Stiftskirche (i.e., Memorial Church) at Tübingen, Germany. It was carved during the Middle Ages and depicts the torture and execution of a criminal, who, it turned out, did not commit the crime for which he was punished. So appalled were the people of Tübingen by the knowledge that they had executed the wrong man that they commissioned this dramatic sculpture for the outside of the church, to be a reminder forever that deterrence by means of capital punishment could involve an irreversible mistake. Deterrence as a principle of criminal justice stands on shaky ground.

Grace, on the other hand, affirms mercy, acquittal, and release. It flies in the face of worldly wisdom and practice and is inevitably accused of antinomianism. Grace always tilts to the side of mercy for the criminal. It tends to relent, to dismiss charges, to look for merciful treatment, to stay the hand of the punisher and also the accuser. It will never rest with a statement like "three strikes and you're out" or "zero tolerance." Such maxims are inconsistent with grace in human affairs.

Do you remember when the Roman Catholic bishops in the USA declared that one case of sexual abuse on the part of a parish priest was sufficient to get him barred from the priesthood? That policy, which was a form of episcopal "damage control" in response to the clergy sexual-abuse scandals, was questioned by the Vatican, and also by one or two American bishops who could not square its terms with what Christ said when he spoke of forgiving your brother "seventy times seven" (Matthew 18:21-22). The policy of "zero tolerance" was a breathtaking contradiction to the historic teaching on all sides of the Christian church.

If I were to try to spell out in concrete terms the implications for criminal justice of "seventy times seven," this theology of everyday life would probably be considered a form of insanity! But Christianity has often been regarded as a form of insanity. When the hero of *The Pilgrim's Progress* awakened one morning and saw a burden on his back that no one else saw, he was immediately thought to be insane. Everyone in the town, the "City of Destruction," avoided the man, until finally he took off on his own to find a way to rid himself of his invisible, real burden.

The same phenomenon takes place whenever grace is lived and affirmed in practice. In practice, grace asserts the principles of mercy, acquittal, and release for criminals, preferring to stand with Paul, who wrote the following words: "Beloved, never avenge yourselves, but leave room for the wrath of God; for it is written, 'Vengeance is mine, I will repay, says the Lord'" (Romans 12:19; Deuteronomy 32:35). The establishing principles of a system of criminal justice founded on grace are mercy, acquittal, and release. Mercy means bending in the direction of compassion for the accused. Acquittal means bending toward the act of forgiveness, by which the accused's status is regarded as free from the external charge of wrongdoing. Release means bending toward the act of un-imprisoning the offender. To practice this in any systematic form would probably be considered insane.

A retrospective dimension to this thinking has to be mentioned. You see it at the end of Howard Hawks's movie *The Thing* (1951). A member of an Arctic research team has betrayed all his comrades and almost gotten them killed. At the end, as the formal report is being filed over a two-way radio, the reporter, Scotty, *covers over* the offense of the betrayer and writes him up as a hero. All the others who are listening say, "Way to go, Scotty." They agree with the imputation of guiltlessness to a man who had wronged them and had died wronging them.

This is acquittal. It often works retrospectively, but it is the only instrument by which the celebrated hope of "rehabilitation" ever takes place. Imagine the scientist who had betrayed his fellows in *The Thing* overhearing the report from Scotty the reporter. He is dead when he is acquitted. Now rewind in order for him to actually take in the power of what his colleagues have done. This is what converts a person. This is what creates decriminalization. It is the way forward for criminal justice.

Grace frames and practices criminal justice differently from the way of the world. When Christianity is vital, the released criminal is taken in and cared for by Christians. Complete release is the reality for which grace holds out.

At the point of mercy, theology is "situational" in the sense that it is worked out in the here and now rather than conceptually. When you think about grace in relation to criminal justice, don't get hung up envisioning the wholesale release of violent offenders or child-abusers. Grace expresses itself in many different ways within the concreteness of everyday life and personal history. Do you remember Jean Valjean? My plea for grace is not unique in the history of culture. Victor Hugo wrote *Les Miserables* (1862) as a hymn to grace in opposition to law. When, in the opening section of his book, Hugo describes the conversion of his hero Valjean, which results from Bishop Bienvenue's mercy, acquittal, and release of the apprehended thief caught in the act by the police, Hugo portrays a man whose crime has been covered over completely. Hugo even depicts Valjean after his conversion *doing it again!* Yes, one more time, Valjean commits an act of petty theft — against a child, no less. The crime occurs *after* his conversion and acquittal. Jean Valjean does it again. But after this second theft, for which he is not apprehended and for which he is not penalized, he is decisively and forever changed. He is the "new being" of the New Testament. That is the way criminal justice looks in the New Testament. Total mercy, complete exoneration, and unconditional release: those are the marks of grace in relation to criminal justice.

Grace in Relation to Social Class

The Universal Reach of Social Class

Hurricane Katrina raised an alarm in the United States of America. The storm uncovered a problem of social class, particularized in the form of race, which had been hidden just under the surface of everyday life.

The movie *Diary of a Mad Black Woman* came out in February 2005. Many African Americans saw the movie, but few white people saw it. When I peddled the movie in the talks and sermons I gave at the time, no one had seen it or heard of it. This was as true in Manhattan as it was in Minnesota. The subculture of that film, joined significantly to the black church, was invisible to white people. That culture has been, to use a contemporary phrase, "hiding in plain sight."

Hurricane Katrina blew the roof off the problem of race in America. Katrina almost touched off a collective nervous breakdown. It would be easy to wish to emulate the novelist Tom Wolfe at this point and try to be a social critic. The problem cries out for Wolfe's approach, or better, for the Gothic approach of Stephen King. This is because there is an ancient crime at the root of it,[7] and the Gothic undertones of what happened in New Orleans are easy to see. But this theology of grace in everyday life is not a work of social criticism. It is a theology of everyday life based on the consistent application of grace to all aspects of life.

What is the impact of grace on social class? What is the impact of grace on racial and ethnic thinking and on the concept of identity as rooted in ethnicity? Class and ethnicity are linked in practice. The prophet of inclusion, St. Paul, mentions them both in one famous breath: "There is no longer Jew or Greek, there is no longer slave or free, there is no longer male and female; for all of you are one in Christ Jesus" (Galatians 3:28). There Paul places ethnicity and race (Jew or Greek) in the same category as economic status and class (slave or free). He leaps to the further point of lumping "gender" with the other two conditions. He proposes the demolition of all three distinctions within what he calls the "body of Christ" (1 Corinthians 12:27), which is his phrase for the Christian church.

How does grace address the question of social class? First, grace exposes the deep stratum of class. Grace understands the appearance of social class in the world, and its enduring impact, as a symptom of original sin. The only way one can account for the impermeability of social class

7. See Stephen King's *Bag of Bones* (New York: Pocket Books, 1998) for a haunting portrayal of a New England town's guilt in relation to a long suppressed racial crime.

as a factor in the battle of life is to consider it under the rubric of intrinsic human nature.

Years ago, I began to notice the impermeability of social class in the Episcopal Church. It was a given that Episcopal ministers, even if they did not come by it "honestly" — by their schooling or upbringing — dressed out of Brooks Brothers; wore tweed jackets and grey flannel slacks in winter, seersucker jackets and khakis in summer; and understood themselves to be chaplains to the establishment. It was not that they especially desired this, or that they were not also capable of sincere concern for the poor. But they were ministers to the establishment in this country as surely as I am writing these words.

Years later, I was speaking at the National Cathedral in Washington and came up to a group of clergy, Episcopal "priests" as they now call themselves.[8] I witnessed something amazing. Now most of the clergy were female, not male; many male and female clergy were gay; some were black. There were few heterosexual white male clergy at all. One thing, however, had not changed. The ethos had not changed. All these priests were dressed out of Talbot's and Brooks Brothers. They were immaculately put together and thoroughly preppy, without a single exception. I had to think to myself: class still rules. These people are still the elite. Race seems to have faded in this context; "sexuality" is no longer an issue; and gender is longer a factor. But class still rules.

Does this take the grace of God by surprise? Fortunately not. The grace of God understands the human situation as so lost and self-serving, and also as so evenly self-deceived, that the persistence of at least one external symptom of original sin, when all others have supposedly been rectified, is no surprise. Hurricane Katrina uncovered this fact and in a less ironic form. The black people of New Orleans were invisible until the storm uncovered their need. It used to be common for people to go to New Orleans for a meeting or professional convention. They would take in the French Quarter and Antoine's, get in a horse-drawn buggy, enjoy a little

8. Until 1979, when a revised Prayer Book came into compulsory use, it was almost universal for Episcopal clergy to refer to themselves as "ministers." The exception to this was "Anglo-Catholics" or "High Church" clergy, who referred to themselves as "priests."

supposed relaxation in the midst of the conventions. But everybody who waited on these visitors, everyone who made up their rooms at the riverfront hotel, was amicably invisible. They were all black people. Underneath the attractive hedonism of the city was this enormous sore of forgottenness and need. Underneath everything was social class.[9]

Five days after Hurricane Katrina struck New Orleans on August 28, 2005, several hundred guests in the Hyatt Regency Hotel were rescued by a surfeit of buses, twice as many as were needed. Nearby, about 6,000 poor people were stuck in the New Orleans convention center. The Federal Emergency Management Agency (FEMA) did not know they were there. It was an astonishing chapter in the commentary on social class that the hurricane became.

A positive theology of grace in relation to social class is to some extent a theology of absence. This is because it is a polemic theology of negation. A positive theology of grace negates the principle of social class and cuts it off at the source. The source of social class is a stratum of original sin that is human power negatively applied. Grace becomes controversial and polemic in relation to social class. It marvels at the depth and intrinsic power of the corruption. Grace, which already obliterated the principle of all distinctions based on class, race, and sex, becomes militant.

Thus grace requires that "everything must go." The results of class power have to be questioned in relation to a theology of grace. When my wife and I were serving a parish in Westchester County, New York, in the 1980s, the car to drive was a Jeep Cherokee. This was the emblem for the upper middle class. I preached about it, in a light and almost ironic vein. In the late 1990s, we served an upper-middle-class parish in the Southeast, for which the Chevy Suburban was the emblem. I preached about it, too, in a light but somewhat more serious vein. People were conflicted about my critique. Some of them sold their cars, others just

9. Interestingly, the artful vampire movie *Dracula A.D. 2000* (2000) caught the problem quite precisely, although no one seems to remember it now. That "sleeper" hit depicted New Orleans as the natural target of a predatory vampire, who took advantage of the city's hedonism to wind his spell around the place. Only Jesus Christ, in the film's wildly unexpected conclusion, is sufficient to banish the Count from the Big Easy. See this movie and think about Katrina.

hoped they wouldn't run into their minister in the parking lot, and others became defensive and a little heated. No one really challenged my principle. Christianity is simply so clear on the principle of not laying up for ourselves "treasures on earth" (Matthew 6:19). The polemic dimension of grace is unavoidable in relation to social class. We are talking about a "fire sale," and grace is able to diagnose the universal hold of class and its emblems on all people. The positive alternative to social class and its emblems is something like a small car. It is something like a small house. It is something like a fairly uniform standard of living. It is a systematic skepticism concerning the things of this world.

In 1987 a short television play was produced in Hollywood entitled "The Card." In it, the main character, an upper-middle-class housewife with a Jeep Cherokee, three small children, and a successful and hard-working husband, acquires a credit card with a few important conditions. She fails to read the fine print. As she acquires a big new refrigerator and several beautiful things for the house, she runs up a debt on the card. At that point things around the house begin to disappear. First the cat goes, and then the dog. Then her children begin to vanish. In this authentically horrifying piece of television polemic, the woman finally grasps the principle to which her greed had blinded her. Her materialism, completely compulsive and overmastering, is wrecking her life. It is taking away everything and finally everyone who is important. At the end, as she herself, together with her house, disappears, we see the card, the deceiving credit card, resting untarnished on the empty lot where the woman and her family and her house used to be.

Social class and its concomitant materialism destroys people. It is a power that attaches itself to the whole human race. No one who has ever been born is exempt from the attraction of social class. As I witnessed at the Washington National Cathedral, it is a "principality and power" that transcends race and sexuality. Talbot's for all!

Grace carries this polemic word of judgment against the pull of class. It comes from John the Baptist:

> "You brood of vipers! Who warned you to flee from the wrath to come? Bear fruit worthy of repentance. Do not presume to say to yourselves,

> 'We have Abraham as our ancestor'; for I tell you, God is able from these stones to raise up children to Abraham. Even now the ax is lying at the root of the trees; every tree therefore that does not bear good fruit is cut down and thrown into the fire.
>
> "I baptize you with water for repentance, but one who is more powerful than I is coming after me; I am not worthy to carry his sandals. He will baptize you with the Holy Spirit and fire. His winnowing fork is in his hand, and he will clear his threshing floor and will gather his wheat into the granary; but the chaff he will burn with unquenchable fire." (Matthew 3:7-12)

Is there a word of comfort here? Is there anything more for us than a blast of scorching heat and obliteration? If we were to imagine a grace-affected *new* New Orleans, what would it resemble? What would the reconstructed city look like?

Or do we rest with David Brooks's words composed for *The New York Times* on September 4, 2005: "Midge Decter woke up in the morning after the night of looting during the New York blackout of 1977 feeling as if she had 'been given a sudden glimpse into the foundations of one's house and seen, with horror, that it was utterly infested and rotting away.'"

Grace Applied to Social Class

Two themes identify a theology of grace in application to social class. The first is what "liberation theologians" such as Gustavo Gutiérrez and Jürgen Moltmann call the "preferential option for the poor." A theology of grace is a theology of the cross rather than a theology of glory, and it looks for the opportunity of God in weakness rather than in strength. This proceeds from what has already been said. The *opus proprium,* or proper job, of God consists in his compassion toward need. God meets us at our point of need. When need is at its breaking point, that is God's point of entry.

The social implication of this is the "preferential option for the

poor." A theology of grace tilts
poor. The form of Christ's Beatitud
Gospel says, "Blessed are you who are
God" (6:20). No qualification is given,
spirit" (Matthew 5:3). Christ said simply, "Bl
The word "poor" may well cover a multitude
and of material things. But the reader is intended
in things has to be reckoned a part of this blank.

The victims of Hurricane Katrina were almost
The newspapers tried to say that they were "mostly" po
African American. But in fact nearly all were poor and th
whelmingly African American. The people who had cars and
cell phones and ATM cards and up-to-date records and the mu
tensions of white middle- and upper-middle-class life were able
bound. They knew how things are done! They knew about frequent-fl
miles and Delta Crown Rooms and getting their way. The African Ameri
cans of New Orleans were not a part of that lifestyle. It was the poor who were hardest hit.

From the perspective of grace, it was absolutely consistent and right that the poor in this material sense should be the focus of relief, at least from the heart. This is not to say that poor people are less affected by original sin and total depravity than the non-poor. The poor in New Orleans were also looters and rapists and takers of advantage. Original sin sits just as heavy on ghetto-dwellers as it does on the white-flight settlers of the suburbs.

A theology of grace invites a non-romanticized preferential option for the poor. The picture of this is probably something like a moderate, non-ideological, and non-utopian form of socialism. Has this sort of socialism ever been put together? People sometimes speak of New Zealand and Canada as if they have reached this goal. There is no less original sin in those two countries than there is in the USA. Certainly New Zealanders and Canadians can be as self-righteous as Americans. But the overall tilt, in terms of Christianity's response to the problem of social class, goes in the direction of social programs such as those of New Zealand and Canada.

ace in relation to
tood because the
love that omits
e idea of doing
l, love requires
one-way love
g for the sins
d be superfi-
original sin
inal sin of
he whole
he theol-
n of the
es no il-
out is not hesitant
mistake is made, if compassion
arding the malfeasance of the very persons to
stretching out its hand, then a high doctrine of the Holy Spirit
is able to take over. The Holy Spirit will make all things right, and the Holy Spirit will handle individual cases of injustice.

A theology of grace in practice is situational within the politics of economic life. In one situation it sees a hopeless housing project and bulldozes it, while anticipating a new and better block of apartments. In another context it sees a hopeless housing project and lets it go in order to help a less hopeless one. A theology of grace in practice may vote for a "liberal Democrat" in a ward full of self-protecting, upper-middle-class white people. Or it may vote for the least self-protecting "conservative Republican" in the hopes that she can actually make a difference with her constituents. A "Mayor Bloomberg" might be right for New York City even if he is one of the wealthiest citizens of a city that is overwhelmingly and extremely poor, while a "Mayor Dinkins" might be wrong for the very same city, even if he represents most of the population. Or it could go the other way.

A theology of grace in practice is situational even as it is always attracted to the weaker and the less "in control." A theology of grace is non-romanticized, anti-ideological, generally socialist, ready to switch political horses (it is never "yellow dog" Democrat or "rock ribbed" Republican), and utilitarian in most cases, providing the theology of the cross is in steady, definite, and articulate antithesis to the theology of glory. These are the predicates for grace in relation to social class.

Grace at the Mall

Grace at the shopping mall takes the form of what the world is now calling "Luddite-ism." This is a term from early nineteenth-century England, where workers known as "Luddites" smashed Industrial Age machines that were stealing their livelihood. Today anyone who resists new technologies and their wide effects is known as a "Luddite." Such people are thought of as resisters of progress who act from a conservative loyalty to the old economy.

Grace is "Luddite" in relationship to the shopping mall. The anthropology of grace considers human beings to be extremely vulnerable to the lure of possessions. If there is one thing certain about human nature, it is its disposition to be dazzled by and attracted to things. Things become idols, substitutes for God, and in this case they are not straw men. Things possess inexhaustible appeal for human beings, and enough is never enough. We all know this.

The biblical authors would have had no question in their minds that the consumerism embodied in the *Dawn of the Dead* shopping malls that stretch from Danbury, Connecticut, to Dhaka, Bangladesh, is a Dagon (Judges 16:23) of the greatest negative significance. Jews of the Old Testament and Christians of the New Testament can be utterly one in their repulsion from these ziggurats of hypnotic power. At best they should be dismantled as *bad medicine.*

Grace is Luddite in relationship to the mall. We understand the power of the seduction. We also understand the lack of "free will" that most people experience in relation to material things. *South Park* captured the bondage to things as a form of primary hypnosis in the 2005 episode entitled "Something Wall-mart This Way Comes." In this segment, the *South Park* boys join their entire town in being drawn at all times, and especially late at night when they think everyone else is asleep, to the new "Wall-mart" outside of town. A binding power pulls everybody into the store. Finally, one of the boys, the one with a little moral grit, makes the effort to discover the secret of the "Wall-mart." He is told to go to the back of the store and open a tiny door. It takes him ages to get there, past all the zombified people and the mountains of discounted toilet paper. When he finally opens the door and learns the secret of "Wall-mart," it turns out to be a mirror! That's all it is: a plain mirror.

Because the theological anthropology of grace is so low, we are not made speechless or undone by this. Human nature drives the mall, it feeds it and extends it, and it finally lies exhausted in the rubble of things that cannot satisfy. If ever there were an axiomatic principle of grace in relation to everyday life, it would be this: destroy the mall if you can; stay away if you cannot; and contest commercialism in a systematic and finally ideological way. Grace applied to the mall is one of the very few issues within this systematic theology of everyday life for which there is an ideological and non-situational result.

Do you remember a *Twilight Zone* episode entitled "The After Hours"? You have probably seen or heard of it at some point in your life. It tells the story of Marcia, a young woman who is strangely drawn to a downtown department store and cannot bring herself to leave when it closes. She is drawn to it but also wants to escape it. It turns out that she is a mannequin who has outlived her allotted month on the outside and is resisting her return. It is a quirky, haunting piece.

In 1987 "The After Hours" was remade. It was remade as a send-up of '80s mall culture in which the "draw" was the pure power of the mall atmosphere. It actually shows Marcia turning into plastic! The feel is completely different from the original. The "tractor beam" of the mall, the seduction of the glass elevators and the bright lights, makes the story real and apt.

It is surprising that in this particular case, the case of commercialism and materialism, a theology of grace should sound such a definite and exception-less note. There is no "nuance" here. The word is prophetic and hastening. The mall must go.

The mall must go for two reasons. First, the mall is an obvious idol that swallows young people. It is more appealing to teenagers than it is even to adults. Consider the plight of security guards in malls. Malls are packed, especially on weekend afternoons, with throngs of teenagers. In inner-city malls there is danger in the air. Beatings and muggings take place, so the security guards are everywhere. Now here is a place that is completely designed to bring out the most self-serving emotions possible, and yet guards have to be hired in phalanxes in order to keep enough control so the show can go on.

One recent evening, I witnessed a young black girl being beaten by fifteen other black girls on the main concourse of the downtown mall in Columbus, Ohio. The ubiquitous security guards were not present, but eventually twelve of them came tearing down the main aisle. The loud beating had interrupted the performance of their main duty, which was to chase away any "Marcias" from staying past their time.

The mall is a molten idol to whose flames the young offer themselves freely. A theology of grace turns its back on the mall. Christian people are just as vulnerable to its tractor beam as non-Christian people. No one is immune. If you spend any time at all in the "suburban happy land" of the mall, you start to feel depressed and unclean. The next time you look up, a new mall has suddenly sprung up on the next hill. And the access routes to the new mall are increasingly complex and hard to navigate.

The second reason the mall must go, from the standpoint of a theology of grace, is that it captures boldly and explicitly the continuing original sin and total depravity that exist below (and above) the surface in all people. The mall *activates* original sin and total depravity to a high degree.

As this theology attempts to show, popular movies and television often tell the truth in ways that moralists and preachers do not or cannot. An episode of a morbid television show titled *Friday the Thirteenth: The Series* emanating from Canada (1987-1990) portrayed this activation grimly. The episode was called "Mesmer's Bauble." In "Mesmer's Bauble," a pimpled, "nerdy" young man was sold a piece of fake jewelry that turned out to be cursed. He was entranced by this piece of red artificial glass. All he could do was hold it in front of his eyes and stare into it, all the time. Gradually it provided him with everything he wanted, which turned out to be the body and life of a girl rock-and-roll singer whom he adored. The hypnotic bauble gave him the apparent ability to have her, with predictably vicious consequences.

Similarly, Stephen King's novel *Needful Things* presents the devil on an extended visit to a small town in Maine. The devil, who takes the form of a kindly gentleman from Old Europe, sets up a little shop on the main street. One by one, his window draws in the residents of the town, who find that this shopkeeper is able to provide them with the material object of their dreams, the possession of which destroys every last one of them.

Most telling for people like me who are professional Christians is the communion chalice that the devil "sells" to the local Catholic priest. It is a fine silver cup with inset stones and detailed carving. The priest is dazzled and ends up sitting by the altar of his church, night and day, staring at this "beauty of holiness." All the time he is focused on this refined ecclesiastical object, the priest's parishioners grow more deeply into their bondages, which results in almost everyone in the town being murdered by his or her own neighbor. Stephen King took his title *Needful Things* directly from Christ's mention of "the one thing needful" (Luke 10:42), which Mary chose in contrast to her busy sister Martha. The need of the "needful things" in King's novel only destroys. The "one thing needful," the grace of God, eludes everyone in the town.

The mall is the crematorium of the young and the beguiler of all. It is a victorious phenomenon to be resisted to the last drop of blood. A systematic theology of grace is absolute in the case of the mall. It is consistent in its seeing the entire enterprise as a graven seduction. Just as this theology opposes the use of war *in every case,* it opposes the construction of malls *in every case.* One can imagine the construction of a "mall" that buys and sells in a normal and necessary way. One can imagine instances of a market that buys and sells, provides, and distributes. But the mall as we now know it is the "green tree" under which the firstborn of the Canaanites were sacrificed.

Thirty years ago my wife and I visited the ancient town of Dan in Israel. It was not a fancy archaeological site but was then rather overgrown and hard to get around. We were told to look for the "tell," the elevated site on which acts of worship had been performed and where we would find the extant remains of the ancient horned altar. My wife found the tell. As we gathered around it to hear an explanation from our tutor, an English Old Testament scholar, we heard the story of what had once been done on the tell, before the religion of Israel had prevented it. We heard about human sacrifice, and the sacrifice of firstborn children. I thought of the many thousands of infant skeletons — human infant skeletons — that have been found at Carthage, where the countrymen of Hannibal created a religion of child sacrifice. And here it all was, high on the tell at Dan.

How can this theology of the one-way love of God in the grace of Christ take such a hard line on a social and economic issue? We are absolutely clear on the "seventy times seven" essence of the grace of God. We are also clear that original sin and total depravity do not respond for a second to the law or to "preaching" in the negative sense of the word. Our theology understands the bondage of the human being and the powerful force of human compulsion. We also understand this compulsion to be spread as evenly among believers in God and Christians as it is among non-believers and non-Christians. Our anthropology is low.

So what is the origin and the enabling principle of consistent judgments on phenomena such as capital punishment, war, and the malls of America? The origin of these judgments is the fruit of the Spirit: "love, joy, peace, patience, kindness, generosity, faithfulness, gentleness, and self-control" (Galatians 4:22). They flow directly from the character of grace-full loving. They see destruction and law, compulsion and aggression, in the obvious evils of these three things.

Simultaneously, we are not surprised at the persistence of these evils. I am not joining the anarchists who throw bottle rockets and smash windows when the G8 meet. I do not believe for a minute that war and capital punishment and the mall can be obliterated from the earth. Yet Christians are hopeful that they can be lessened and their influence diminished. These are hurtful, not needful, things, and they require opposition.

Such opposition is a fruit of the Spirit, the consequence of grace. It is the unpopularity of the prophet, and a polemic toward the Pharisees. This grace-full opposition is not ideology, because it holds out no hope in human terms for its own completed work. It is persistent opposition to what kills, an opposition that flourishes in the name of one-way love. It is also undeterred by its incompleteness. It is not laboring under a false view of people. It beholds the bondages that permit no escape.

CHAPTER FIVE

Grace in the Church

Grace in Church Politics

I have no ecclesiology. "Ecclesiology" is a word that means doctrine of the church. An "ecclesiology" is a teaching or concept concerning the Christian church: what it is, what it consists of, what is important in it, and how it relates to other ideas about the church. When I say, "I have no ecclesiology," I am not really saying that. I am simply saying that "ecclesiology" is unimportant to me. It is low on my list of theological values.

Why Is Ecclesiology Unimportant?

Ecclesiology is unimportant for two reasons. The first reason is positive: the other themes of Christianity are infinitely more important than the "church idea." No one has ever awakened in the middle of the night anxious about ecclesiology per se. You may wake up worried about your child or upset about something someone said to you during the day. But you never wake up worried about your concept of church. This lets us know that ecclesiology is a secondary value, at most, in human life, and in Christian engagement with human life. You worry about guilt; you dread certain things. But you never worry about ecclesiology. Ecclesiology is therefore unimportant because other things are more important, such as the saving inherent in the Christian drama and the poignancy of life in relation to loss.

Ecclesiology is also unimportant for a negative reason. Ecclesiology is an actual ill! By definition it places the human church in some kind of special zone — somehow distinct from real life — that appears to be worthy of study and attention. The underlying idea is that the church is in a zone that is free, or at least more free, from original sin and total depravity than the rest of the world, but the facts prove otherwise. The facts of history run counter to ecclesiology. They reveal a grim ersatz thing carrying the image of Christ but projected onto human nature and therefore intrinsically self-deceived. The gospel of grace, based on relational love that is entirely one-way, is at odds with ecclesiology. Whatever "ecclesiology" comes in the train of grace is variable, secondary, contextual, and contingent. It varies hugely with local circumstances and needs, and it cannot be universalized.

I was talking with a Swiss church historian several years ago. He was gruff and rough-edged, as Swiss people can be. He told me that he had left the official church (the Reformed Church of Zürich) and was on neither its tax rolls nor its membership rolls. That sounded harsh, so I asked, Why? He answered me, "The church here has long lost the fire of Zwingli and his justification by grace of sinners. It cares only for its own survival, so I am done with it."

At that time in my theological development, I would not have gone so far. Nor would I go so far today. Yet the wind of grace blows in that direction. This is because grace-based people are focused more on salvation and the problem of being human than they are on any institution, especially on an institution that evinces amnesia about its origin. You can see why Luther found himself, despite himself, protesting the church. Read "The Grand Inquisitor" parable from *The Brothers Karamazov;* almost everyone you know can identify with Fyodor Dostoevsky's view of "church."

Emil Brunner's little-read book *The Misunderstanding of the Church* (1953) is a devastating critique of the idea of church. Brunner can find almost no evidence in the New Testament for anything like what many

Christians consider to be the church. For Brunner, the New Testament describes a fluid and Holy Spirit–filled movement of people gathered together within an experience of God that involves massive individual changes of plan. There is a collective dimension to this: all the early Christians experienced the same thing. Like alien abductees, the first Christians had a shattering experience in common. This brought them together. But this experience was not an institution.

To Have No Ecclesiology Is to Have an Ecclesiology

To say we have no ecclesiology is not just a negation. *To have no ecclesiology is to have an ecclesiology.* What sort of ecclesiology is this? It is a noble one. It puts first things first. It puts Christ over the human church. It puts what Christ taught and said over the church. It puts grace over the church. It puts Christ's saving work and the acute drama of the human predicament over the church. It puts the human hope of change over the church. It places the Holy Spirit over the church.

Not long before he died, a retired presiding bishop of the Episcopal Church said something memorable in this vein. Presiding Bishop John Allin said, "I regret that for much of my ministry I put the church over her Lord." The problem of "ecclesiology" is that it — like the bejeweled, beguiling, silver communion chalice in Stephen King's *Needful Things* — has a false brightness, the shine of fool's gold. The human church evokes an aesthetic as well as a controlling or *handling* spirit in its admirers. In this controlling, handling spirit, they lose the one thing needful, which is the grace of Christ.

The controlling spirit affects both those on the Catholic side of Christianity and those on the Reformed or Genevan side. On the Catholic side, the church becomes the source of authority. We need an authority to tell us how to live and think, and a central church institution gives us that. On the Reformed or Genevan side, the church becomes the source of pure doctrine. The church tells us how to think and how to live, and a "teaching" church gives us this. In both cases, it is all about law. Not much grace comes through, and even less of the Holy Spirit.

Having no ecclesiology is to possess a proper ecclesiology. Whatever form an emerging church takes, it cannot be dried for observation. It is a pneumatic, Spirit-led movement, always, like mercury in motion. Church is flux. A systematic theology of grace puts church in its right place. Church is at best the caboose to grace. It is its tail. Ecclesiology, on the other hand, makes church into the engine.

The Impact of Grace on Church

Given this weighting of "church," how does grace criticize and amend church? What is the impact of grace on church?

Its impact is considerable. One way of putting forward an ecclesiology of negation would be to entitle it an ecclesiology of suspicion. Because we believe in the depth of sin and in the impossibility, until death, of any "original sin–free zone" in the world, we are skeptical of any church idea that ascribes to church a distinctive authority or requirement that it be obeyed. A systematic theology of grace is, in respect to church, irreducibly Protestant. The Protestantism of grace's church idea, which is church by negation and church from suspicion, is important for all Christians to come up against, because it delivers them from the skepticism and finally the voluntary abandonment to which all church fealty finally leads when the lights go on.

In one sense, this theology is "culturally Christian" rather than "church Christian," because it is skeptical of the exemption that Christian churches have usually argued for themselves from the pull and taint of the world. The observation of churches, from Orthodox to Roman Catholic to mainline Protestant to evangelical and Pentecostal Protestant, always ends in disappointment. I repeat: *the observation of churches always ends in disappointment.*

Moreover, as Brunner demonstrated in his neglected masterpiece (unarguably, if you take the time to read the book), the church of the New Testament is a charismatic movement, twisting and pulling. It is subject to no one's possession. The church of the New Testament is a tornado movement. If you plot the history of revival and renewal in

Christianity all through the world, you see the same thing. It "touches down" in England with George Whitefield and John Wesley, then in Northern Ireland in 1859, then in East Africa during the 1930s. It touches down in the black slave population of the United States almost from their first involuntary steps there. The "touch down" is not entirely quixotic, for it must be preached from and to weakness; it must be in touch with the grace of absolution without conditions; and it usually springs from "the least of these" (Matthew 25:40).

As a thirty-year veteran of political wars in the Episcopal Church, I have been forced to think a lot about "church." It is a clammy and betraying kind of an entity on its own terms. "Church" is a tank that rolls over rank upon rank of its servants. There is an old allegorical painting entitled *The Conquerors.* It depicts Napoleon, Alexander the Great, Genghis Khan, Pompey, and a few others riding toward the viewer on beautiful white horses. Underneath the hoofs of these white chargers are dead bodies, hundreds and thousands of dead bodies, stacked like the bodies in a photograph from a concentration camp. In my opinion, it is not too strong to say that the church, as a human institution, treads over its servants in its "original sin–free zone" of self-protection and its possession of full rights and privileges. The visual image of *The Conquerors* is not too strong. This is why I am a traditional churchman, Episcopal in this case, only by chance — biographical chance — and not by conviction. Those Christians I know who are churchmen by conviction are skating on the thinnest of ice in light of history and in light of the Bible. Churchmen desired the death of Jesus (Matthew 27:1-2; Mark 15:1-4; Luke 23:1-5).

This applies to the Reformed side of Christianity as well as to the Catholic. A very Reformed Presbyterian theologian told me once that Presbyterian church government is mandated in the New Testament. I asked him to cite me the best example of this. He said, "The Sanhedrin, in the Gospels. The Sanhedrin, the temple consistory. It was a piece of pure Presbyterianism." I was speechless. Did he remember what the Sanhedrin did?!

The negation of ecclesiology explicit in this theology of grace puts the protagonists of grace in a powerless position in relation to the human politics of churches. It puts the protagonists of grace in the loser's position immediately, and places them at the mercy of the victors. There are numberless examples of the *de iure* loss to which believers in grace are exposed and which they suffer. The famous martyrdoms of Christianity are obvious examples. The theme here, however, is the martyrdoms to which believers in grace are exposed because of their negative ecclesiology, *from the church*. Joan of Arc is a more instructive case. George Bernard Shaw called Saint Joan "one of the first Protestant martyrs."[1] When proponents of a zero ecclesiology run up against the proponents of a high ecclesiology, the former are ground into the dust.

An instructive case of this suffering, a case of active engagement and after-the-fact reflection on the part of this author, and the case I know best, has occurred in relation to the loss of status on the part of the "orthodox" or "conservative" minority of the Episcopal Church in relation to the struggle over human sexuality. The case has had a high profile. The interest of it here is not in the issue of Christian social ethics that precipitated it, but in the political defeat of a minority by a majority in an institutional church, and the way this defeat played out. No mercy was given. The result was total loss and splitting.

This is what happened. A victory in the form of a political vote was won, and the winning group was unable to assure the losers that a place would remain for dissidents within a comprehensive church. The minority appealed to the majority for "space" or toleration: a place of safety, a "no-fly" sector within the American Episcopal Church. This was not granted, and the spin-out of the long process of applications for such a place of safety is a paper trail worthy of study. But the victors, to whom the losers constantly appealed, did not give grace. Formal concession was never granted. The result of this was a species of martyrdom for "conservative" Episcopalian Christians. The formal result was a long-term hemorrhage, and the end of what had once been an uneasy but official unity.

There are many instances in the history of Christianity of such a disillusioning turn on the part of the formal church. What happened in the

1. George Bernard Shaw, "Preface to *Saint Joan*," *Saint Joan* (Baltimore: Penguin, 1966), p. 7.

Episcopal Church was the turn of the "victors" in the direction of church law to establish their "victory," and the complete rout of the losers. It was all law, in other words. Traditionalists had argued that their political loss within the Episcopal Church could become the occasion of a powerful grace if the victors could give them some ground. I myself talked about Abraham Lincoln's views of Southern "Reconstruction" after the Civil War, for which he was prepared to give enormous concessions in the interests of long-term reconciliation. I spoke of concessions given by Northern Irish Protestants to their Catholic neighbors, concessions I had witnessed and actually participated in directly, as models of grace that might be offered from winners to losers. I quoted the "Christ hymn" of Paul's letter to the Philippians (2:5-11), the "ground-zero" text in Paul concerning the humiliation of the victor in favor of the losers. I pleaded with the victors in the church battle to follow suit. These examples, right down to the last one, were disregarded. The result was the exodus of "traditional" Episcopalians from an institutional church they had loved and thought they knew.

Grace in church politics is a "losing" proposition by definition. It is a losing proposition because it is solid with Calvary and the historic loss of all things undertaken by the Founder of the religion. If you have a "zero-sum" ecclesiology, then you are safe from disillusionment with the core of the movement that predated and "founded" the visible church. If you have a higher ecclesiology than this, you will eventually go the way of atheists, for whom disenchantment with the church means disenchantment with God. A theology of grace, with its ecclesiology of suspicion, is the tonic and antidote to the church behaving badly.

I can write this in my own blood. Disenchantment with my own branch of the institution has not affected my conviction that Christ is the light of the world and that God's grace is the way of human freedom. Had the ecclesiology of grace been higher than the anthropology of original sin and total depravity permitted it to be, the result of the loss of the Episcopal Church would have been a loss of hope in God. The negation of ecclesiology from grace permits the survival of faith in Christ as the Wound of the world to stitch the wounds of the world.

Grace in the Pulpit

One-way love takes aim from the pulpit with a flagrant strategy of demolition: "I'm a steamroller, baby" (James Taylor). Anything short of a killing yet accurate anthropology fails to make contact with listeners of any kind, believers as well as non-believers. Anything short of blood-substitution is insufficient to bring healing.

It is easy to swing out at the hortatory and defeating sermons one normally hears in almost all sectors of Christianity. They are a non-moving target. I hear them almost every Sunday, and, as a seminary dean, on most days of the week. The sermons I usually hear are long and inaccessible stacks of Bible verses tied together by a so-called "expository" method, with little of the preacher's own struggles in evidence. They appear to instruct but carry little impact. These are often sermons in the Reformed tradition.

Other sermons I hear are strings of *Reader's Digest*–type anecdotes that probably aren't true but carry a theme of goodwill. Other sermons, especially in the Episcopal Church, have to do with society's issues and problems, but they tire out the poor congregation with lists of worthy things to do that they have not done.

Every so often you hear a sermon that connects with your actual struggles. Bishop T. D. Jakes of the Potter's House in Dallas almost always connects with his hearers, black and white, female and male, poor and rich. Bishop Jakes talks about real things. There are a few others like Bishop Jakes, but you will search in vain, from Sunday to Sunday, in most cities and towns.

The fundamental problem is the same everywhere. You hear the law and not the gospel. What you hear, if you distill the many words, is always the same: Here is what you should do, you are not doing it, so get out there and try harder. This is the "three-point sermon" of the churches. I sometimes suggest to clergy that they carve over the main door to the church the following words: "Abandon hope, all ye who enter here." If you are looking for comfort and release, you had better hold *that* hope until you leave church. From the pulpit, what you are likely to get is the law.

It is easy to tax the churches and their preachers with the exhorting and depressive substance of their sermons week to week. The situation is that bad and that widespread. But there really is another way. What is the meaning of grace for the pulpit?

A Personal History of Grace

In the first place, preachers require a history of grace in relation to their own personal sin and sorrows. Unless preachers have individual knowledge of their own form of original sin and total depravity, they have nothing to offer to which anyone else can relate. Grace has to be the core of preachers' own story in order for their sermons to carry any impact. If this is not so, they will preach the law and exhort. Then they will become angry at their own dispirited and paralyzed listeners. Ministers who start to despise their own congregations — and many do — do so because "their" people are not doing what the minister is telling them to do. The minister assumes they have "free will" because he thinks he does. Therefore, when they exercise their "freedom" in the direction of not doing what he preaches, he starts to dislike them.

This drama is repeated in churches of every type across the country, Sunday after Sunday. I once asked Jürgen Moltmann what happens when a pastor preaches the law on Sunday morning. He answered, "Schwierigkeiten Sonntag Nachmittag" (difficulties Sunday afternoon). Herr Moltmann meant this two ways: The pastor will know that he has preached demand rather than comfort and he will not be able to nap; *and* the people, without knowing it, will be walking around in a mild state of depression for the rest of the day.

Preachers need a history of grace in relation to their own individual sin. This is the thing that qualifies them to speak to sufferers. The English novelist George Eliot published a novelette in 1858 titled "Janet's Repentance." It was part of her first book, *Scenes of Clerical Life*. In it, her genius, which had departed from the evangelical religion of her youth, nevertheless understood the dynamic of grace in Christian ministry. She wrote her novelette about a Church of England minister named Edgar Tryan, who is evangelical in theology and therefore controversial in the small village where he has come to serve. Mr. Tryan is young and zealous, and he riles quite a few of his staid and "culturally Christian" parishioners. But he preaches grace from the pulpit, and gradually one after another person is converted to his "born again" version of belief. This all takes place in the 1820s.

Mr. Tryan's greatest success, however, is the impact of his words and his life on the young wife, Janet Dempster, of an abusive drunk. Janet is in complete despair, and Mr. Tryan sees immediately into her situation. When she is beaten one night and seeks help from him, he ends up telling her his own story. He describes how he seduced and then abandoned a young girl in the city of Cambridge, where he was a student. Later he discovered that the girl had died after going into a life of prostitution. It was his fault. This sin, forgiven by the grace of Christ, is what led Mr. Tryan to enter the ministry. He tells his story, briefly but leaving out nothing important, to Janet.

She now realizes that she is not alone in her plight and in her sorrows. As a result, Janet is converted. Her husband dies of complications relating to alcoholism, and so does Mr. Tryan, who has contracted tuberculosis partly through overwork. The point is simple: grace to Mr. Tryan becomes grace to Janet Dempster. He would have had nothing to say to her plight if he had not had an answered plight of his own. The first point of grace in the pulpit is personal experience of grace on the part of the preacher.

Humor in the Pulpit

Another indispensable aspect of grace as applied to the pulpit is humor. Humor is a vital part of the theology of the cross, which is the blood of Christ de-mystified and connected to real things. Humor is an embodiment of humility, because it demystifies human importance and transfers this importance to God. Humor in the pulpit says that the preacher takes his or her own role with a grain of salt. It also lowers the walls of denial that people bring to any form of public address and builds up what we today call the "comfort level."

A contemporary example is the plays and movies of Tyler Perry. When you see a Tyler Perry play, and you have been warned that it is a "Christian" play, you at first cannot see the Christian aspect. The humor, almost always involving a female character named "Madea," played by Perry himself, goes on and on. It is broad and boisterous. But it serves to soften up the audience. After twenty minutes or so of slapstick and even vulgar hilarity on stage, Perry uses a plot device to get himself off the stage. He arranges for something to happen that removes him physically from the stage. *Then* the tragic and also the grace-full issues that are the pumping heart of what the play is really about come to the fore. They come to the fore so directly and with so little segue or mediation that you move from laughter to tears in about twenty seconds.

Humor plays two roles in the pulpit. First, humor deconstructs the preacher. He or she is just a fool and martinet and narcissist like everybody else. The preacher needs humor for the sake of humility. This is a requirement for speaking the gospel. Second, humor takes down the defenses of the listener. When you laugh, you are then ready to cry. Your emotions are working. Humor is part of the "heavy lifting" of preaching.

Knowledge of the Difference between the Law and the Gospel

The preacher is required to know the difference between the law and the gospel. If the sermon ends in ethics, if its "application" (a word that needs to be avoided in sermons) or "bottom line" amounts to something that I should do, it is a sermon of law and not of grace.

You can pick up the difference between law and grace in the body language of the listeners on a Sunday morning. My job places me in a different church almost every Sunday, where I am often listening and not speaking. Most Sunday mornings I can actually see the congregation moving west, that is, away from the pulpit and altar, during the sermon! What I mean is that the body language of the people as they listen to the "challenge" of the sermon shows me they are heading for the door, at least in their hearts and minds. I want to go with them.

Whenever you hear a preacher invoking concepts like "accountability" or "discipleship," you can be sure you are hearing the law. Whenever you feel comforted or elated or absolved or "fresh as a foal in new mown hay," then you know you are hearing the gospel.

The Necessity of Illustrations

The Sunday sermon must be heavy on illustrations. When you attend church services in Britain and Europe, you almost never hear an illustration. You hear quite a few conceptual and scriptural propositions, and possibly — but rarely — a literary allusion. Over the thirty years or so that my wife and I have listened to sermons in England, Switzerland, and Germany, I think we have heard maybe five actual illustrations from everyday life, and perhaps two from the preacher's experience of life.

The illustration *earths* the concept. What the illustration does is connect to common experience. This is why Christ used parables. He was seeking to offer access points to his listeners, most of whom were farmers, shepherds, and fishermen. The parable was Christ's approach to the illustration.

Incidentally, one of the most successful sermon illustrations in history is the prophet Nathan's story of the ewe lamb (2 Samuel 12:1-15), which he told to King David after David had committed adultery with Bathsheba and arranged to have her husband killed. Nathan "got through" to David because he distanced his message to David in the form of a common story, and then, by the Holy Spirit and a very few timely words, made the connection. Without the sermon illustration, the sermon is just a form of words.

Brevity in the Pulpit

Another *sine qua non* of grace in the pulpit is brevity. This is important. The reason most sermons are too long is that they are exercises in narcissism on the part of the preacher. A current label for original sin is one used increasingly by psychotherapists to give words to what their patients are encountering in everyday relationships gone wrong: "Narcissistic Personality Disorder." I laughed when I first heard that one! Is it really a "disorder"? Or is it original sin?

The point is that many pulpit performances on Sunday mornings are exercises in what is now called "NPD." This is the real reason why many sermons are too long. In the first place, preachers may carry so much need to express themselves for the sake of self-expression that they do not focus their thoughts into a straight line. Everything becomes discursive and non-linear. "It's all about me." Or preachers may just "like to preach." They like being up front and being the "star," so by definition the longer the "star turn" the better.

Students and candidates for jobs in ministry sometimes come to me to be interviewed. When I ask them what they like to do best in ministry, some of them say, "I like to preach." Immediately my inner thoughts rule them out as far as the job is concerned. What they are saying is, "I like to be the star of the show." Who doesn't? Have you been to an audition in New York City lately? Who does not wish to be the star? For this to be the motive in preaching is death. Preachers who feel this way and think this way preach long sermons.

Sermons should be brief. When the message of grace is being channeled through a normal human instrument, it is best when it is brief: a minimum of ten minutes and a maximum of twenty. This has everything to do with the humility and the grace-full deference of the preacher.

Grace Is Not Expository

Grace in the pulpit is not expository. This sounds like a technical point, but it has become important in contemporary Christian perspective. Conservative or "orthodox" Christians are in search of interpretive tools for Scripture that do not depend on "liberal" criticism of the text, but rather allow the Bible to speak for itself. Reacting against the dominant schools of biblical interpretation or "hermeneutics," as it is now called, which seek to subdue the Bible by means of an interpretive matrix, conservative or "traditional" Christians want an approach that lets the Bible speak on its own terms. This is to the good. It is a listening approach, a receptive one.

The problem is that the whole evangelical Christian world seems to have fled to the *Reformed* version of hermeneutics. The Reformed version wants to see each verse of the Bible as being of equal weight and value. What the Reformed do is to take the Scripture verse by verse, even word by word, in the belief that the cumulative effect will amount to something powerful and transforming. The idea is that detailed treatment of every single verse, which checks the verse against all other parallel or comparable verses of the Bible and tries to get the meaning right using cross-comparison, will carry an incremental power that transforms.

There may be a few "expository" preachers who are able to do this and pull it off with connecting effect. But most of the time, the effect is dry. The Bible *in itself* needs a listener. It needs contact. It is not a thing to enjoy in itself. Nothing is to be enjoyed in itself. Things and beings can be enjoyed only in relation. The Bible needs a listener who is hearing and understanding. The Bible and the listener need an interpreter. In the book of Acts, the Ethiopian eunuch is reading a passage from the prophet Isaiah but does not understand what he is reading. He requires an interpreter. Fortunately, Philip overhears, and Philip becomes the man's interpreter (Acts 8).

The Bible is not the Qur'an. It should not be reified. It is the Word of grace to a respondent, to the passive listener to which the Word speaks. The preacher is not a reader of the Bible in a public place. The preacher is the interpreter bearing the Word of biblical one-way love to the listener. Scripture stands over the preacher but also depends upon the preacher.

Grace in the Pulpit as Interpretation

What does it mean to be an interpreter and not an expositor? Grace in the pulpit is interpretation, not exposition. This is because the listener to Scripture is a listener to life, and life breathes condemnation. People *hear* judgment. I have already observed the common fact that we are so susceptible to judgment that we infer it. We infer it everywhere and in everything. The word of grace is the opposite of judgment and thus the opposite of what we are accustomed to hear.

Therefore, grace in the pulpit has to interpret the Bible and not simply expound it. There is a riveting theme in Scripture, from Genesis to Revelation, of God's *proper* work of one-way love. But it is sometimes concealed within the *alien* work of dismantling and deconstruction. In other words, there is law, which is demolition, and there is grace, which is lifting up. This dialogue between two words, the second of which is always superior and conclusive, is almost omnipresent in the Bible. But it requires interpretation. Exposition alone is not enough. The grace theme requires discovery and unveiling. It is not automatically discerned. This is why St. Paul made such a point concerning preachers in Romans: "How are they to believe in one of whom they have never heard? And how are they to hear without someone to proclaim him?" (10:14).

Grace in the pulpit will absolve and strengthen the drooping spirit. Law in the pulpit will depress the already depressed and send them along their way with nothing but the unconscious resolution not to return. Grace in the pulpit will make you laugh and cry in the same proportion. Law will make you ask yourself why you ever came to church this Sunday. Grace in the pulpit will elicit things inside you that you did not know you had. Law will suppress what little you think you did have and shrink you down to the size of a microbe. Grace will draw you out to see the Big Story. Law will make you want to retreat to your small unfocused impressions of daily general discontent.

In short, grace will grow the fruits of love and extension, while law will stunt you and hold you in. Grace in the pulpit, aided by grace in pastoral care and grace in prayer, is the secret of church growth. Keep your ecclesiology running at a steady zero, and your ministry may just have a chance.

Grace in Pastoral Care

The main feature of pastoral care rooted in grace is *non-proactivity*. This is another way of saying that the main feature of pastoral care rooted in grace is passivity. Grace in pastoral care eschews control and acts out of response rather than action. This means that pastoral care from grace consists mostly of listening and watching.

Two symbols of pastoral care are decisive. The first symbol of pastoral care is the three monkeys who see no evil, hear no evil, and speak no evil. God sees, hears, and speaks everything. Nothing eludes God: no data, no motives, no skulking. But God *imputes* good, "seeing" good, "hearing" good, and "speaking" good. Pastoral care is exactly this, a kind of full-time life of encouragement to the world, which ordinarily hears defeating judgments.

The second symbol of pastoral care, and one that bears the same idea, is Mr. Magoo, the cartoon character. Mr. Magoo walks through life blind, or rather extremely near-sighted. All around him, terrible things are happening. Ladders are crashing down, buckets of paint are falling from window ledges, cars are screeching to a halt. Everything is a near miss. But Mr. Magoo sees none of it. He walks through life as if nothing whatsoever bad is taking place around him. This is a symbol of the imputation involved in pastoral care.

Many Christian ministers understand what is happening around them. Because they understand original sin and total depravity, they are diagnosticians of the human life cycle. They see within and beyond, because the Bible has given them a matrix of perception. They are like the cathedral dean in Lloyd Douglas's long-forgotten novel *Green Light* (1935), who understood the heart and inner life of everyone he ever talked to in his study, but kept it to himself. They are like Christ in this way: seeing all things, yet maintaining a silence in relation to sorrow until the sorrow comes to them. Christian ministers are like Mr. Magoo. They walk through their busy and conflict-riven lives, but these lives are *simul iustus et peccator.* They see and do not see. They discern and yet are stupid. They pierce the veil and look the other way.

Three Monkeys

Ministers see no evil, and yet they see everything. This is the reality of imputation. Pastoral care is not "proactive," a big word in our lives today.

Pastoral care observes, yet decides not to see. This is the essence of grace in practice. You look out on a group of people on a Sunday morning and observe bickering mothers and daughters, sullen and resentful sons, sexually frustrated men and misunderstood wives. You feel the rising infidelities and the hurt feelings and the palpable mourning for mothers and fathers who are no longer present. You see all this if you have an eye to original sin and total depravity. Yet you speak the word of imputed righteousness: "God did not send the Son into the world to condemn the world, but in order that the world might be saved through him" (John 3:17). The blanket of condemnation that the discerning eye cannot fail to see is replaced by the "garments of salvation" (Isaiah 61:10).

This means that pastoral response is always the response of listening and passive reception. It is not the response of trying to fix things. Every conversation you ever have in ministry is a piercing conversation from the standpoint of the pastoral listener. He or she has heard it all before, many, many times. Yet it has to come out. It has to be heard with full acceptance, even sorry acquiescence. Grace never tries to fix, but trusts God to do this. Grace listens.

In caring for people in the setting of a local church, the idea is first to relax control and the idea of control. No more micro-managing! This relaxation of control makes room for the Holy Spirit to work, work that only takes place in the vacuum provided by the absence of human control. It is the fruit of the Spirit to create love where there was resentment, and creativity where there was blockage. This happens among everyday people when the control of the law is lifted.

The beginning of this fruit of the Spirit is the imputation of good to people where there was clear evidence of bad in people. An example of this comes at the conclusion of the popular Disney movie *Lilo & Stitch* (2002). The berserk alien Stitch finds a home in a broken human family that consists of two orphaned sisters. Otherwise completely aggressive, Stitch experiences grace within the caring of the bereft (and equally aggressive) Lilo. Two "ugly ducklings" have found each other! In the concluding moments of this animated film designed for children, Stitch declares his adoptive family to be "little and broken, but good." Stitch's pursuers from outer space are touched. They let him stay in the place where he, lost and "out of control" earlier, has experienced grace.

The animators conclude the film with a series of snapshots from Stitch's future. They are snapshots of Christmases and birthdays, elementary school classrooms, weddings, and little children to come. They are in every visual sense the fruit of the Spirit. The grace of Stitch's adoption produces decades of fruit. The last snapshot to be shown is an old torn one of Lilo's original family, of her and her sister happy long ago with their parents. A picture of Stitch has been glued onto the edge of the photograph. The adoptive family has replaced the lost original family.

I invite any adult to watch this and not be touched. It is grace superseding law, and it results in the very things law had tried to achieve but failed. *Lilo & Stitch* is a minor masterpiece of the world's instinctive grasp of grace. It puts most church preaching to shame.

In pastoral care, imputation is the tool by which grace is applied. The pastor relaxes control. It is as much a matter of tone and motive as of anything that is materially done. The minister lets be, so that the people over whom he or she has "responsibility" become free. The fruit of this is beloved-ness and love outreaching and creative, new ideas that are not ideological but rather rooted in the real situation, and a freshness and vitality that are instinctively missionary. In thirty years of parish ministry, I have seen this grace of pastoral care take place again and again. It is in proportion to my own graced-ness, from God and people, for certain. And it is in a perpetual counterintuitive conflict with my instinctive "Type A" personality. But this grace has happened.

The three monkeys on my desk are a metaphor for imputation. They see, hear, and speak only good. They are a metaphor for grace in pastoral care. They embody the center of the ministry of Jesus, which was absolution, and the fruit of human freedom through fruitful love.

Mr. Magoo

The famous cartoon character, voiced by the late Jim Backus, is the perfect clergyman. Terrible and real things happen all around him, but he just presses on, unseeing. The only difference between Mr. Magoo and the wise minister is that the wise minister pretends to be blind while fully seeing. He or she practices *simul iustus et peccator.* The wise minister is tuned into the human, sinful dimension of life, yet sees the "justified sinner." This pastor proceeds on the basis of imputation, but doesn't miss the diagnostic deficits of the situation.

Ministers who visit the hospital do not need to know what is wrong with the patients they see. What they listen for is what the patients are thinking and feeling. For pastors, that is the only important thing. They do not need to know the details, whether it be cancer or a swollen hip or the now universal description for a proto-stroke, the TIA. A patient may tell the minister, or a member of the family may brief him or her outside the room; but, like Mr. Magoo, the pastor does not need to know where the suffering comes from. All he or she needs to do is focus on the patient and what the patient wishes to say.

How often I have been with clergy who think they have to become doctors with an opinion about the treatment. This is a form of control. The pastor is there, rather, to see both nothing and everything. That makes him or her a wise guide as opposed to an ersatz practitioner or an ecclesiastical gossip.

The same thing is true in pastoral counseling. The minister does not need to ask questions, at least not questions of fact. Let the facts emerge in their own time and under the guidance of the Holy Spirit. The minister is there only to listen with concentration and vertical silent prayerfulness. The clergy who do the most good in pastoral counseling are clergy who say the least and pray the most (silently), and thus elicit the true case of the sufferer who has come to them. The honest admission of the sufferer is the equivalent of the theological experience of repentance. The grace-full focus of the pastoral listener is the equivalent of theological absolution. It is more than the equivalent! It is the divine absolution itself, made concrete in practice.

When you "run" a parish, run it like Mr. Magoo or like the three monkeys who see no evil, hear no evil, and speak no evil. These are symbols of the relaxation of control upon people, subtly and beneath the surface. You do not judge, but you know what goes on behind closed doors.

You are the silent diagnostician who misses nothing but is all about grace.

When diagnosticians like that bring their infrared wisdom into the pulpit and into their illustrations of the way grace works, they help people. Their churches are filled, and their working days are like the days of Christ. They can barely steal away from human need for a single hour. Their diagnostic wisdom is anchored in their own suffering and their own experience of God's grace at the point of suffering. Not everyone has to know this. But the minister's own story is the root of his or her success in the cure and care of troubled people. The minister resembles an old (wise) monkey, wiry and weathered. But this pastor has a life's work: the piercing and effective look of imputation upon all human beings who are, in the Christian view, totally human *(peccator)* and totally loved *(iustus)*.

Grace in Church Administration

In the Anglican cathedral on the Island of Antigua, there is a brass plaque to a former bishop of the diocese, an Englishman who served there five decades ago. It reads, "To the Memory of Bishop 'Smith' [dates of life and dates of service]. He was a good administrator." That is all the plaque says. (I have changed the name.) It is one of the best examples on record of damning with faint praise. Obviously whoever wrote the text had to come up with something to say, and the bishop must have been unpopular and unloved. The best that could be said were the words: "He was a good administrator." There is not a pastor on earth who would wish for such an epitaph. Maybe "Beloved of all" or "He walked with God" — but "He was a good administrator"? No one would desire such "praise."

Administration is low on the list of desiderata for any post. Sometimes parish search committees *think* this is what they want, perhaps because the rector they knew most recently was an alcoholic or became depressed at the end of his or her tenure and let things go. But good administration is not the most important characteristic of a pastor. What parishes want is affection and some depth in the pulpit. Everything else is secondary.

Administration is low on the list in pastoral care. The point is important because within a theology of grace, administration, like everything else, flows from the source, which is the preached Word of one-way love. If the minister is "Type B" and disorganized, grace will raise up someone else to do the administering. Or grace will change the minister's heart, so that some degree of administration will become rewarding or even fun. Grace always places administration in the secondary line of interest and significance. It is a minor theme.

Grace and the Difficult Person

Most members of the clergy will tell you that the phenomenon most damaging to their morale is the emergence of the difficult person. You can take a lot of stress and a lot of pressure on many fronts, even simultaneously. But the biggest chronic headache of parish life is the difficult person. If you talk to parish ministers who have left a ministry for reasons not related to scandal, they will often tell you that they were driven away by a few, and rarely more than two or three, members of the congregation.

How does this work? I can give numerous examples from my own life. In the first parish where I was rector, a man appeared at every vestry meeting who looked every inch the New York City commuter. He was articulate, personally devout, and had some "command presence." He was usually quiet for the first two hours of the long vestry meetings that were the rule in that parish. But toward the end of each meeting, he would invariably become contentious, even harsh. He would cause fights over tiny things, let nothing go, and get positively vitriolic by eleven at night. Naturally, I took it personally. Moreover, as a young parson of little experience, I was hurt and discouraged by this man's continual harping. I had no idea what was going on.

As time passed and I acquired a little more experience, I began to notice that he sweated profusely during the first hour or so of the meeting.

His initial silence during the first two-thirds of the meeting also baffled me, in comparison with his volatility during the last third. Then it struck me: he must be an alcoholic. He arrived at the church with two or three martinis under his belt and was afraid people would notice. So he sat tight while the alcohol worked its way through his system. That accounted for the beads of sweat pouring off the back of his neck. Then he started to want a drink. At that point, about 9:30 or 10:00 P.M., all the vitriol of the alcoholic, and a good portion of the addiction, came out. The man was furious, in the second stage of his nightly detox, and was dying for a drink.

My growing picture of what was really going on was soon confirmed. It turned out that this man was known, in our little commuter belt, for being a drunk. Like the woman who is the last to find out her husband is cheating on her with her best friend, I, the parish parson, was the last person to find out what everyone else apparently knew already. At least I knew now. At that point my wardens (the leaders of the vestry) came in to handle the problem for me.

What happened in this parish to clue me in concerning this difficult person served me well later. It made me ask the question, *why* is this particular man or woman being so impossible? There must be some original sin in the picture. There must be a deeper cause than the appearance of things.

Later on, in a church in South Carolina, the same thing happened: a chronically difficult man on the vestry made my life miserable. Again, sadly, it was alcoholism. I was no longer so surprised by his outbursts, and, aided by others, I helped him to get treatment. In South Carolina we also had a racist. The man was devout and very nice in almost every way. He had lost an arm during a teenage accident with a shotgun. I found it easy to forgive him his racism and his anger because of his (lost) arm. Grace helped me there, together with a clearer understanding of original sin, which stands behind every tall tree and every high thicket.

A theology of grace is necessary when dealing with a difficult person. It is necessary because it gives you the tools for understanding what is going on, for recognizing a provocative form of original sin. A theology of grace helps you have compassion for the difficult person. It also helps you see the problem as a *compulsive* one. You need help to face it and deal with it. You cannot do it yourself, partly because the problems of the difficult person are not aimed at you personally. They are aimed at "life" and finally at God. This is why the difficult person is at church in the first place. The very fact that he or she is there is an expression of the suffering, a real cry for help. It is just a peculiarly alienating and provocative cry for help. So you need help, help from your other leaders in the parish family, help from the God who alone has enough heart for such a person. Grace helps you understand what is happening in the case of the difficult person, and grace helps you find help in facing that insoluble chronic problem of life and ministry, the difficult and deliberate antagonist.

Concluding Unscientific Postscript

When I speak of the primacy of grace in theology, and specifically of the supersession of the law by grace in theology, colleagues sometimes become nervous. They think that the grace position goes a little further than the Scriptures do. They want to lease grace to law, at least somewhat. Their idea is that the full-bore grace position discounts some of the law-oriented parts of Scripture and thus may be running in front of the "whole counsel of God."

I have already underlined and advocated the one-sidedness of grace above. For me, it is the overwhelming theme of the whole Bible, provided that the theological distinction between grace and law is consistently understood. I have now stated this position, and not every interpreter will agree. Certainly, the issue is an old one, and you can marshal Christian thinkers on either side of the case.

There is, however, an important "concluding unscientific postscript" (the term derives from Søren Kierkegaard) to this penultimate section of my book. The concluding unscientific postscript is this: *It works.* The theology of grace works. It relieves people of burdens and births a new view of their future. It creates the spontaneous and unself-conscious response of works of love. It engenders what the law demands.

I have seen it happen repeatedly for thirty years. At a downtown church in the East Village of New York City, in a John Cheever-esque parish in the high suburbs of that city, in a "sea island" parish on the coast of South Carolina, in a traditional cathedral parish in Birmingham, Alabama — in all of these churches I have seen grace work.

In New York City and Westchester County, the preaching of this message caused rapid long-term growth. On the "sea island" it caused initial quakes and then settled in for sustained steady growth. In Birmingham, it created massive growth, both in numbers and in money. Grace applied, in the pulpit and in pastoral care, brings about that which it intends. The law stunts growth, begrudges it, puts a damp cloth over it, and finally kills it.

Here is a maxim, a concluding unscientific postscript for all who are concerned for the mission of the church: Grace applied will grow your church. "Every valley shall be lifted up, and every mountain and hill be made low" (Isaiah 40:4; Luke 3:5). Grace will grant to your church joy and humor and love and generosity. Law, on the other hand, will clip your wings and will add insult to injury in a declining situation. It will create resentment, sourness, self-absorption, and penury. For parish life, that is the maxim of this theology.

Grace in Prayer

In a ministry driven by ideas, there is a tendency to speak as if the ideas were the thing. In a systematic theology of grace applied in everyday life, there is a tendency to regard the idea of grace as the paramount thing. In the rush to think existentially about theology, there is a tendency to believe that the idea is the lever, that the idea of grace is the grace. This is not right. Ministry *is* idea-driven. But it is animated the way the "dead bones" became animated in the prophecy of Ezekiel (37:1-10). Ministry is animated by the action of God, who is outside the situation and enters the situation to revivify what is limp and what is dead. Ministry from grace is about resuscitation — or better, resurrection — from the dead.

This is why a theology of grace runs parallel to a high and strong theology of the Holy Spirit. We do nothing; God does everything. We relax control; God takes control. We are dead and deadened; God is alive and enlivening. The message is either/or. Human people are either dead without grace or alive with grace.

Joined to this high doctrine of the Spirit of God is a high concept of prayer. Prayer is not the expression of an idea. It is not the embodiment in speech of the position of absolute dependence that is assumed within the theology of grace. Prayer is the expression of a relationship. This is easy to say, and sounds a little trite. But prayer is one word: "Help!" That is what prayer is. It is the cry for aid in the circumstance where there is no aid and no resources to provide aid. Prayer is the "Help!" of the person whose intrinsic givens offer no way out. Prayer within this systematic theology of everyday life makes possible the conceptual travel "from a whisper to a scream" (Allen Toussaint, 1970).

The Holy Spirit causes concepts to come alive. It animates ideas. Prayer from human beings is the voice of God's Spirit making real the idea of grace in practice. I pray from need, and I rarely pray from thanks. It is an untrue conception to believe that people are full of prayers of thankfulness. We think they should, and we believe we should. But when a good thing befalls us or a bad thing escapes us, we sigh with short relief and then simply move forward with our preset plans for ourselves. I am unconvinced that thanking comes naturally. I have to force myself to do it.

What comes naturally, however, in the language of prayer, is the cry for help. The more dire the circumstance or checkmate is, the more heartfelt and spontaneous the prayer for help. This cry for help is always grace-prayer, because it is spoken only when you see nothing natural, nothing *within the situation,* coming to you with aid. You pray deeply when you pray with a death-resurrection model of life. In this theology of grace in everyday life, a person prays for help when there is no help in the air. Prayer on this model discerns nothing helpful within the needy situation, but vaults and projects the whole need to the outside possibility. It is the grace-prayer of faith.

How do I pray, in practical words, for something that can come only from outside myself, something that can come only from God? Examples of grace in prayer are rare. This is because most prayer — that is, most spoken prayer that is extemporary and spoken with others present — is horizontal. By "horizontal" I mean prayer that conveys information to another person rather than makes a request to God. You know what I mean: "Lord, we just pray for our sister Nancy. She is upset and miserable and we feel for her terribly. We want so much for her to feel better and so we commend her to you now, hoping that . . ." This is a horizontal prayer because it is really directed to Nancy. It is a message of sympathy sent to Nancy, who is on the other side of the room.

Or this: "Lord, we know Bill is in trouble. Will you help him find his way? Give him the power not to be so angry all the time, and help him to know that whenever he wants to smoke that cigarette, you are with him to stay his hand. . . ." That is a sermon couched in a prayer. It is a sort of judgment, however well intentioned and sincere. Can Bill himself hear it in any other sense than judgment?

Other horizontal prayers are informational lectures. I first observed this in an evangelical parish of the Church of England in the aftermath of a horrific plane crash in the Midlands. The rector prayed as follows: "Father, we are in prayer today concerning the victims of Thursday's airplane crash near Nottingham. We understand it was caused by wind shear, with possible faulty maintenance on the part of the British Midland maintenance crew. Help us now to understand why such things happen, and please comfort the . . ."

I turned to my wife after the minister's lengthy "pastoral prayer" and said, "Now at least we know what caused the crash and whom to blame it on." The prayer was didactic. It contained no real asking and simply served to let all the members of the congregation know that the rector had been listening to the radio on the way to church and wanted to let us in on "breaking news."

Other horizontal prayers are liturgical. Episcopalian priests, ministers, and bishops almost always begin their prayers before church services, within the little huddle at the back of the church consisting of acolytes, torch bearers, flag bearers, and lay readers, with the salutation, "O Gracious God, we . . ." It is a mantra and puts the listener into "liturgy-speak." A switch is flipped inside your head: "Oh yes, we are getting ready to have church now, so no normal words, please!"

Once when I was getting ready to process into a big and carefully planned liturgical service, the host rector offered a "liturgy-speak" prayer, redolent with inherited phrases but no sense of connection. By chance, the preacher for the service, who happened to be a Pentecostal woman of a different denomination, was in a different room at that moment. She herself was asked to pray a few minutes later, in front of the whole procession, when we had formed up by the main door of the church before the first hymn. Her prayer was so simple and heartfelt that all of us mainstream liturgical types felt like hiding behind her skirt. She had talked to God.

A prayer of grace is simply plain speech addressed to God from the standpoint of human need. "God, I am so upset I don't know what to do. The situation is beyond me. If you don't do something about this, nobody will. And I can't. Please, dear God, help me, for Christ's sake. Amen."

I almost never hear prayers of grace being prayed. What I hear is prayers of judgment, prayers of horizontal sympathy, prayers of information (including those that bring glory to the messenger), or prayers of formula. We seldom hear prayers of grace. Just about the only prayers of grace we hear are prayers we say ourselves that no one else hears. Those are the prayers of heartfelt and spontaneous need. They are vertical emergency prayers. They are from need to aid. They are the prayers of grace.

CHAPTER SIX

Grace in Everything

The disconnect between theology and everyday life is nowhere more prominent than in the disconnect between grace and law in everyday Christian life. The classic and common experience is for a sufferer to be saved through an experience of God's grace, only to be lectured and "taught" the moment he or she becomes a part of the Christian church. This is to take away with one hand what has been given by the other. The purpose of this book has been to show this disconnect for what it is — the supersession, in everyday life, of law for grace — and to state the alternative, which is the supersession of law by grace. "Christ is the end of the law . . . for everyone who believes" (Romans 10:4).

For ecumenists, bondage to sin and consciences bound to law do not seem as relevant as ecclesial solidarity and unity in the face of Christianity's apparent marginalization. In contrast, this study affirms that a visibly unified church is not nearly as important as delivering God's gifts of forgiveness of sins, fresh life, and salvation. The former quest, noble as it seems, is accountable to the latter.

Grace as a Wall of Separation from the Church

A theologian of grace has no ecclesiology. The ecclesiology of a theologian of grace is a negation of ecclesiology. The problem with the church as institution, humanly and historically understood, is that it almost always seeks to confine and control the word from the cross, which is the word of grace and one-way love. The human church cannot help itself. To use contemporary language, "This is what it does. This is who it is." The church, being in no sector free from original sin, clings closely to sin and exercises will. This is the will to law, which becomes the will to power. In almost every moment of historical time, the church has come down on grace. It has been fearful of it, competitive with it, and hostile to it. Church is typically the enemy of grace.

I have witnessed this so many times during my own ministry that it is depressing to number the occasions. From church bishops squashing the Spirit in vital local parishes or parasitically siphoning off its vitality; from church conventions that typically pull back from strong or countercultural statements; from the "churchiness" that worships form and shuns substance (a particular vice of Episcopalians); from the will to control that church bureaucrats seem constitutionally unable to resist — I have witnessed all these things during three and a half decades of service.

I have witnessed the punishing "brain centers" (the phrase is Rod Serling's) of church administration crush good things among the Protestant people of Northern Ireland and in western New York. I have seen the punishing "brain centers" take their pound of flesh from humble rectors in the English Midlands, and then form up in queues of obsequious time-serving to bless the Labor government in England as it attacks Christianity root and branch. I have seen too much to desire to have an "ecclesiology." Ecclesiology is an ill the world cannot afford. It is an ill the Christian world of grace cannot afford. To paraphrase St. Paul in Romans 10:4, "The church is the end of God's grace . . . for everyone who believes."

Theologians of applied grace pull away from "ecclesiology" at the very mention of the word, *for the sake of the sufferers they seek to help.* A "strict wall of separation" is required between the gospel of grace and the church. This negation of ecclesiology, pronounced so emphatically from the standpoint of grace, is provocative. But it is no more provocative than my own teacher Ernst Käsemann's negation of church as the incessant and proven corrupter of grace. Käsemann returned again and again to this theme in his theological work. Here is a classic quotation from Käsemann, who always saw the "turn to ecclesiology" as the return of a will to control the uncontrollable, the Spirit of Christ's grace:

> The church as the real content of the gospel, its glory the boundless manifestation of the heavenly Lord, sharing in it being identical with sharing in Christ and his dominion, his qualities being communicable to it — we know that message. It has lasted for two thousand years, has fascinated Protestantism, too, and is today the main driving force of the ecumenical movement. If only the theology of the cross were brought in to counterbalance it! But the church triumphant, even if it starts from the cross and guards it as its most precious mystery, has still always stood in a tense relationship to the crucified Lord himself. . . . The church's introversion puts it into the sharpest contrast with the crucified Lord who did not seek his own glory and gave himself to the ungodly.[1]

Käsemann taught us to think antithetically rather than dialectically concerning the adversary, church.

While the conflict between a systematic theology of applied grace, on the one hand, and the notion of a settled ecclesiology, on the other, results in a radical negation of the church idea, this should not scandalize us. It is the essence of Protestant belief in demystifying and deconstructing the human church.[2] This book is only a contemporary expression of an enduring if intermittent plea within the history of Christianity: grace trumps church every time.

1. Ernst Käsemann, *Jesus Means Freedom,* trans. Frank Clarke (London: SCM Press, 1969), pp. 89-90.

2. The extreme end, perhaps, of faithful Protestant deconstruction of the "official church," as Kierkegaard called it, is this description taken from a sermon preached at the end of his life: "[the church is] the clerical gang of swindlers who have taken forcible possession of the firm 'Jesus Christ'" (*Attack upon "Christendom,"* trans. Walter Lowrie [Boston: The Beacon Press, 1944], p. 117). I owe this quotation to the Rev. Ted Schroder, of Amelia Island Plantation Chapel.

Grace as a Wall of Separation from the World

A surprise in the life of grace is the fact that it not only tends to separate you from the church but also builds a wall of separation from the world. The usual implication of grace's extremist compassion is that it pushes one toward the world's suffering. The last thing grace should imply is a wall of separation between the Christian and the world for which Christ died. But in fact, grace is quite jumpy in relation to the world *on its own terms*. This is because the world on its own terms is bound under the law, paying tribute to it on every side.

Do you watch "reality TV" shows? They are full of young, beautiful/handsome yet also real people. Because I believe that youth often speaks things that adults are afraid to say, I watch for flashes of insight, unsublimated observations about life that may hold promise. But I never hear one. What I see is unsublimated self-preoccupation and self-protection. Christians will watch "reality TV" in vain if they wish to see demonstrations of altruism or mercy. What they will see is mercilessness, self-congratulation, and self-serving neediness writ large. The world on its own terms, young or old, is governed by the law, original sin, and total depravity. The puppeteer, the "ancient adversary," is the devil.

Theologians of grace are in flight from the church. This is the way it has always been. St. Patrick, threatened with excommunication by the leaders of his church in France, fled back to Ulster where he could work in peace. John Wesley was barred from most pulpits of his own denomination and addressed people in the open air. Joan of Arc, the "first Protestant martyr," won all for France, was then captured through the church, tried for heresy, and burned to death. There are long books of martyrs, Protestant and Catholic, Sudanese and Japanese, women and men, who have died because of the church. This does not mean, however, that we should trust the world.

There is a revealing moment in Roberto Rossellini's 1945 film of the Italian Resistance, *Open City*, in which a leftist priest, captured by the Nazis, is in an execution cell with a communist partisan. The priest is a hero, true to his Christian convictions in fighting the Gestapo, and prepared to give the last full measure. The communist is also selfless. But the communist tries to tell the priest something disturbing. After this is all over, he says, "when we have won, we [the communists] will . . ." He can't complete the sentence. What he means is, "We will wipe you Christians out."

The requirement that a theology of grace retain a wall of separation between grace and the world is not heard often enough. Again and again I witness colleagues of grace discovering that their skepticism about the church pushes them in the direction of the world. This is what I hear them say: I see more of Christianity, understood as a religion of compassion and acceptance, among people in the world than I do among the so-called "Christians" and church people with whom I have been living my life. Therefore, sayonara, I'm out of here. I will spend my disillusioned life at the homeless shelter, among Doctors without Borders.

There is an instructive illustration of this natural movement to the world and away from the church in the novel *Catherine Furze* (1893) by the English novelist Mark Rutherford (writing under the name William Hale White). In *Catherine Furze,* a sincere young pastor of grace, an evangelical vicar in a small town, has a fall from grace in which he almost leaves his wife for a member of his congregation. In coming to himself, this man, the Rev. Theophilus Cardew, sees deeply into the shallowness and selfishness of what he had thought were important evangelical Christian convictions. Cardew finds himself disillusioned with the church and with the Simeonite version of faith that had given words to things he thought he knew. At the end of the book, he returns, sheepishly and deeply ashamed, to his wife; leaves off preaching; and after ten years, returns quietly to a secluded rural parish where "his sermons were of the simplest kind — exhortations to pity, consideration, gentleness, and counsels as to the common duties of life. He spent much of his time in visiting his parishioners and in helping them in their difficulties."[3]

The author of *Catherine Furze* is explaining that Mr. Cardew fled from the church into a mode of low-profile helping that eschews Christian language. It is the area of "common grace" and requires no trumpet. This ending is a little disturbing and also a little off the mark. In fact of

3. William Hale White [Mark Rutherford], *Catherine Furze* (London: T. Fisher Unwin, 1913), pp. 365-66.

life, the world is no better than the church. Original sin is no less distributed among the "salt of the earth" than it is among the leaders of a visible Christianity. We do not need to go to Lambaréné in our justified reaction to the pharisaism and falseness of Christian institutions. That is what Albert Schweitzer tried to do, but the truth is he had lost the plot long before he traveled to Africa. Schweitzer was living in the world long before he exited the church.

The world will kill us with just as much effect as the church will kill us. This is why a theology of grace requires the low anthropology of the New Testament. We do not harbor illusions about the world. There is only one good man, "Jesus Christ the righteous" (1 John 2:1). The crucifixion of our life will come from the church and it will come from the world. Neither environment is safe. This is why I wish to stand in only one specific place, even if it continually moves. This is the place of God's one-way love and its imputing accuracy, which rescues the human situation in every case where it is given play. It witnesses no sector of human affairs immune to the disease, but also none immune to the cure.

Epilogue

Stevens: The salvation of the world is in man's suffering. Is that it?
Nancy: Yes, sir.

William Faulkner, *Requiem for a Nun*

God's grace exists in relation to the human world only because of the substitutionary defeat of Christ's final love on the cross. If God had not been defeated in a moment of time, then our own defeats would have implied the possibility of victory. But the beginning of wisdom comes when individual human beings put an end to the possibility of overcoming. Only then are they able to deliver their life over to God. If there is the slightest chance of a person doing it for himself or herself, God's grace is made null. And the death of human hope in the death of God makes it possible for a person to trust the Outsider.

Grace in practice is a hopeless theology and therefore extremely hopeful. It is like this: When you are in a taxicab in New York City and find yourself in gridlock, especially if you're a "type A" person, you can't help becoming increasingly anxious to the point that you ask the driver if you can pay your fare and hoof it on your own. Terminal gridlock in Manhattan touches deep "out of control" feelings. The response to this original sin is to think that it is better to take the situation into your own hands and walk the forty blocks than to sit there dependent on the traffic forever. The fact that the traffic eventually starts to move, and that you still always get there faster if you stay in the taxi, is just a detail. Control is better on any terms, at least on my terms.

If Christ had not died on the cross, there would remain at least the narrowest sneaking suspicion that I could still wrest life from the jaws of death. But I cannot. And Christ died. He acquiesced to the narcissistic wound, the highest possible narcissistic wound that he must cede his own life away, down to its roots. But Easter was related to this, not to his decisive acquiescence but rather to the simple fact that it took place. The paradigm of life is always from death to resurrection, not from action to consequence. Jürgen Moltmann has said that for years, and I think it is a Zen-style truth, a Christian Zen-style truth.

The human predicament, the conflict of existing between demand and reality that takes no naming because it is simply there all the time, is intractable without an external life preserver thrown to you. The crucifixion is the Word that this is true. God's defeatedness is vicarious. I could not admit the extreme seriousness of the plight unless it were that vividly portrayed and demonstrated to me.

I saw a man whom I had not seen for thirty years. He had been a devout evangelical Christian and also a reflective one. He could not have been more intellectual in his faith, and at the same time utterly and consistently devoted to God. Yet he had lost it all. He had lost his faith, as the saying goes. His wife tipped me off before I saw him. She said, "I guess you could say Bill has burned out."

This is absolutely possible. There are thousands of religious people for whom the un-broken-through "box canyons" of their lives have proven too much for them. They have failed to discern any help that comes from God. The wiltedness of the man's face, the face I had loved once and still do, was overwhelming. It was the expression of people in *Invasion of the Body Snatchers* (1956), as their bodies begin to shrivel after being inhabited by an alien intelligence. They have shriveling faces and shriveling limbs because of the disappointment that life could, with God's help, have been improved by means of just the right insight or just the right action.

But God is defeated, and this means that our defeat is complete. This is important because now the victory can come from the only source possible. It can come from the Outside. This is the total eclipse of the Son of God, by which the "Happy Morning" is achieved within the defeated life.

Index of Proper Names

Index of Biblical References